WARRIORS OF ARTHUR

John Matthews & Bob Stewart

Illustrated by Richard Hook

'Days as dark as night....'
(*Annales Cambriae*)

WARRIORS OF ARTHUR

John Matthews
& Bob Stewart

Illustrated by
Richard Hook

BLANDFORD PRESS

LONDON · NEW YORK · SYDNEY

First published in the UK 1987 by Blandford Press
Artillery House, Artillery Row
London SW1P 1RT

Distributed in the United States by
Sterling Publishing Co, Inc,
2 Park Avenue, New York, NY 10016

Distributed in Australia by
Capricorn Link (Australia) Pty Ltd
PO Box 665, Lane Cove, NSW 2066

British Library Cataloguing in Publication Data

Matthews, John, 1948
Warriors of Arthur.
1. Arthur, King
I. Title II. Stewart, Bob
398'.352   DA152.5.A7

ISBN 0 7137 1900 1

Typeset by Asco Trade Typesetting Ltd., Hong Kong

Printed in Portugal by Printer Portuguesa

THIS ONE FOR GRAHAEME

(because it's the first he will really like)

AND FOR KATHLEEN HERBERT

(explorer of the Heroic Age of Britain)
J. M.

Contents

ACKNOWLEDGEMENTS
9

AUTHORS' NOTE
10

INTRODUCTION
11

1 · THE LEGENDS OF ARTHUR
The Basic Legend; Geoffrey of Monmouth; Wace; Chrétien de Troyes;
The Vulgate Cycle; The Morte D'Arthur; Chivalry; Courtly Love;
Henry II; Edward III, The Order of the Garter; The Knight
Lugh Strong-Arm and the Three Queens (by John Matthews)
15–41

2 · THE CELTIC CAMELOT
The Romans in Britain, and their Withdrawal; The British Church; Gildas;
Vortigern; The Saxons; Ambrosius; Merlin; Dux Bellorum; Historical Sources
The Blundering Hero (by Bob Stewart)
42–77

3 · WARRIORS MALE AND FEMALE
The Celtic Warrior; Warrior Women; Goddesses; Minerva; Celtic Gods
and the Druids; Queen Boudicca; The Hag; Scathach; Riddles
The Abduction and Rescue of Gwenhwyfar the Queen (by John Matthews)
78–97

4 · BATTLE ON LAND AND SEA

Nennius and the Battles; Conflict at Sea:
Arthur and Naval Warfare; Camlan, the Last Battle
Kei and the Giant (by Bob Stewart)
98–124

5 · MAGICAL WEAPONS AND WARRIORS

Legend and Archaeology; Celtic Traditions; Kingship;
Weapons and Mobility; The Heroes; The Original Knights of Arthur;
The Warriors of Arthur; Merlin and the Druids; Origin of the Name 'Merlin';
Magicians, Priests and Spies
The Beheading Game (by Bob Stewart)
125–166

6 · CELTIC FRENZY

Arthur Through Time; Arthurian Miracles;
Arthur in Politics; Nationalism; Paradoxes
Owein of the Ravens (by John Matthews)
167–184

ENVOI
185

BIBLIOGRAPHY
186

INDEX
189

Acknowledgements

UR GRATITUDE and thanks go to all the authorities who allowed us to reproduce materials to which they hold the copyright. Neither could we possibly have written the book without the efforts of all those countless scholars who have laboured to throw a little light onto the so-called 'Dark Ages' in which Arthur and his warriors lived.

A special note of thanks goes to Caitlín Matthews, who aided us tirelessly with our researches, enabling us to deliver the book on time, and who drew the map which appears on page 99.

We should also not like to forget our three illustrators, Richard Hook, Chesca Potter and Miranda Gray, who laboured so diligently to breathe life into our own descriptions – that they succeeded is to their credit and not to ours.

Thanks also go to John Rogers, who made several trips to the West Country to take photographs, and Rosemary Wright, who managed to deal with a multitude of requests for obscure papers without tearing her hair out.

The quoted material at the beginning of each chapter is taken from *The Bardic Museum*, by E. Jones (see Bibliography).

J.M. and R.J.S.
London and Malmesbury, 1987

AUTHORS' NOTE

The colour illustrations in this book are based upon extensive research into details such as costume, armour, weapons, and general cultural background for each scene. We do not, however, claim any authority or precisely dated reference for the contents of each picture; often this is impossible for the events concerned. The illustrations are imaginative reconstructions based upon research, rather than firm visual evidence in their own right. Greater imaginative scope has been given to the illustrations for the stories and greater detail to those for the factual chapters; but the cultural background has been kept constant and coherent throughout.

There is some variety of spellings of names and places in our text; some names may appear in several variant spellings. In choosing our quotations from early sources and major reference works, we retained original spellings without any attempt at a standard of our own making. Throughout, we felt that the original spellings and style are more important than any editorial imposition. To the reader familiar with Arthurian names, the variant spellings will present no difficulty. For the reader encountering Arthurian themes for the first time we have tried to give sufficient information and modernised spelling in our factual chapters and individual stories to enable recognition of variants wherever they arise.

John Matthews
Bob Stewart

Introduction

GAINST THE VAST backdrop of a dusk-laden sky, a ship with a single bright sail vanishes slowly from sight. A final glimpse shows a man's body stretched out on the deck, with three white-clad women standing over him like ghosts. . . . It is almost the last frame of John Boorman's 1982 film *Excalibur*, and the audience in a packed London cinema have been watching the story of Arthur and Merlin, Lancelot and Guinevere, for nearly two hours. The king has been wounded in a terrible battle against his own son, in which most of his followers have fallen with him; now he is being carried off to a place where tradition says he will be healed of his hurts, to return when his country needs him.

The cinema audience has been very quiet during the last thirty minutes, and there are some who are visibly moved by the dark ending of the tale. Shortly they will go out into the streets again, having been deeply affected by the story of the once and future king.

There the images were of medieval knights, clad in fantastic armour or masks of gold; but the Arthur discussed in this book is a very different figure – at least outwardly. This Arthur is a fighting man rather than a great king, a warrior tried in battle and a leader of men who share his strength and skill. In a brief span of less than 50 years he made such an impression upon the times in which he lived (sixth-century Britain after the departure of the Roman Legions and before the creation of Anglo-Saxon England) that he will probably never be forgotten.

Indeed the story of Arthur is still not completed. Though he and his warriors perished long ago, their names and deeds have been kept alive through the art of story-tellers, of which *Excalibur* is only one example among many hundreds of others: medieval, Renaissance, Victorian and modern.

Just what it is that keeps these stories alive we hope to show in the following pages, in which we shall attempt to see through the images of medieval splendour and chivalry to the dark days when the legends were born. In order to do this we shall look, with the eyes of modern archaeological expertise, at the times in which the events described in the legends took place, and we shall consider the historical evidence, accumulated over years of careful study of the fragmentary records which remain to tell the real story of Arthur and his times.

We shall try to place before the reader a fresh perspective of those times, of the warriors who fought with Arthur, of the kind of weapons they used and the kind of armour they wore, and of the world in which they lived. Because it was the nature of the Celtic peoples who made Arthur their hero to award the gifts of magical powers or weapons, we shall also discuss the nature and skills of the magical warrior, and find that even here are echoes of the real world of the sixth century.

Finally we shall show how the methods of battle practised by Arthurian men and women (for there were female warriors also in those days) have been preserved into almost contemporary times through the nature of the Celtic spirit, which has itself changed hardly at all since Arthur's day. Because above all the people of those times loved stories, we shall tell some of the best-loved tales again, in our own words but faithfully as far as possible to the spirit of the times.

THE STORIES

HERE ARE SIX stories in this book, three by each author, and each with a short introduction. We make no excuses for these re-tellings as they are directly within the mainstream of Arthurian legend and history. Nevertheless, before the tales were written some firm rules of conduct were established, and these are worth outlining in advance.

Firstly there is no obscure stylism, none of the quirky pseudo-medieval linguistics that editors call 'Arthur-speak'; the language is intentionally direct and simple. Secondly there is no Celtic twilight glimmering around the vocabulary; we have not employed obscure Welsh terms, for example, that might mean little to the modern reader. Any such terms have been given modern English equivalents. This is the root of the matter, for any story is, or should be, utterly contemporary to the people within it.

A few Roman and Celtic terms do appear, but they are related to matters in our six chapters of history and Arthurian research, as are many of the details in each story. The reader will recognise many elements in the stories which are given factual detail in the chapters. We have aimed to re-tell a selection of classic Arthurian legends without any derivative medieval or later accumulation; they are set in a period between the fourth and sixth centuries, and the matters of which they speak are those which concerned the people of that period.

To come to some understanding of Arthur and his warriors and people we must always remember that they revived a genuine culture of heroic imaginative dimensions; the magical elements were not merely grafted onto obscure semi-history by later writers, but are inherent in the British Celtic inspiration and traditions. Arthur was perhaps the first consciously British (Celtic) king after the collapse of Roman influence . . . it is this revival of native culture, so strong in the fifth and sixth centuries, that caused numerous legends and traditions to become magnetically drawn to the figures of the king and his warriors and their consorts. Stories would have been central to the daily life of the Arthurian court; both stories and songs preserved the original legends well into the medieval period, and certain themes have persisted in folk traditions even into the nineteenth and twentieth centuries.

It would not be too excessive to say that a culture such as that of sixth-century Britain was held together by its songs, tales, and communal store of education and imagination. In times of stress and invasion, such elements of the shared consciousness come even more strongly to the forefront of family, group, tribe or national activity. We know that extensive Welsh and Scottish traditions were preserved well into the twelfth century, and for many years beyond, as we have written records such as the *Mabinogion* or the ubiquitous *History of the British Kings*. Apart from the resurgence of national identity in a historical context which supports a culture held together in time of stress, we have a direct modern parallel in the famous behaviour of the English during the Blitz. Personal concerns were temporarily laid aside, and without an enduring store of tradition people still created unity through popular songs and entertainments. This is a typical example of how communal tradition supports people in difficult circumstances; it remains to be seen in the future whether or not widespread television has finally destroyed this communality that appeared in such an attenuated form during the Second World War.

In the re-tellings of Arthurian legends, we selected six themes which have quite widespread variants, both primitive and literary. They are told in such a way that both reader and teller are supposed to be part of a living culture . . . there is no suggestion of alienation or separation or academic speciality. The stories are to be enjoyed, not dissected. In some cases there are stories within stories, and they are told by people already in a historical Arthurian setting; examples of this are dealt with in our brief introductions which give basic historical connectives where necessary. As one might expect, two major themes emerged when we began to work on the tales: battle or warfare on both individual and national scales; and the magical or otherworldly elements which are fundamental both to Celtic culture in general and to Arthurian lore in particular.

We have not neglected the essential aspect of feminine power and awareness; later medieval legends moved towards the theme of courtly love, but this is firmly rooted in a more ancient source, where women are equally as powerful as men . . . and in some cases superior. There is little doubt when we examine Celtic tradition that while action and heroism come from men, wisdom, education and initiation are the gift of woman. In later literature, this potent feminine influence, once defined as the power of ancient goddesses, is heavily corrupted sometimes to the extent that Arthurian heroines are merely wilting stereotypes being alternatively courted, seduced and abused by muscle-bound mail-clad knights. The same corruption has crept into the tales regarding Merlin, who in his earliest records is guided and advised by a feminine power, but by the Victorian era is shown as being seduced and enervated by a ludicrous vamp. No such stereotypes were allowed when our tales were planned and we trust that they have not sneaked their way into the final tellings.

As has been repeatedly proven by the success of historical novels, the imagination is greatly fired by details of the past brought to life from a factual foundation. The sole aim of this book is to bring together many disparate elements of Arthurian studies and bring them to life for the general reader and specialist alike. By creating an alternating rhythm between factual discussion, illustrations, and re-tellings in a genuine cultural context, we have tried to compose a holism . . . a natural unity of parts in harmony with one another.

This exercise of holism is, in itself, an important aspect of Arthurian lore. On a historical level Arthur tried to revitalise and unify a British culture, and out of this obscure historical period emerge legends and mythical patterns of human unity, even of spiritual vision, which are unquestionably holistic. The fight against savagery, the order of honourable warriors, the Round Table, the essential significance of feminine power, the ultimate quest for truth in the form of the Grail . . . all attempt to fuse historical and imaginative elements together and pass them on to future generations.

Our aim has been less exalted, of course, and if we have given the reader some insight into the true nature of the roots of Arthurian history and tradition, we are temporarily content. Why temporarily? Because, like the famous *Prophecies of Merlin* which are given fresh meaning as each generation considers them in retrospect, Arthurian studies and developments will always change and expand. Hence our statement at the opening of this section, in which we claim that our re-tellings are directly within the mainstream of Arthurian legend and history . . . for it is a source, a cauldron of inspiration, for the historian, archaeologist, sociologist, psychologist, and most important of all for those who tell and those who read and listen to stories.

1 · The Legends of Arthur

Tri Marchawg gwyry, cedd yn Llys Arthur: nid amgen; Galath, ab Ilaunfelot dy Lac; Peredur ab Efrog, Iarll; a Bwrt ab Bwrt, Brenin Gafgwyn: pa le bynnag i delai y rhain, lle na bei na chawr, na Gwyddan, neu ryw beth anysbrydol er cadarned vai cu herfen, a dded vai eu Calonneu ni ellynt ddim ou haros.

Three immaculate, (or unblemifhed) Champion Knights, were in Arthur's Court: *Bwrt*, the fon of *Bwrt*, King of Gafcoyn; *Peredur*, fon of the Earl of *Evrawc*; and *Galath*, the fon of *Lanfelot du Lac*: where ever thefe men came, if there was either a giant, a witch, or an enchanter, they could not endure, either of thefe pure Knights.

THE BASIC LEGEND

HE STORIES OF Arthur and his warriors consist of many strands woven, sometimes inexplicably, into the mesh of history and myth. To untangle these strands is by no means easy, so deeply enmeshed are they, one with the other. To most people Arthur is a splendid figure whose face and form are unclear. Even now, just as in the Middle Ages, when he was seen as inhabiting a distant, semi-mythical past — though in contemporary trappings — there are those who believe in the actual existence of a medieval Arthur who fits somewhere into the line of English kings, including Richard Lion-Heart and Henry II. So great has been the influence of this extraordinary figure that both he and the warriors who surrounded him have attained their own kind of immortality — a reality as much at variance with their actual selves as with received historical fact.

Everyone seems to know the famous stories: how the boy king pulled the sword from the stone and proved himself heir to a kingdom; how he founded the Round Table, where all that was brightest and best among the chivalry of the age could meet and talk and share their adventures, and how they were dedicated to the service of the weak and all those falsely oppressed or imprisoned. Well known, too, are the stories of Merlin, the great enchanter and prophet who raised Stonehenge and helped Arthur to found a realm of civilization and culture, but whose passing was as mysterious as his beginning. Who has not also heard the tales of those great lovers, Lancelot and Guinevere, or Tristan and Isolt, whose passionate liaisons hastened the destruction of Arthur and the breaking of the great fellowship?

15

Equally memorable is the great Quest for the wondrous vessel, the Holy Grail, which appeared floating in a ray of sunlight in the hall of Camelot, and which all the knights pledged themselves to discover; though of that whole company only three were to find their way to the holy city of Sarras, where the final mysteries of the Grail were celebrated before it was withdrawn forever from Arthur's realm.

After this, the stories agree, nothing was ever the same: the passion of Lancelot and Guinevere (in abeyance during the Quest) waxed hot again, and the coming of Arthur's bastard son, Mordred, signalled the beginning of the end for Camelot. Secular values overcame sacred, set briefly aflame during the Quest, and it was not long before the end came – civil war, the banishing of Lancelot, the death of Gawain at the hands of his old friend, and the final carnage of the last battle at Camlan. The story might indeed have been an episode from actual history.

Nevertheless, it was not. Arthur did not die; sorely wounded, he was carried to the otherworldly realm of Avalon, where its mysterious queen promised to heal his wounds and where he still waits the call to return to his country's need.

Such is the great story, in briefest form. Much is omitted: the stories of Gareth, nicknamed Beaumains or 'Fairhands', the scullery-boy who became one of Arthur's greatest knights; of Owein and Lunet; of Tristan and Isolt, whose story mirrors that of Lancelot and Guinevere; of Gawain and his encounter with the fearsome Green Knight, who offered his neck for an axe-blow and lived to invite the young hero to seek him a year later for a return blow. These are only a few of the literally scores of stories told of Arthur and his knights – but who told them, and when were they first set down in written form?

To answer this question we must first say something about the time in which the Matter of Britain (as stories of Arthur came to be known) was at its most popular – during the period between 1100 and 1500, at the height of the Middle Ages. Then, the seemingly endless darkness which had descended upon the West after the fall of the Roman Empire had at last come to an end. Despite numerous wars, Crusades and plagues, despite the poverty of the peasant class and the ruthless oppression of the nobility, a kind of stability had been established in Europe. Kingdoms, carved out by determined and ruthless men, had defined the shape the Western world was to follow for several decades, and in the rich and culturally active courts of the kings of England and France, Germany and Spain the arts flourished. Stories which had hitherto circulated by way of wandering *conteurs* and ballad singers now began to be written down, often in brilliantly illuminated MSS which told their stories in both word and image. As though a dam had burst, a veritable flood of tales appeared, and, not altogether surprisingly, these reflected the main interests and concerns of the age: Religion, Chivalry and Courtly Love.

Aside from a few smaller areas of interest, there were three cycles of stories which reflected these concerns: the Matter of Rome, which consisted of stories about the Magician Virgil, Alexander the Great and the Nine Worthies; the Matter of France, which concerned the deeds and battles of the Emperor

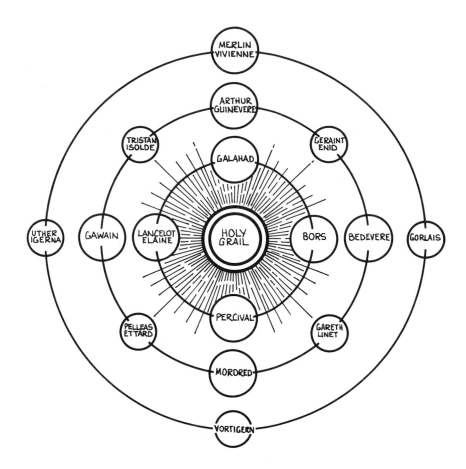

A diagrammatic representation of the Arthurian epic Cyclus, according to the narrative of the Anglo-Norman trouvères (from *The Arthurian Epic* by S. Gurteen).

Charlemagne and his peers; and the Matter of Britain, which talked of Arthur. This last, as existing MSS attest, far outstripped its rivals in popularity. Soon, as one medieval writer claimed, there was no part of the world which 'knows not the name of Arthur the Briton'.

GEOFFREY OF MONMOUTH

ᴀMONG THE FIRST writers to deal with Arthur was the monkish fabulator Geoffrey of Monmouth (*c.* 1100–1155) whose *Historia Regum Brittaniae* ('History of the Kings of Britain'), written in 1132, became a bestseller of its time. In this very first recital of the Matter of Britain Arthur is treated very much as a historical figure, one of a line of great kings stretching back to Brutus, son of Anaeas of Troy, who founded the first dynasty of Britons – including, among others, Shakespeare's Lear – and whose blood still ran in the veins of Henry II, to whom Geoffrey dedicated his book in extravagant terms.

Already the historical figure of Arthur, whom we shall be seeking to uncover in the next chapters, had become overlaid with the trappings of the medieval world. Geoffrey painted a brave picture of his hero as kingly conqueror, ruling a kingdom which included Iceland, most of Scandinavia, and much of Brittany and France, and which brought him finally to the gates of Rome itself. In this, as we shall see, Geoffrey was dealing out a mixture of tradition, oral tale and plain literary invention; though it is worth noting that recent scholarship has shown him to be less of a romantic than a 'decorator' of history. There was still little of the ornate richness of the later versions of the story – there was more of battle and politics than was ever to be the case again in the world of Arthur. Yet already we begin to see, in descriptions like this, a first glimpse of the glittering figures of King Arthur and his knights:

. . . he invited unto him all soever of most prowess from far-off kingdoms and began to multiply his household retinue, and to hold such courtly fashion in his household to begat rivalry amongst peoples at a distance, in so much as the noblest in the land, fain to vie with him, would hold himself as nought, save in the cut of his clothes and the manner of his arms he followed the pattern of Arthur's knights. At last the fame of his bounty and his prowess was upon every man's tongue, even unto the uttermost ends of the earth.

(*Historia*, Bk IX, Ch.2)

Geoffrey was also responsible for drawing into the circle of Arthur the figure of Merlin, arch-mage of Britain, prophet and magician. In this, it now seems likely, he may have been recalling a tradition of some antiquity, but, howsoever, he succeeded in making Merlin forever a part of the Matter of Britain, and gave us also several books of prophecies, which have recently been shown to be of considerable authenticity, and which establish their author as one of the truly great prophetic figures of all time.

WACE

 ROM GEOFFREY'S day the legend of Arthur grew rapidly. A Norman, Robert Wace, retold the *Historia* in octosyllabic couplets, calling it the *Roman de Brut* (1205) and making his hero the epitome of the Norman gentleman. (To Wace also we owe the concept of the Round Table, which he describes as seating 50 of Arthur's knights.) He was followed in turn by Layamon (*fl.* 1189–1207) who wrote for the first time of Arthur in English, thus ironically becoming the first Anglo-Saxon to write of the British king whose chief fame lay in his defeat of the original invaders from Germany and Frisia.

By now everyone seemed to be talking or writing of Arthur and his knights: the story is told that a certain Abbot, addressing a group of novices, saw that they were nodding off, and declared loudly that he was going to tell one of the stories of the renowned Arthur of the Britons . . . at which they were suddenly all attention.

The ramparts of Cadbury Camp, Somerset. Archaeological evidence shows that this Iron-Age fort was re-fortified in Arthur's time. It may have been the site of the original Camelot.

CHRÉTIEN DE TROYES

HE ORIGINAL Celtic stories, transmitted to Europe in the sixth and seventh centuries by refugees fleeing these shores for Brittany, had taken root in the imagination of a new breed of storytellers, the *trouvères* and *conteurs* of France and Germany. One of these, Chrétien de Troyes (*fl.*? 1160–1190) wrote the romance of *Erec and Enide*. In this, Arthur is holding Easter court at Cardigan in Wales, where he decides to revive the custom of 'the Hunting of the White Stag'. Here, whoever is successful in catching or killing the stag was permitted to kiss the most beautiful maiden at the court. While following the hunt, Queen Guinevere is insulted by an unknown knight, and Erec, who is accompanying her, sets off in pursuit. A number of elaborate adventures ensue in which Erec meets and falls in love with Enide, the daughter of a poor vassal. Eventually, he returns to court, and all agree that Enide is the most beautiful maiden present and automatically should be the recipient of the kiss from the knight who has won the test of the stag-hunt. Erec then marries her and lives for some time in conjugal bliss until Enide reminds him of his forgotten knightly duties. Furiously, Erec forces her to accompany him on a series of adventures to prove his manhood and chivalric splendour. Finally he is crowned king in the presence of Arthur and his men.

Here, with one bold stroke, the warlike, wonder-ridden world of Arthur, which in Geoffrey and his successors still looked back to the time of the historical reality, became transformed into the elegant world of courtly epic. Knighthood became an almost dilettante affair, designed to equip men for amorous adventure as much as for war. The concept of the 'knight errant' forever roving the land in search of wrongs to right or deeds of daring to achieve, had come to stay.

Chrétien went on to write four more romances: *Cliges*, in which he dealt with the romance of Tristan and Isolt; *Lancelot, or The Knight of the Cart*; *Yvain, The Knight of the Lion*; and finally *Perceval, or the Story of the Grail*, which he left unfinished at his death. With these five works Chrétien totally changed the face of the Matter of Britain, and established the pattern to be followed by most story-tellers who came after.

In *Lancelot* he introduced the figure of the great French knight, who was to become the greatest representative of the chivalric way of life in the world; and, in a bold stroke, invented (or some say retold) the story of his illicit relationship with Arthur's queen.

In *Yvain*, drawing on fragments of Celtic lore and story, he fashioned an elegant tale of magic and love, in which the hero, successfully overcoming the perils of a magic fountain in the wood-world of Broceliande, overcomes a black knight who is its guardian and himself becomes the successor of his defeated adversary, falling in love with and marrying his daughter.

Finally, Chrétien embarked upon his last great tale, that of the mysterious and wondrous object known as the Grail. Much argument has raged amongst scholars as to the origins of this *Perceval*, some holding that Chrétien worked from a lost original, others that he structured a series of fragmentary oral tales into his own version of the quest. What does seem certain is that Chrétien drew on numerous Celtic stories of a wonder-working object which had the power to restore life to the dead and which was guarded by a number of strange personages. Comparison of Chrétien's text with the Welsh *Peredur*, which although written down after *Perceval* nonetheless contains much of a more primitive order, suggests that there may have been more than one source. Chrétien must, by then, have been familiar with a huge range of stories, both written and oral, and it is not hard to imagine him working these into a more coherent whole.

Here, then, are many of the basic concerns of the Grail story as it has come down to us. Perceval, brought up in ignorance of the world, is an innocent youth and something of a fool in his dealings with life. He comes to the splendid Arthurian court and is immediately drawn into a series of adventures which culminate in his visit to the mysterious castle of the Fisher King, wounded and unable to recover his strength until a knight comes who witnesses a procession of mysterious objects, including something called a 'Grail', and asks about their use. Perceval himself fails to do so on this occasion, and thereafter wanders for seven years in the Waste Lands which surround the castle. Reminded at last of his duty, Perceval is about to attempt the mystery of the Grail again when the poem breaks off.

The enigma posed by this curious work caused several writers of less distinction than Chrétien to attempt a completion of the story. They extended the text by several thousand lines but failed to give it a satisfactory conclusion. By now, however, the story of the Grail had come to occupy a central point in the Matter of Britain. As further stories were added which traced the history of the mysterious object back to the time of Christ (incidentally making its association with Christian symbolism, which was *not* present in Chrétien's original, part of its heritage), and immensely elaborating the original story until it was almost unrecognizable, the secular adventures of the Round Table became almost totally subordinated to those of Spiritual Chivalry. The qualities of the knights were judged upon their degree of success or failure on the Quest, and a seemingly endless series of new adventures were invented to act as vehicles for moral and theological teaching.

Culhwch at Arthur's court, a nineteenth-century engraving.

THE VULGATE CYCLE

ERHAPS THE greatest single cycle of stories, known as the *Vulgate Cycle*, was compiled between 1215 and 1235 by Cistercian clerics – some say at the direction of their founder St Bernard of Clairvaux himself. It included everything, from the origins of the Grail as the vessel in which Joseph of Arimathaea had caught some of Christ's blood, to the death and departure of Arthur to Avalon; and, in between, the whole splendid panoply of the heroes, their tournaments and amorous adventures, their Quest for the Holy Grail, and the intricate stories of Lancelot and Guinevere, Tristan and Isolt, Gawain, Galahad and Bors. These themes were elaborated into a vast, sprawling edifice, kept going through the use of a technique known as *entrelacement*, which consisted of beginning one story, interrupting it with another, interrupting that in turn and finally returning to the original. In its modern edition the *Vulgate* stretches to eight large volumes.

An Arthurian warrior. Arthur was the first Romano-British war leader to use mounted warriors against the invading Saxons. Lightly armed, carrying a small round shield and with a cavalry lance, these horsemen were the prototype of the later medieval armoured knights.

THE MORTE D'ARTHUR

T WAS UPON THIS version that the most famous and very probably the best account of the Matter of Britain is based. Sir Thomas Malory's *Morte D'Arthur*, completed in 1485, is a monument to the age of chivalry which he saw gradually dying around him as a result of the internecine horrors of the Wars of the Roses. Written in prison, where Malory was held for various unprovable crimes, it has the ring of a death-knell to the age in every line. It also contains some of the finest examples of English prose ever written, and it is no surprise that to this book and its author we owe most of what is generally known of as 'Arthurian' in our own time. It has been edited, re-edited, cut, bowdlerized, re-written and retold for children and adults countless times. It has almost never been out of print since its first publication by William Caxton in 1488. (Caxton himself was the first editor to impress his own stamp upon it, by cutting the original manuscript in several places and dividing it into chapters rather than the division into stories which seems to have been Malory's original intention.)

There are so many unforgettable passages in this book that it is hard to find one that best represents its unique flavour. One of the most famous and often quoted is Malory's threnody for the days that were – the mythical days of Arthur when life was better than in his own day, and better than it would ever be again:

And thus it passed on from Candlemas until after Easter, that the month of May was come, when every lusty heart beginneth to blossom, and to bring forth fruit...and in likewise lovers call again to mind old gentleness and old service, and many kind deeds that were forgotten by negligence. For like as Winter rasure doth always erase and deface green Summer, so fareth it by

unstable love in man and woman . . . therefore, like as May month flowereth and flourisheth in many gardens, so in likewise let every man of worship flourish his heart in this world, first unto God, and next unto the joy of them that he promised his faith unto . . . and such I call virtuous love. But nowadays men cannot love seven night but they must have all their desires . . . Right so fareth love nowadays, soon hot soon cold: this is no stability. But the old love was not so; men and women could love together seven years and no lycours lusts were between them, and then was love, truth and faithfulness: and lo, likewise was used love in King Arthur's days.

(Malory, Bk XVIII, Ch.xxv)

And so with chivalry and other values, Malory implies, which were once so different from what they had become.

CHIVALRY

HIVALRY WAS the great dream of the Middle Ages; an idealization of reality which paradoxically influenced reality itself. The image of the knight in his metal skin, plumes tossing and harness a-jingle is, perhaps, a romantic one. Yet the ideas behind the code of chivalry, which saw the knight as a champion of the downtrodden or oppressed, expressed a genuine desire for the betterment of the human state. Just as there are clear examples where the veneer of chivalric behaviour remained no more than a veneer, so there are instances of men behaving in a more civilized manner because they were aware of the example of knightly manners as evidenced in the romances. Thus, out of the overlapping of the real world – which was, we know, far from glamorous – and the idealized world of Lancelot, of Roland, or of the Cid, came a realization of human life and understanding which is the real foundation of the chivalric ethic.

Two conflicting ideals underpinned this further: the overtly Christian aims which saw the knight as receiving his commission from God (he took his sword from the altar and kept vigil in a church); and the ethic of Courtly Love, which gave its energy to the idea of knighthood as a means of winning the favour of one's lady through feats of arms or acts of daring.

The strange and fantastic stories of Arthur and his knights, initially circulating orally, began, as they were written down, to serve as a reflection of the requirements of knightly behaviour, turning them into:

. . . a history which had a compelling interest for a knightly audience, because it seemed to catch the very essence of chivalry, to offer a reflection of themselves and their world not quite as it was but as they would have had it be in terms of prowess and riches, and spiced with magic and magnificence to add to the excitement.

(Maurice Keen, *Chivalry*)

This expressed itself clearly in the example of the Nine Worthies, figures held up to the medieval world as the epitome of all that was best in a knighthood which took its lead from Christian precepts. Arthur, of course, was numbered amongst them, as was Charlemagne, but, significantly, a contemporary and

Medieval knighting.

very real figure, Godfrey of Bouillon, was included in the nine as a living example of earthly chivalry.

Again, in the *Parzival* of Wolfram von Eschenbach (*c.* 1170–1220), which told the story of the Grail in a elaborated version of Chrétien's original, the élite guardians of the holy place which contained the Grail were called 'Templars'. They were named without doubt after the senior military order of the time whose members earned the description 'warrior monks' from their unwavering dedication to the religious disciplines alongside those of military origin. They became virtually the police force of Europe and the Holy Land during the period of the Crusades, and until their fall from grace in 1307 were the most highly respected force of men in the Western World. From them, understandably, inspiration for the depiction of the knightly guardians of the Grail was drawn; just as, in turn, their kind of spiritual chivalry derived in some part from the romances themselves.

COURTLY LOVE

GAINST THE IDEA of spiritual chivalry was set that of *Amour Courtoise*, or Courtly Love, which successfully mimicked Chivalry. Knights were instructed to devote themselves solely and utterly to a single lady, irrespective of whether she was already married or returned their amorous desires. Echoing actual proceedings, several 'Courts of Love' were set up, in which intellectual noblewomen like Eleanor of Aquitaine, wife of the same Henry II who promoted the 'discovery' of Arthur's grave at Glastonbury, and her daughter Marie de Champagne, for whom Chrétien wrote his elaborate tales of love, held trials in which the actions of lovers of both sexes were judged and punishment meted out according to an elaborate set of rules. These were formalized in a textbook written by Marie's chaplain Andreas in 1175. *The Art of Courtly Love* detailed the proper way of approaching or addressing the lady or gentleman of one's choice, and the intricate observances of class, whereby a noblewoman might speak to a man of the middle classes, or a person of higher station address one of a lower order. This in turn both influenced Chrétien in the composition of his Arthurian romances and caused a revolution in the chivalric code of behaviour throughout the courts of Europe. At its worst Courtly Love became an excuse for adultery; at its best it furthered a new respect, almost amounting to idolatry, for women – hitherto little more than chattels.

HENRY II

UST AS THE mingling of tradition and literary artifice form an entanglement through which it is often hard to find a way, so the overlap and interface of history with the romantic world of Arthur and his knights is equally intricate. Several times this enters into actual historical events. During the reign of Henry II, at a time when the Welsh were talking eagerly of the prophesied return of Arthur and the imminent fate of the upstart Plantagenets, a tomb claimed to be that of Arthur and Guinevere was discovered in the grounds of Glastonbury Abbey. This convenient event, which reflected the traditions that

The defences of Cadbury Camp. The steep ramparts would have been additionally strengthened by having massive wooden defences built onto them, making them virtually impassable.

Glastonbury was the original of Avalon, helped stabilize the situation, and Henry was quick to visit the site and arrange for a magnificent marble tomb to be erected before the High Altar in which the bones of Arthur and his queen could be re-interred.

In 1486, another Henry, the VII of that name, specifically arranged matters so that his queen, Elizabeth of York, could give birth to their first child at Winchester — then widely believed to be the original site of King Arthur's fabled city of Camelot.

When the ensuing infant proved to be a boy, it received the name Arthur; but once again the choice proved ill-omened as Arthur, Prince of Wales, died in his sixteenth year.

More than 300 years earlier, during the reign of King Stephen, chroniclers wrote that God's angels had closed their eyes against the horrors of the age. One of these horrors was the marauding Marcher Lords of the Welsh borderland, who virtually held the king to ransom and challenged his right to rule. The parallels between Arthur's early reign, when he had to defend his crown against a rebel alliance of subject kings who each sought to rule in his place, could not have been lost upon the story-tellers of the time. But then, the

Howard Pyle's depiction of the Royal Bard entitled 'Sir Tristram harpeth before King Mark'.

country they envisaged as ruled over by Arthur was very far from actual reality in a number of ways. For, once he had secured his kingship against the rebels, Arthur's reign was one of lasting peace. Logres was a land of plenty, where right triumphed over might and the rule of law over that of individual strength, unlike the world of the medieval romancers themselves, where, as a poem written during the troubled reign of Edward II has it:

> For might is right, the land is lawless;
> For night is light, the land is loreless;
> For fight is flight, the land is nameless.

That it was still a feudal land was another matter; we scarcely ever read of peasants in the world of Malory and his like.

The feudal system in which overlords supplied men and arms to the king, to

Arthurian chivalry as portrayed by Howard Pyle: 'Sir Tristram cometh to ye castle of Sir Nabon'.

whom they had pledged fealty by the traditional act of placing their hands between those of the sovereign, was very different to the kind of organization represented by the Round Table knights. They came from all over the world for the honour of becoming one of Arthur's men, and not only in times of war; they came to a peaceful land which stretched into mythical dimensions wherein an adventure or quest, or a wrong to be set right, awaited around every bend in the forested roadways.

The oath, sworn by every knight who took his place at the Round Table, was very different to the kind of oath of fealty usually expected of the medieval knight:

. . . then the King stablished all his knights . . . and charged them never to do outrageously nor murder, and always to flee treason; also by no means to be cruel, but to give mercy unto him that asketh mercy, upon pain of forfeiture of their worship and lordship of King Arthur for evermore; and always to do ladies, damosels and gentlewomen succor, upon pain of death. Also, that no man

29

take no battles in a wrongful quarrel for no law, nor for no world's goods. Unto this were all the knights sworn of the Table Round, both old and young.

(Malory, Bk III, Ch.xv)

This indeed was the chivalry to which Malory looked back at the end of his long book, with sorrow for something which had once existed, but which did so no longer. That it had never really existed at all, adds in some measure to the sadness of the final pages.

Night of the Long Knives. Vortigern, usurper of Britain, called the leaders of both Celtic and Roman factions to meet peacefully with the Saxons at Stonehenge. At the start of the council the Saxons rose up and massacred the Britons.

EDWARD III, THE ORDER OF THE GARTER

 OMETIMES CHIVALRY owed its historical manifestation to direct Arthurian influence. The career of Edward III, who became something of an Arthurian 'fanatic', had many surface parallels with that of Arthur. This may well have reinforced his preoccupation with the chivalric exploits of the Pendragon. As the son of the mismatched Edward II and Isabel of France, his minority was served out under the dominion of numerous barons including that of the unscrupulous Roger Mortimer, his mother's lover. But by the age of 19, Edward had rid the kingdom of the odious Mortimer's influence, re-established a firm government, married a pretty wife and fathered a son. Like Arthur, Edward had troubles abroad and was the first to put himself in the field against the French, determined to pay homage to no foreign power. In a series of brilliant and chivalric engagements, Edward returned to England covered with glory – a strong, popular monarch who yet harboured a romantic desire.

In 1344, he had sworn a solemn oath in the Chapel of St George, Windsor, that 'he would follow in the footsteps of King Arthur and create a Round Table for his knights,' but it was not until his return from the victories of Crécy and Calais that the Order of the Garter – Edward's own Round Table Fellowship – was formally established on St George's Day, 1348.

Interestingly, this idea seemed to have been borrowed from Roger Mortimer who, together with his grandfather, had set the precedent of holding Round Table tournaments, possibly as a reminder of the Mortimers' supposed descent from Arthur and Brutus. Nothing averse to converting the bad memory of Mortimer (whom he'd had executed in the years of his minority) into a grand chivalric ideal, Edward instituted the Order of the Garter to be:

. . . a Society, Fellowship, College of Knights in which all were equal to represent how they aught to be united in all Chances, and various Turns of Fortune; co-partners both in Peace and War, assistant to one another in all serious and dangerous Exploits; and through the course of their lives to shew Fidelity and Friendliness the one towards the other.

The new Order was exclusively composed of 26 knights, appointed by the king. It was to prove the inspiration for many other such orders, including the Burgundian Order of the Golden Fleece, but none was to have the prestige value

attached to the Order of the Garter. Like the inauguration of the Round Table Fellowship, there was an undoubted cachet in being a Garter Knight.

Edward's self-made chivalric image extended to his own son, Edward, the Black Prince, whom he was fated to outlive. Each were described as 'the most valiant prince of this world throughout its compass that ever was since the days of Julius Caesar or Arthur.'

While the exploits of Edward III prove that chivalry was not confined to the tournament field, it is nonetheless more realistic to regard the Middle Ages as mainly non-chivalric when it came to the battlefield. This is particularly noticeable when we turn to the military context of Malory's era – the Wars of the Roses. This bloody civil war between the rival Yorkist and Lancastrian factions to gain the crown undoubtedly gave Malory pause. Literature was not then apprised of social realism, and there is no finer antidote to the bloody doings of those times than the chivalric exploits of King Arthur and his knights. Within the framework of everyday life, the news was all too gory.

1460: Edward, Duke of York, and his son Edmund of Rutland executed and their heads set up on Micklegate Bar, York. The Duke's brows set with a paper crown in mockery of his regal ambition.

1471: Edward, Prince of Wales, the Lancastrian hope, slain at the Battle of Tewkesbury, aged 18. The Yorkist, Edward IV, breaks sanctuary in order to flush out his enemies, and executes them by military tribunal.

1485: the body of anointed king, Richard III, is summarily brought from the field, naked, on a pack-mule. His men are declared traitors to the realm by the expedient of pre-dating the accession of his opponent, Henry VII, to the *day before* the latter's victory at Bosworth Field.

The parallels between history and literature are almost too clear to need redefinition: the hard-won peace of Arthur's realm obliterated in a savage civil strife which totally destroyed the old order of chivalry – such was the state of late fifteenth-century England, and Malory knew it. The shimmering glory that was Camelot was to be remembered again in later ages by other writers, but none bade it fonder farewell than Malory, who wrote the epitaph of his age:

> Alas, most noble Christian realm, whom I have loved above all other realms, and in thee I have gotten a great part of my worship and now I shall depart in this wise . . . and that is my heaviness, for ever I fear after my days that men shall chronicle upon me that I was flemed [*banished*] out of this land.
>
> (Malory, Bk XX, Ch.17)

So speaks Lancelot as he prepares to leave Britain and his king's service forever, and many knights standing by lament with him:

> For we all understand in this realm will be now no quiet but ever strife and debate, now the fellowship of the Round Table is broken; for by the noble fellowship of the Round Table was King Arthur upborne, and by their noblesse the king and all his realm was in quiet and rest. . . .
>
> (Malory, Bk XX, Ch.17)

The strength of Arthurian tradition in the Middle Ages is evidenced from the preface attached to Caxton's first edition of *Morte D'Arthur*. In this he mentions

King Arthur, from the bronze statue at Innsbruck, designed by Albrecht Dürer.

Warrior from the tenth-century *Silos Apocalypse*: a stark and practical figure.

that he had produced a book about the deeds of Godfrey de Bouillon, who was numbered among the Nine Worthies, which he had presented to Edward IV, only to be told that he ought not to make books about foreigners — however famous — but rather of Arthur 'considering that he was a man born within this realm, and king and emperor of the same'. Caxton duly complied with his royal mentor's request, and in the same preface made it clear in what light he intended the book to be read:

> ...to the intent that noble men may see and learn the noble acts of chivalry, the gentle and virtuous deeds that some knights used in those days, by which they came to honour; and how they that were vicious were punished and oft put to shame and rebuke.

The world of Arthurian chivalry was very much that of the individual, the 'knight-errant' who rode in pursuit of adventure for both his own honour and that of his king. In the real world, however, honour was more likely to come on the battlefield and adventure in the bedchamber!

THE KNIGHT

HE FIGURE OF the knight himself, typically accoutred in the elaborate plate armour of the fifteenth century, mounted upon a splendid war-horse with the fantastic decorations of heraldry on his helm and the language of his personal device painted upon his shield, is still, to this day, the way most people see the Round Table knights of Arthur's realm. Many pages in the works of medieval writers like Malory are taken up with descriptions of tournaments and jousts, the war-games of the Middle Ages, with lists of who unhorses whom, and how many spears they broke: in short what T.H. White, in his wickedly funny, though loving, portrait of Arthur's time, called their 'batting averages'.

Yet, even by Malory's time, the heavily armoured knight was already becoming anachronistic. The introduction of cannon, the blatantly un-chivalric weapon which Malory significantly attributes to the arch-villain Mordred, and the terrible carnage wrought by the longbow at Agincourt and Crécy, signified the demise of the knight; even though it was not for several decades that the last great tournament, 'The Field of the Cloth of Gold', was held by Henry VIII in 1520.

The fantastic golden armour worn by the king on that occasion can still be seen today: it is a monument to an already obsolete figure, whose deeds henceforward became the subject purely of romance and fantasy. The image became solidified and has remained virtually unchanged, resurfacing in the eighteenth and nineteenth centuries only as an even more romantic vision of knightly and chivalric pursuits. The reality of Arthur's time, and of the warriors who fought at his side, is very different.

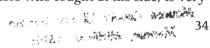

Lugh Strong-Arm & the The Three Queens

In the medieval romances which we have been examining, the figure of Sir Lancelot of the Lake is in the forefront of Arthur's knights. He displaced earlier heroes, such as Gawain and Kei, and became the premier Knight of the Round Table, unbeaten in each single-combat or tournament until the coming of his strange and saintly son Galahad, the Grail winner.

Many scholars have followed the belief that Lancelot was an invention of the fertile brain of Chrétien de Troyes. However, an alternative theory suggests that behind the tremendous figure of the medieval knight stands a succession of older, Celtic heroes, of the kind more appropriate to the historical Arthurian period.

Amongst the most prominent of these are Lugh Loinnbheimionach and Llwch Llemineawg, originally the same character but subsequently split into Irish and Welsh aspects. Both were noted for their strength, fiery disposition and the possession of magical weapons — a spear which roared for blood in the case of the Irish Lugh, and a flaming sword in that of the Welsh Llwch.

In the story which follows is told one of the most famous episodes from the life of Lancelot — his encounter with three magical women of Arthurian Britain. However, in this version, which should be seen as told by one of the wandering story-tellers likely to have been found at Arthur's court, it is Lancelot's earlier self who is the protagonist.

The three queens themselves, in the medieval version Morgan le Fay, Morgana and the unnamed Queen of Norgalles, can be seen as representing ancient Celtic matriarchal themes, or at a deeper, still more ancient level, as debased aspects of the Triple Goddess, worshipped throughout the Western world during the Bronze Age and after.

The description of the otherworldly realm in which Lugh/Lancelot is imprisoned is consistent with details to be found in numerous Celtic stories — as is the belief that while the denizens of Faery may capture the body of a human being, they have no power over his or her soul, and therefore cannot compel either to act against their will.

Time is either without meaning or of a different order in Faery. When the Irish hero Bran son of Febal visited the Land of Women (a place not unlike that in which Lugh is here confined), though he remained there for what seemed to him only a few months, when he returned to the real world he found all whom he had known were long dead. He himself had become legendary.

The final paragraph of the story refers to another episode from the life of Lancelot — how a maiden from the land of Astolat fell in love with him and how, when her passion was unrequited, she died and her body was ferried downriver to the walls of Camelot, together with a letter which told her story. In Malory this has become part of the world of chivalry and courtly love; Tennyson retold it in the nineteenth century in his poem *The Lady of Shalott*; the version offered here is merely a speculation as to the origin of the story.

A genealogy of Lancelot's literary descent from Lugh is on page 138.

The story I have to tell is of Lugh of the Strong-Arm in the days before he became one of Arthur's men and of that company the greatest champion and most feared warrior of all. Even then he had the kind of face that drew the attentions of women and led him into adventures from which only the swiftness of his sword-arm – and sometimes of his feet – drew him whole.

On this occasion of which I speak the hero had gone hunting alone, and such was his success that by noon of the day he had enough meat to feed even the Cauldron of Dwrnach the Giant for more nights than one. Now in the heat of the day there came upon him a great desire for sleep, for he had hunted well and come far from his home-run. And so, having stacked his hunting spears carefully against the bole of a great tree, Lugh cast himself down in its shade and fell into a light sleep – though always his hand lay near to his sword, and he twitched in his sleep like a hound before the fire.

While he lay thus, there was a movement in the forest, and there came into view as strange a procession as any you might see in that time and place. First there came a dwarf carrying a great spear on which was set a freshly severed head – the mouth still gaped in its death shout and blood darkened the shaft of the spear. Behind this came four ill-shaped creatures, dressed in skins, who seemed as though they had once been tall men, but who now shambled and dragged themselves along like broken beasts. Above them they supported a canopy of rich cloth, finer than anything seen in those parts, and beneath its shade, sitting upon three white ponies, with saddle-cloths of softest sheepskin, were three women of such beauty you would have thought they came of the Underland itself. They were dressed in such richness as might have shamed the court of Melwas, King of the Summer Country, himself.

Now when these three saw where Lugh of the Strong-Arm lay beneath the tree, they stopped, and seeing how his hand lay close to his broad-hafted sword and how his spears stood close at hand, one of them raised her hand and drew upon the air a sign that caused the hero at once to fall into a sleep from which none could have wakened him, save she who cast it upon him.

Lugh and the Three Queens. The warrior, Lugh, sleeping beneath a tree, is discovered by three Otherworld queens.

Then the three got down from their mounts and came nearer, and when they looked upon the sleeping youth and remarked upon his beauty and the play of his muscles beneath his breathing skin, they at once fell to arguing. For, said she who had laid the sleep-without-dreams upon him, this was surely the most beautiful creature they had seen this long while and he must surely be intended for her. And she had hair the colour of a raven's wing and secret eyes, and her mouth was the colour of rowan berries and her form was fair, and her name was Morgana, though in those days she was not so well known in the Lowlands as now she is.

And her sisters, who were called Morgause and Argante, were equally fair, and the first had hair like a sunset and the second like a bright golden net; and they were all three touched with the gleam of twilight and the radiance of inner earth. And when they looked upon Lugh where he lay they all three cast lustful thought towards him, and began to dispute with each other – for it seemed to them that all might have sport with this young hero; but as to who should have him first they could not agree. And so at last Morgana, who was the eldest, said: 'Let us take him to a safer place than this and, when he wakes, let him decide which of us three he shall have first.' And by their arts – for they were indeed partly of Elvish stock and well-versed in the magic arts – they went from that place to another, deeper in the woodwards of the forest, taking the sleeping hero with them, so that when he woke at last, stretching and turning like one who has slept overlong, he found that he was in a place where branches of hawthorn met over him, and that a barrier of thorns was on every side, so that he was as much a prisoner as he had been held in a room of stone. Further, he saw that his weapons had all been taken from him while he slept, but that food – fair, small cakes and a bowl of good beer – had been left by his side. And though he knew the prohibition against eating the food of Faery, yet he was young enough to put the needs of the belly before thought of danger, so he ate and drank his fill and then sat down upon the ground and drew his knees up to his chin and waited for what would occur. . . .

And what did occur was this: there came a high, clear, far-off seeming voice that said words which Lugh could neither hear nor understand – except that it made the hairs on his neck stand up, while a shiver ran through him like one who sees his own grave. Then there came into his prison – though how, he could not see, since there seemed no entrance or exit – three beautiful women (for such at least he supposed them to be) who stood close together as though they were each part of a whole, and looked at him. Then Morgana – though he did not know it was she – said, 'You are called Lugh of the Strong-Arm, and you will be the greatest warrior ever to walk in the halls of the Lord Arthur.' Now this meant nothing to Lugh since the name of Arthur was little known at that time; but he stood up slowly and looked at the three women in the eyes as unflinchingly as he could; though he could not help a small gleed of fear that needed little to fan it into flame. 'As to that,' he said, 'you seem to know well enough who I am; but I would as soon know who it is that has brought me here.'

'We are the Queens of the North and of the South and of the East,' said Morgause, 'and we have brought you here that you might choose which of us you will have for your lover.'

'As to that,' Lugh replied, 'if I truly have a choice, then I might refuse you all.'

The three queens drew even closer together and it seemed for a moment that Lugh saw before him a great serpent whose scales shone green in the strange light of that place, and that it hissed and spat at him. Then Argante, she of the hair like a spun-gold net, spoke up for the first time: 'Listen well, warrior,' she said, 'it would be easy for us to compel you to our need, but it is our will that you choose one of us to lie with. Therefore we shall leave you to think upon this, since we understand that it is no easy thing for any mortal to choose from three such as we. But we shall return shortly and you must choose by then.' And before Lugh might protest further he found that he was alone, though the manner of the three women's exit he still could not guess. Then he fell to thinking, and he remembered the four broken creatures who had carried the canopy above the three, and in his mind he understood that such would be his own fate if he took any one of the queens to his bed – for though he was young and lusty enough to feel desire for all three, yet he knew also that to love such as they brought only pain and fretful longings, and in that place of thorns and dim, un-focused light, he felt a great longing to feel the air of the outside world upon his face, and to see the sun again. And his spirit felt heavy and chill, and he chafed to hold a sword in his hand with which to cut his way out of that place. . . .

Then he heard a voice which spoke to him from beyond the imprisoning hedge, and which asked him how he fared. 'Not well,' he answered, 'nor is it likely to get better.' At that there was an audible sigh and a small hole appeared in the spiked thickness of the hedge, and through the hole came a slim white arm and hand, offering a dish of food and a vessel of beer. Lugh took these and said, 'Who is it that asks after my well being?'

'A prisoner, like yourself.' 'And have you a name, fellow-prisoner?'

'I had . . . once, but one soon forgets.' 'Then do you know where this place is?' 'O yes, this place is nowhere and everywhere and somewhere.'

'That is no answer.'

But the arm and hand withdrew and at once the hole closed up, leaving Lugh alone once more. He ate and drank and walked around the confines of the hedge and tried to see what lay beyond it, but there was only uniform greyness where there were chinks in the living wall of his prison; and there was only silence save for the sound of his own breathing. . . .

In that place time had no dimension, so that Lugh had no way of telling how long he remained there. Twice more the three queens came to visit him, and each time he refused them. Once, they showed him pictures in his mind of the methods they would use to persuade him; and once they showed him what pleasures he might enjoy if he gave in to their desires; but in spite of this they did nothing to compel him, and in his heart Lugh began to believe that they could not, that he must give willingly what they sought.

And when next the hole appeared in the hedge, and the owner of the slim white arm came with food and drink for him, he asked if this was true.

'It is true that they cannot take what you do not give; but in time you will be glad enough to do what they desire.'

'Is that why you do their bidding?'

'Yes.'

'But why do you not try to escape?'

'Why do *you* not try?' 'Because I am a prisoner behind this hedge of thorns.'

At this there was silence for a time, but at length the voice spoke again. 'There is no hedge; our bonds are of another kind.'

'But if there is no hedge, then how is it that I can see and feel it; and how is it that all I can see of yourself is an arm and a hand?' But all the voice would say was that there was no hedge.

But in a while he heard the voice again, and this time it said, 'The Three have been talking together and they have decided that if you do not choose one of them today they will kill you.'

'What can I do?' Lugh asked.

'Do you wish to escape?'

'There is nothing I could liefer do.'

'Then take my hand and believe that what I say is true,' and once again the slim white arm and hand appeared through the hedge and Lugh took it. But still he hesitated. 'Hurry!' came the voice, 'Why do you hesitate? The Three are coming.' At which Lugh closed his eyes and in desperation pressed himself upon the hedge of thorns. But where he had thought to feel their harsh pricking he felt nothing but air, and when he opened his eyes, he found that he stood upon a green mound and that his hand was clasping that of a slender girl whose black hair and red mouth and bright eyes reminded him of a blackbird. She pulled hard at his hand and urged him to hurry. 'For the Three are near, and once they discover that you have escaped they will surely pursue us to the very edge of the world.'

Lugh looked behind him and saw only a featureless greyness on every side, and nowhere that might be called an end to the sky or the land, if such indeed there were. 'How may we escape?' he said.

'There are twelve gates to this place, 'said the girl, 'and if you will but trust me I shall lead you through them all.'

And Lugh looked at her and knew that this was no trick, and when she offered him her hand again he took it in his own without hesitation and followed where she led.

And that was the strangest journey that Lugh Strong-Arm ever took, even in time to come when he undertook many deeds in the name of Arthur, but he never forgot it, though if you were to ask him the how and the where of it he could not tell you. Only that there was much that seemed real and much unreal. Faces and voices and hands challenged them, but always the girl had answers for them where he would have had none, so that they came past each one until at last they stood in what seemed the entrance to a wood and there were two great trees on either side of it like sentinels and here his guide stopped.

'This is the last gate of all,' she said, 'and through it I may not pass. But to you I will teach the way so that you may depart.'

'But surely if I may pass then so may you?' But the girl shook her head. 'I have been here too long. If I were to step beyond that gate I should at once crumble to dust,' and Lugh remembered a story he had heard of a warrior who had returned after what seemed only a few days in the Land of Dreams and it was in truth a hundred years that had passed. 'Then how may I thank you?' he asked.

'I ask only that you remember me,' said the girl. 'Who knows, perhaps I may find a way to escape. If not, I shall be here when *you* are dust.'

And then she taught Lugh the secret words by which he might pass by the guardians of that last gate, and when he had spoken them he found himself in a part of the wood that he knew. But of the entrance to that strange world in which he had been a prisoner he could see nothing.

And it is told that Lugh Strong-Arm was changed from that time forth, and began to follow the course which brought him to the place of Arthur's greatest hero. But it is said also that of that time came the sealing of his fate, for when the three queens found that their prize was gone, they laid this geasa upon him: that he should find love only with one woman, and that one, another's. But the gift of forgetting they withheld, so that even when Lugh became the lover of Guenhwyfar the Queen, he might not forget she who had rescued him from prison. And this was the reason (though none knew it then), that when, long after, a barge drifted down to Camulodunum the Great, bearing within it the body of a fair young girl with dark hair and white arms crossed upon her breast, that Lugh wept long and bitterly for what had been stolen from him when he scarcely knew what he had lost.

2 · The Celtic Camelot

Tri marchawg aurdafodiawg oedd yn Llys Arthur: nid amgen, Gwalchmai ab Gwyar; Drudwas ab Tryffin; ac Eliwlod ab Madog ab Uthur: Canys nid oedd na Brenin, na Iarll, nag Arglwydd ag i delai yr rhain attynt nas gwrandewynt arnynt o flaen ereill; a pha neges bynnac a geifent hwy, yntwy ai mynnynt, naill ai o fodd, ai o anfodd; am hynny i gelwyd nhw yn aur — dafodiawg.

Three Golden-tongued Knights were in King Arthur's Court: *Gwalchmai*, the fon of *Gwyar*, (Lord of Pembrokefhire;) *Drudwas*, the fon of *Tryffin*; and *Eliwlod*, the fon of *Madog*, fon of *Uthur*. Thefe three heroes were fo wife, fo candid, and eloquent, and proffeffing fuch power of language, that neither a King, nor a Lord they went to, but would give them audience before any others; and whatever bufinefs they went upon was attended with fuccefs. which they never failed of obtaining, by fair means, or otherwife. Their oratory dropped as gold from their tongues: therefore, they were called the Three Golden-tongued Knights.

THE ROMANS IN BRITAIN, AND THEIR WITHDRAWAL

HE TRUE STORY of Arthur's Britain may never be told. It is certainly a tangled web which is by no means easy to unravel. Even to find a beginning is difficult since there is no real break between the period of Roman rule and the age of Arthur — despite the artificial label attached to the period by early historians who regarded the sixth century as a recession into barbarism. In fact, rather than a Dark-age 'trough' situated between the high points of Roman rule and the establishment of the English monarchy, we should be better advised to see Britain at this time as a far more stable and unified whole than the rest of Europe — then suffering repeated attacks from Visigoths, Franks, Ostrogoths and their like. Indeed, as one writer has recently stated:

> Even when the imperial structure had gone, the Britons still regarded themselves as citizens of the Empire. Although it was not a state in the sense we would give the word today, Britain did form a nation. And despite continuous domestic quarrels, there was that sense of belonging to one nation which enabled the British to form a united front against the Saxon, Pictish and Gaelic invaders.
>
> (J. Markale, *King Arthur King of Kings*)

Nor is it surprising that the Britons should continue to see themselves as part of the Empire. The Romans were in Britain for nearly 400 years, during which time they established a machinery of government which must have seemed unshakable. They left their stamp upon everything — on people, on culture, on the landscape itself.

We must not imagine for a moment that this disappeared overnight, that with the departure of the last Roman galley from the island all contact with the

The Roman General
Stilicho, who responded
to a call for help from
Britain, with his wife.

Empire or things Roman ceased. Britain had been virtually self-governing for 50 years, and continued to regard herself as an outpost of the Empire for a long time to come. Indeed, the term 'Romano-British' is far more accurate than 'Arthurian-British,' which is really a blanket term for something which scarcely existed. The period between AD 500 and 600 may contain the events of Arthur's regency, but this in itself is only a brief episode within a much larger framework.

To begin with there were many Romans who remained behind when the last legion departed in AD 407. These were a mixture of retired soldiers who had been given lands in Britain as reward for service and had settled there and

43

married into British families; and merchants who plied a steady and surprisingly, scarcely interrupted trade through Gaul with the rest of Europe. Others, of high rank, had married into British aristocracy, forming a nucleus from which the governmental and administrative class was drawn.

They would have spoken both Latin and British, and been very much a part of the cultural milieu. There would, of course, equally have been members of the old British royalty who, once links with Rome had been officially severed, would have sought to reassert their claims. These two parties form the centre of a power struggle which was never to cease, and which in the end spelled an end to Romano-British autonomy, and brought about the birth of English rule throughout most of the island.

That this did not come about more swiftly, and with consequent destruction of both language and culture, we owe to a handful of Romano-British leaders, of whom Arthur is only one, who held back the influx of barbarian invaders and colonists long enough for them to feel the influence of Romano-British culture and become part of a new racial mixture – the Anglo-Saxons or English.

All this was, of course, still far off in 407 when the last of the legions had departed. An appeal by the British civil authorities to the Emperor Honorius was met with a vague response telling them to hold out and look to their own affairs. To all intents and purposes from 410 onwards, Britain was independent.

Again, however, matters were so muddled and unclear that it was some time before the fact began to register on the native population, and in the mean time government remained in the hands of administrators, drawn from both British and Roman families who had been appointed by the last official governor of the island. Since all personnel had been appointed to the province by the rival emperor, Constantine III, who had summarily withdrawn and subsequently weakened the province's garrisons by turning his attentions to the Rhine frontier and to consolidating his position in Spain, it is assumed by historians that the letter to Honorius asking for troops and support presupposes the deposal of Constantine's officers and officials. The Emperor's reply was vague for the best of reasons – the Sack of Rome by Alaric the Goth left the Empire reeling with shock. 'In the one City, the whole world dies . . .' wrote St Jerome, extravagantly.

Under Roman administration, Britain had been divided into four provinces whose capitals were probably Cirencester, London, Lincoln and York, each individually administered by vice-prefects. The whole was under the jurisdiction of a Praetorian Prefect. Two military commanders were appointed: the Count of the Coast (later called Count of the Saxon Shore) who commanded the forts from Portsmouth round to the Wash, and the *Dux Britanniarum* who was based at York and responsible for the garrisons along the northern frontier. It is logical to assume that these administrative areas still obtained after Rome relinquished its authority in Britain.

So, to imagine Britain as a kind of wasteland, torn by internecine strife, would be a mistake. The garrisons had been indeed sadly depleted by successive military commanders intent on defending their rights in Europe rather than defending the Empire's Ultima Thule, but it is still possible to envisage wealthy

Cadbury Camp from the west. Rising above the flat Somerset plain, Cadbury dominates the area around. It was ideally suited to act as a base for Arthur's cavalry squadrons. Local legend tells that on St John's Eve (23 June) a figure in golden armour rides around the hill and (sometimes) casts a silver horseshoe.

merchants and retired veterans with farms and villas operating very much along Roman lines. Writing, literature, the cultivation of vines and agricultural methods introduced during the occupation continued without interruption long enough to influence the Saxon incomers as late as the sixth and seventh centuries.

Not that Britain was by any means at peace. Rebellion and armed insurrection had been rife for a hundred years before the departure of Rome. The chieftains of the British royal houses had not waited to reassert their independence, and the mountainous areas of Wales had never fallen totally under Roman rule. Beyond the Wall build by the Emperor Hadrian, the savage tribes of Picts were massing, many already driving deep into northern Britain; while, as early as 407, Irish pirates (then known as the Scoti) had begun to raid along the western seaboard, led by the colourfully named Niall of the Nine Hostages.

The dissolution of the Empire was itself a very long-drawn-out affair, and its effects were already being felt in the fourth century, during which period there were widespread rebellions in Britain and Gaul. Although a degree of settlement was re-established by 410, this was only short-lived, and the province never acquired the same degree of stability as it had once known. Effectively,

Roman rule had already begun to die as the Empire itself tottered on the brink of collapse.

THE BRITISH CHURCH

HE PERIOD OF Roman withdrawal saw the consolidation of the British Church and the active spread of Christianity to the outlying and barbarous regions of Ireland and Scotland. The active missions of Palladius, Patrick, Germanus and Ninian were to have a powerful effect throughout the British Isles and subsequently throughout Europe due to the agency of their devoted disciples. The British Church itself had been sufficiently co-ordinated to send four representatives to the Council of Arles (314) and remained in touch with the European bishops and Rome until the mid fifth century at least, at which time our certain knowledge lapses due to lack of documentation. How Christianity survived into the time of Arthur may be suppositional. John Morris has suggested the following:

Children who had been born and baptised just before the revolt (442) who had seen their first Christian services in sophisticated Roman buildings . . . were aged sixty or seventy when Arthur was emperor and the monastic reformers of the sixth century were growing boys. The continuity of ideas is obscured, Roman Britain and the Welsh monks are made to seem unrelated worlds, by the break in historical tradition, as savage in the history of the church as in the history of laymen. Yet the older teachers of Gildas and his fellows were themselves children of an undamaged Roman Britain. To the young, ruined buildings and tales of the life lived in them were meaningless ancient history, ghosts of a dead past; but old ideas of the relation of man to man and man to God still mattered.

(John Morris, *The Age of Arthur*)

It has been assumed that Arthur's personal relationship with the British Church was less than pacific since he goes unmentioned by the chief monkish chronicler of his age, Gildas.

Of course, the mystery cults introduced by Rome still survived vestigially, side by side with vigorous native cults of gods who were the direct ancestors of some British royal families, and whose exploits were a matter of familial pride in the relation of poetic genealogies.

These factors show that life — at least on the surface — continued much as it had always done in Britain. However, in areas like Wales, where Roman rule had always been most tenuous, a new generation of British chieftains was beginning to assert itself. Many were descendants of tribes which had been planted by Roman overlords along the old border country between Britain and the Pictish tribes (in much the same manner as Cromwell planted Presbyterian Scots in Northern Ireland in the seventeeth century). There they had grown strong, and some, like the famous Cunedda, had migrated to Wales, where they drove out the few settlements of Irish pirates and settled there, firmly entrenched behind the natural defence of mountain ranges like Snowdonia.

Reconstruction of Sutton Hoo warrior and Celtic warriors based on a manuscript at Clonmacnoise.

Once these petty kings understood that contact with Rome was finally severed, they began to come down from their mountain fastnesses and establish territories in the Midlands.

GILDAS

HE RESULTING mayhem caused a ripple of panic which spread rapidly throughout the whole province. It was this which, together with the steady influx of the Picts and continued raids from Ireland, may have prompted the leaders of the Romano-British faction to call for help from a Gaulish magistrate and general named Aetius, whom Gildas calls 'Agitus'. We learn of this from one of the few surviving sources of information we possess for this period. It comes in the writing of the British monk, Gildas, whose chronicle *De Excidio Britonum* ('The Ruin of Britain') is really a long diatribe against various native 'tyrants' – one of whom, though unnamed, is probably Arthur – and the general state of decay and ungodliness then rife in the island. The letter to Aetius begins thus:

47

To Agitus, thrice consul, the groans of the British. . . . The barbarians push us back to the sea; the sea throws us back to the barbarians; thus two modes of death await us, we are either slain or drowned.

But Aetius was unable to help. Under his not-inconsiderable leadership, the Gaulish Roman forces had been able to consolidate sufficiently to unite the warring tribes into a loose-knit confederacy which later drove back Atilla's Huns. But this left him no opportunity to respond to 'the groans of the British' and the crumbling administration was left to organise its own defence against both the northern barbarians and the fast-growing strength of the native British tribes.

Arthur's Camelot. The sixth-century reality was a far cry from the medieval splendours depicted in later romantic retellings. Here instead we see the royal magnificence of the Celtic mead-hall where the War-Lord, Arthur, and his queen held court, surrounded by their warriors.

VORTIGERN

I T IS AT THIS point that the first among a number of more or less discernible characters emerges from the darkness of post-Roman-Britain. This is the man usually known by the name Vortigern (though in fact this name may mean no more than chieftain) who bore a British name but claimed Roman parentage. His wife is believed to have been the daughter of the great Magnus Maximus (who proclaimed himself emperor in 383 and marched on Rome). Vortigern may also have been able to claim British descent, since he is later shown as (unsuccessfully) attempting to unite the opposing Roman and British factions against their common enemies from the north and west. Certainly by 441–2 he held high office among the administrative hierarchy, and when the still very Romanised nobility looked to Roman inspiration to aid them Vortigern seems to have been able to fit the bill.

At any rate, when no response was forthcoming from Gaul (it may have been Vortigern who sent the letter to Aetius) the Britons were forced to take action for themselves. They succeeded, possibly under the leadership of Vortigern, in putting an end for a time to the worst of the Irish raids, and in containing the Picts beyond the Wall. But this was a state which could not last, and the recurrent threat of attack from the native rulers of Britain was a continual nagging thorn in the side of the Roman administration.

It should be understood that Vortigern was almost certainly not a king in the general sense of the word, although he is called this by later writers who saw him as a paramount figure among the numerous petty rulers of the time. Like Ambrosius and Arthur, who followed him, he was an able administrator and leader of men who did his best to restore some semblance of order to his ravaged land.

Unfortunately, history has not served him well, and he is remembered as at worst a tyrant and at best a fool whose blunder caused the final breakdown of all that remained of Roman rule in Britain.

Whether this image is a true one is no longer easy to say with any certainty. For what happened next in the history of the war-torn island is crucial and at Vortigern's door, one way or the other, the blame must be laid.

When the 'call for help' sent to Aetius elicited no response, Vortigern (or someone with similar responsibilities and authority) called in a group of Saxon *federati* to help. It is possible that these were already settled in part of southern Britain (probably Kent) or that they were a remnant of one of the old Roman legions recruited in Europe years before. Gildas as well as other sources speaks of three shiploads of men under the leadership of a chieftain named Hengist ('Son of Wodan, "God forbid!"') who were given lands in Kent and Essex as a reward for their services.

Initially, at least, they were active in aiding the Britons against the Picts, but having once seen the richness of the country they had come to defend (compared with their own sparse holdings along the coast of what is now Holland) they sought lands in which to settle more permanently.

Based on the evidence of Gildas, repeated in Nennius and Bede, we are able to establish a date of *c.* 443–4 for the initial advent of Saxon settlers – though these were still confined to the areas 'gifted' to them by Vortigern or his like. By 449 they were well established along the western seaboard and Nennius tells us they had taken the Isle of Thanet and were seeking still larger holdings. Nennius also tells us that Hengist saw that he had only simple 'savages' to deal with (though the boot could well be said to be on the other foot) and brought another sixteen shiploads (keels) of men to Britain, along with his daughter, with whom Vortigern conveniently 'fell in love'. In fact, it was probably an arranged deal sealed over several pots of wine. Octa and Ebissa, Hengist's cousins, were given the whole area beyond the Wall, which they would have to secure for themselves, and this seems to have opened the way to more widespread colonization. The Saxons promptly took the Orkneys and attacked the Picts from the north, effectively calling a halt to their attack on Britain for some time to come.

However, it seemed that by inviting these men from across the sea the British administration had replaced one menace with another. As Bede's account puts it:

It was not long before such hoards of these alien people vied together to crowd into the island that the natives who had invited them began to live in terror. Then all of a sudden the Angles made an alliance with the Picts, whom by this time they had driven some distance away, and began to turn their arms against their allies. They began by demanding a greater supply of provisions; then, seeking to provoke a quarrel, threatened that unless larger supplies were forthcoming they would ravage the whole island.

When they did not get what they wanted (one suspects that Vortigern's supporters baulked at the idea of giving anything more away) 'they were not slow to carry out their threat'.

In desperation, with his military position weakened and his popularity waning, Vortigern sought to make a new treaty with his 'allies'. A gathering was arranged at which a hundred British leaders were to meet a similar number of Saxon nobles. Somehow, Vortigern persuaded them to come unarmed as a gesture of good faith; he himself had by then agreed to marry Hengist's daughter. The result was the terrible episode known as the 'Night of the Long

Pictish warriors from an eighth-century Celtic cross slab.

Knives', in which the Saxons, having hidden knives in their boots, at a given signal rose up and massacred the Britons, presumably before Vortigern's horrified gaze.

He himself managed to escape and, pursued by both Saxons and Britons, fled to Wales where he eventually met his death. With his going, any semblance of organisation crumbled almost to nothing. The Saxons were left to run free, marauding through the length and breadth of the land, only a few of the larger fortified towns being able to withstand their onslaught, hurriedly throwing up new defences and recruiting militia from the local areas. By 435 things looked bleak enough to merit the first entry in the *Annales Cambriae* – 'days as dark as night'.

THE SAXONS

BUT WHO WERE these Saxons, the implacable enemy invited into Britain by Vortigern? The term actually includes a number of loosely-related Teutonic tribes: Angles, Frisians, Gauls and even some Franks. They were culturally backward, savage and ruthless; they were also driven by desperation. Overcrowding, endless feuds, and the poorness of the overworked lands where they scraped an existence, led them to look elsewhere at the possibility of conquest abroad. The Gallo-Roman historian, Sidonius, describes them as 'canny'. They appear not to have been governed by kings, but were bound together in loose-knit bands, each having a chieftain, to whom they owed absolute devotion and obedience. They were also brave, fearless, strong and terrible fighters. Jack Lindsay describes them thus:

51

The Roman road across Wheeldale Moor, North Yorkshire.

The image that keeps coming out of [their] songs is tragic; the figure of the lonely fighter in a hopeless place who goes down without a flare of regret. A haunting loneliness is the profoundest note, as at the heart of the fierce exultation there was a deep sense of loss, of nothing more in a shifting world.

They were, in fact, not unlike their Celtic adversaries, minus the Roman influence which gave the Britons an advantage in the use of tactics and weaponry and, of course, horsemanship. It is they who, in the end and after many years of intermingling with the native British, produced the Anglo-Saxon race which, blending finally with the Norman-French, gave us our own ancestors.

Between the Saxons in the south and east, the Picts (still active though temporarily penned beyond the Wall), warring factions among the British party, old federate army officers 'gone native' and raising their own levies, the land was divided. But were things *really* as bad as they seemed? In fact there is no evidence to show that any of the larger cities in Britain ever fell to Saxon, Pictish or Irish assault. They were re-fortified after the Romans departed, as indeed were some villas, and town-leaders continued to recruit local militia.

There is also evidence to show that various dikes were either strengthened, or in some cases freshly constructed between the middle of the fifth and the beginning of the sixth century. Wansdyke, Berkeley and Grimsdyke were made specially to keep out the Saxons. At the same time, the old Iron-Age hillforts, for the most part deserted, were refurbished and in some instances had extensive additions made to them. They were to form the backbone of Romano-British

52

defence, and many were rebuilt according to Roman specification and standards; impressions of Roman legionary-issue hob-nails in the mud at such sites, together with remains of pottery, indicate this.

It required the energy of a remarkable man to bring all this about, and the figure most generally believed to have carried out this rebuilding programme was a man named Ambrosius Aurelianus – the 'last of the Romans' as he is called by several writers. More than one portrait has been painted by recent historians of a last stand by Roman civilization against the incoming Saxons. Ambrosius' title alone makes it clear enough what kind of order and efficiency he stood for. In some cases he is even made to outshine Arthur, and there may be a certain amount of overlap between the two characters, who were certainly contemporaries (though of differing age and background) and probably formed successive bridge-heads against the invaders.

AMBROSIUS

 ILDAS WAS UNUSUALLY lyrical when he came to this point in his story. He describes how 'a remnant to whom miserable citizens gather from various lairs on all sides as keenly as a hive of bees under threat of storm . . . take up arms and challenge [the Saxons] under Ambrosius Aurelianus.' He then describes their leader thus:

He was an unassuming man who alone of the Roman race chanced to survive in the clash of such a tempest (his parents, indefatigably clad in purple, having perished in it) whose offspring in our own times have greatly fallen away from the ancestral virtue . . . to these men with the Lord's assent victory came.

A Scottish warrior from the *Book of Kells*.

Elsewhere Gildas calls Ambrosius *Dux* (duke), but we are told little else of him in the existing chronicles; however, there is, in the story of Vortigern's final days, a clue which suggests that we may well know him under another, far more familiar, title.

The story first appears in Nennius, where Vortigern's flight from both Saxon and Briton is described. Together with a handful of followers still loyal to him, he reached the mountainous fastness of Wales, where he attempted to erect a tower in which to take refuge. Every attempt to complete the work was frustrated, however, since each night whatever building had been completed fell down. In desperation, Vortigern consulted his advisors, who are generally portrayed as 'wizards', but who were, more probably, a last surviving remnant of the native, Druidic priesthood. It was they who instructed Vortigern to seek out 'a child without a father' and sacrifice him in the foundations of the building, which would then stand; but when the youth was brought before them he confounded them all by revealing the presence of two dragons, hidden beneath the stones of Vortigern's tower. Their nightly battle was the cause of the falling stones, and they symbolically represented the struggle of Briton against Saxon.

All that the child had prophesied proved to be true, and he added to his foretelling that though the Saxons held power then this would not always be so. Fascinated and not a little afraid of this strange boy, Vortigern asked his name. Nennius continues:

He replied, 'I am called Ambrosius,' that is, he was shown to be Emrys the Overlord. The King asked, 'What family do you come from?' and he answered, 'My father is one of the consuls of the Roman people.'

Can this be the same Ambrosius Aurelianus who was also of Roman stock and was an 'overlord' in Britain?

Swearing fealty. King Arthur stands upon a sacred stone and accepts the oath of fealty from a Celtic chief, a Pict and a Saxon.

MERLIN

HE NAME EMRYS is simply a Celticized form of Ambrose, but it is also found attached to another personage, along with the story of Vortigern's tower. In Geoffrey of Monmouth it is Merlin, later known as Arthur's magician and advisor, of whom this tale is told. Its application here to Ambrosius is interesting and suggests something which may have been overlooked in previous works dealing with him. Merlin is later made out to have been a British prince and to have taken a leading role in several battles. Even in his later, more wizardly guise, he is still a military advisor to Arthur. If we take these facts together, an interesting thought arises: did Ambrosius lend some of his character and deeds to the stories circulating about a wondrous child-prophet named Emrys? If so, we have to revise our picture of Ambrosius, the Last of the Romans, to form a different pattern. In one version, Merlin is made to fall mad after seeing his family killed in battle, and as a result becomes gifted with prophetic insight. If Ambrosius had the same gifts, then the luminous nature of his story is somewhat explained and the reason for his preferral before Arthur over his nearest contemporaries becomes clearer.

Whatever the truth, Ambrosius cemented the broken shards of Vortigern's reign in a way which was to prove lasting. When he met his death (of some unspecified sickness, rather than in the field) he left behind a reconstituted system of government across a good deal of the country; he had refortified many of the ancient hillforts, strengthened dikes and re-opened a number of the old Roman roads which had fallen into disrepair from lack of use. He had even re-opened trade-routes with the continent and established a reasonably stable economy. Neither, it seems, had he neglected to prepare for the future. It is almost certain that Arthur was a protégé who had already begun to assume many of Ambrosius' tasks towards the end of the older man's life. Whatever the exact train of events we can be certain of one fact: with Ambrosius gone, the Britons turned to Arthur for leadership and a legend was begun which was to outlast them all.

DUX BELLORUM

HEN WE COME TO it, so little is known about Arthur that he threatens to remain an insubstantial figure whom only the action of the imagination can flesh out. We do not know when he was born, or where (various sources suggest Wales or Cornwall, the Midlands or Scotland, making him truly a son of Britain); neither can we say where or when or how he died. Lacking these two pivotal points, the years between fade into a mist which only an occasional flash of light illuminates.

What is clear is that someone – whom for the sake of argument we may *call* Arthur – drew together the last remnant of Romano-British defence, as Ambrosius had begun to do before him, and added to this the wilder less-disciplined forces of the native kings, welding them into a force powerful enough to push back the Saxon advance to the coast on every side and there to contain them. We also know with reasonable surety that this force consisted largely of mounted men, armed like the Roman cavalry, known as *cataphracti*.

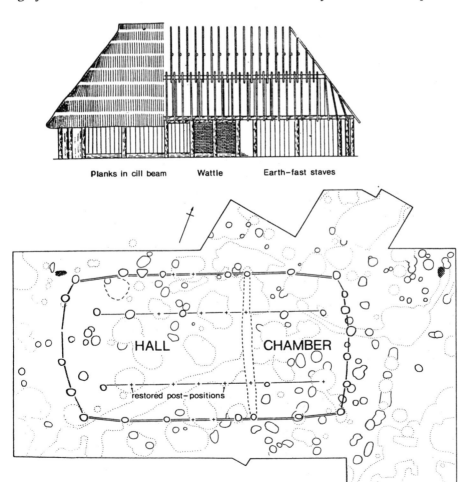

Reconstruction of the Timber Hall at Cadbury Camp.

Planks in cill beam   Wattle   Earth-fast staves

HALL   CHAMBER

restored post-positions

The sheer mobility, as well as the power, of this force enabled Arthur to be literally 'everywhere' at once, and this probably accounts for the widespread sites of his battles. Certainly he fought over a huge front and in so doing inflicted such losses upon the Saxons as to preclude their attacking again in any serious way for perhaps as much as thirty years; during this time they ceased to be wholly invaders and became instead settlers, intermarried with the people they had originally come to conquer and thus seeded the beginnings of the Anglo-Saxon people.

This much we can say with some assurance. The rest must be added from hints scattered through often fragmentary and sometimes fictionalized chronicles; from ancient literary sources preserved in medieval manuscripts; and from the vast sprawl of legend and myth which gathered, almost from the start, around the figure of Arthur.

To begin with we must forget the idea of Arthur as a kingly figure. The earliest sources refer to him as *Dux Bellorum* (Duke of Battles) or sometimes as *Comes Brittanorum* (Count of Britain), while the fact that his name does not appear in any of the surviving king-lists relating to the British monarchy, suggests that he was not of royal lineage at all. Certain old Welsh texts refer to him as *Amerawdwr* (Emperor), but this dates from a later period than the chroniclers and almost certainly reflects a more heroic image.

Gildas also refers to Ambrosius by the title of *Dux*, from which we may infer that he, and Arthur after him, revived the Roman title as part of their campaign to restore something of the old ways to Britain. Certainly the title establishes Arthur as the leader, initially at least, of the Romano-British party. That he later extended his influence to the native British forces may indicate that he assumed a more royal status – but this can only be speculation.

HISTORICAL SOURCES

ET US LOOK MORE closely at what we *do* have by way of sources. As always for this period, written accounts are scarce. Gildas, whom, as we have seen, is not always to be trusted and who may indeed have had personal reasons for the omission, does not mention Arthur by name, though he does describe a nameless leader who fits the bill. Nennius is as enigmatic as ever, despite giving a list of the twelve famous battles, apparently fought by Arthur against the Saxons (see Chapter 4). Bede, in his *History of the English Church and People* follows Gildas more or less exclusively and is anyway writing from the standpoint of an ecclesiastic over 150 years after the event. Apart from these, and a few brief mentions in the earliest Welsh poetry, and various (often conflicting) anecdotes in the lives of British saints, there is nothing. Even here there is a certain legendary quality about the stories which already – even at this early date – portray Arthur as a larger-than-life figure; which he may indeed have been.

Certainly those who recalled him within as little as 50 years of his disappearance saw him as 'the stuff of legend', a figure who stood head and shoulders above the rest of his contemporaries, and whose deeds were already touched with an aura of magic.

Certainly, a great deal of speculation, both historical and general, has been lavished on the figure of Arthur, and many different contenders have been put forward as likely candidates on which to base an understanding of his remarkable hold upon the imagination. Some very ingenious attempts have been made to fill in the gaps of history in this dark period (some of which we shall deal with later in this book). We now know, from archaeological discoveries made over the last 30 years, that life continued in a remarkably undisturbed fashion from the time of Vortigern to the disappearance of Arthur. Certainly, commerce continued in parts of Britain more or less unaffected by the Saxon wars. The high quality of imported pottery and glass found at sites as far apart as Tintagel in the south-west and Dunnad in western Scotland bears witness to continued trading with Mediterranean countries. This would seem to devolve on the areas where a residue of Roman civilisation was retained. In the rest of Britain, where the return to a more tribal existence was marked, there is little or no evidence for a continued presence of such luxury goods.

However there is evidence, from the surviving literary remains of the period, of a flowering of culture among the Celtic peoples of Wales and the Midlands. Much of the poetry attributed to the early Welsh bards, Taliesin, Aneurin and Llwyarch Hen, dates from this period and demonstrates an increasing complexity and richness of language.

There is evidence also for a strong resurgence of native religion about this time. While Britain, like the rest of the Empire, was nominally Christian, there are new shrines dating from this period, such as the one to the god Nodens or Nudd at Lydney, or those of an apparently druidic origin like that at Maiden Castle in Dorset.

Whether Arthur supported this religious revival we do not know, though the stories of him which appear in saints' lives of the period, suggest that his relations with the Church were at least strained, if not openly hostile. It is reasonable to suppose that as the leader of the Romano-British contingent he may have subscribed to the state religion, and in both Gildas' and Nennius' accounts he is described as bearing either the 'image of Our Lady' or 'the Cross of Christ' on his shield at the Battle of Badon, where he crushed the Saxons.

Taken over all, this renaissance of culture, religion and economic life of AD 480–530, suggests that a form of stability had returned to Britain; while archaeological evidence supports this by showing a distinct check in the decay affecting towns and cities after the severence from imperial government. Britain had always been the least Romanized of the colonies, with a strong contingent of the native royal houses (however subject) apparent at every period, and substantial areas in which the British tongue continued to be spoken. With Rome gone in all but a few areas of determined resistance, something like a true intermingling of the two cultures took place, and here again the stability and influence of our Arthur-figure must be given credit.

THE
MODENA ARCHIVAULT

The Archivault of the Cathedral of St John in Modena, Southern Italy, contains what is probably the earliest representation of an Arthurian story yet discovered (i.e. 1100). It almost certainly predates Geoffrey of Monmouth, proving that earlier versions of the legendary tales existed before the *Historia* was written. The story here concerns the rescue of Winlogie (Guinevere) from the castle of Mardoc (Melwas?) by six knights: Galvaginus (Gawain), Galvarium (Gaheris?), Che (Kay), Burmaltus (Durmart?), Artus de Bretagne (Arthur) and Isdèrnus (Ider). Against them are ranged a nameless churl armed with a steel-shod hammer (*martel-de-fer*, *baston cornu*?) and a knight named Carados (Caradoc?). Several attempts have been made, notably by R.S. Loomis and K.G.T. Webster, to identify the scene depicted as originating in either the *Prose Lancelot* (Vulgate Cycle) or the *Lanzelet* of Ulrich von Zatzikhoven. However, both of these post-date the carving, and despite the similarity of some of the names, this precise combination of characters does not occur in either text. The inclusion of Durmart, Ider and Carados does suggest that there is a strong element of the European Arthur tradition, but the origin of the story seems more likely to have been a version of that found in the *Life of Gildas* by Caradoc of Llancarven. The interest of the archevault lies chiefly in its being the earliest known representation of an Arthurian theme, and for the very precise details of armour and weapons twelfth-century) which shows how these were adapted to the times in which the carving was executed.

The Modena Archivault.

In the final analysis, we can only state, along with many other commentators before us, that if Arthur did not exist it would have been necessary to invent him. There is, indeed, always an Arthur-figure in some senses — brought into being, perhaps, by the need of the time. This, before all other legends, and after stripping away all the historical or pseudo-historical facts, is what keeps his story eternally green.

It is perfectly possible, as both Geoffrey Ashe and Mildred Leake Day have shown, to suggest a much earlier date for Arthur's reign. Ashe's theory, as set forth in his book *The Discovery of King Arthur*, may be summarized as follows. According to various European historians of *c.* AD 600 a certain 'King of the Britons' named Riothamus (the word actually means something like 'Great King') crossed the channel in about the year 468, with twelve thousand soldiers, to join forces with the recently-named western 'Emperor', appointed by Leo I. There they fought bravely against Saxons from the area of the Loire, and the Visigothic King Euric, until they were betrayed by the then prefect of Gaul, Arvandus. Riothamus escaped from a battle in which many of his followers were killed, and shortly afterwards 'vanished' from sight and from the pages of history.

This may, Ashe thinks, have been the origin of the stories of Arthur; certainly Geoffrey of Monmouth seems to have heard the story of the British king who fought in Europe, and he makes Arthur a contemporary of Leo I. Whether Riothamus was actually British or, as some have believed, a Breton, is hard to say; but he could have been the original Arthur, in which case we have

to fall back on the figure of Ambrosius to fill the gap left by his successor. It is perhaps still too soon to decide one way or the other about this new contender for Arthur's crown; but interestingly the theory is supported by details in a thirteenth-century Latin romance of the boyhood of Gawain, *De Ortu Waluuanii* ('The Rise of Gawain'). Here Gawain is the illegitimate son of Arthur's sister, brought up abroad and trained in the army of the Roman Empire. His adventures include single combat against a champion of the Persian army then besieging Jerusalem, and, significantly, offering military support to his uncle, Arthur of Britain, who is fighting a rearguard action against raiders on his northern borders. Gawain is specifically described as a cavalry officer in the Roman army, and the picture of the events described are such as would fit very well into the framework of fifth- or sixth-century Britain. We may, without stretching credulity too far, see Gawain as the leader of a relief force from Rome (or Gaul) to aid the stricken Britons – perhaps even that this was the help requested but supposedly not sent in response to the urgent pleas of the Romano-British party. This story is told nowhere else, and in other romances Gawain performs a very different role. Yet he is generally described as Arthur's nephew, and is one of the older figures associated with the legendary king. It may well be that we have here a lost fragment of history which has been preserved in this romantic form while the original version, like so many of the Arthurian sources, has been lost. Once again the setting seems to place Arthur at an earlier time, but we cannot be sure. Until evidence of a more conclusive kind is discovered (an unlikely but not impossible event at this late date) we must consider both possibilities as viable, accepting or rejecting one or the other as we seek for a face behind the mists of heroic British history.

The Blundering Hero

The Quest for the Grail is central to Arthurian literature, but much of the Grail material was added slowly, accumulating mainly in the Middle Ages, several hundred years after the historical Arthur. There is, however, one theme (found in the *Mabinogion* in the long complex tale of *Peredur*) which seems to be the foundation of the highly sophisticated Grail legends. That theme is retold here as the tale of the Blundering Hero, and his name has been kept as Peredur even though he might have had many names during his heroic career in generations of retelling.

The theme behind the Grail legends is very ancient indeed, involving a series of mythical or religious motifs which were central to Celtic culture, in particular that of the cult of the sacred head. In early Celtic sites archaeologists have found sanctuaries for preserved human heads, plus carvings of heads of later date. We also know from classical sources that the early Celts were head-hunters who preserved their trophies in cedar oil or by some similar means. This savage ritual behaviour evolved into a cult and pattern of magical-religious thought which is still mysterious to us today; it also laid the foundations for one of the most profoundly sophisticated spiritual legends of the world, that of the Quest for the Holy Grail. Not until the twelfth or thirteenth century did the fusion of esoteric Christian and pagan Celtic traditions flower as the Grail legends.

How might such mystical or magical lore have been presented and preserved in the sixth century, and how might it have related to the historical Arthur? We can be sure that tales and customs involving sacred heads or skulls were active at that time, and that they were connected to themes of the health of the land, or to the sanctity of certain wells and springs. Furthermore, we may reasonably assume that some of these ancient practices were active within the early Christian Church, as so much effort was made on the part of the political Roman Church to suppress heresy in Britain and Gaul from the fourth century onwards.

Our tale, therefore, is set initially in a Celtic church sanctuary or chapel, in which an acolyte is being taught by a rather strange saint. It is this elder, Father Melchior, who actually tells the tale of Peredur to his anonymous pupil.

Some of the matters touched upon in his retelling would have been crucial to sixth-century Britain, as they involve the relationship between pagan traditions and Christianity, and the dramatic issue of the Roman Church versus the native Celtic Church . . . a matter that was not to be resolved for some centuries. While the Church in Britain and Gaul held to many peculiar practices, defying the political concept of a state Church with firm materialistic ends, the Church in Rome increasingly became an organ of suppression and control. Thus Father

Melchior utters a number of obscure heretical prayers and rituals which are either Celtic or Gnostic, and certainly would not have found favour with the Pope. Some of his utterances, incidentally, were preserved in oral tradition in Gaelic-speaking areas well into the eighteenth and nineteenth centuries, and none of them are mere fabrications or fantasies.

The chapel in which the story is told is built from the remains of a stone circle or sanctuary, as was often the case. In this chapel resides a curious relic; a skull is kept and associated with a water ritual. Customs of this sort are recorded in Scotland and Wales as recently as the present century, and a contemporary example of magical therapy in traditions associated with a skull is given by Dr Anne Ross in her book *Folklore of the Scottish Highlands*. The Celtic reverence for the head, and for skulls connected with water and magical practices is not simply a curiosity from the distant past; it has a deep significance which endures in actual tradition. It conceals and at the same time reveals a profound mystery. In the tale of Peredur certain objects are displayed during a ritual procession in a hall or castle; one of these is a dish containing a severed head. This sequence, with the gradual exclusion of the head in favour of the vessel alone, gradually became the central vision of the later Grail legends . . . yet the head remained in Welsh traditional tales from which the *Mabinogion* known to us today derives.

In the re-telling, the adventures of Peredur are used by the old saint to encourage his pupil to learn about the mystery of the head, to visualise otherworldly locations and beings, and to ponder and meditate upon the role and power of woman. In this last context it is Peredur's mother who lays a *geas* or binding magical condition upon him regarding arms and armour; it is an otherworldly maiden who initiates him into the subtle arts of what is possibly swordplay; and it is an old hag who finally tells him how to lift the *geas* while battling an adversary of terrifying power and appearance.

These are all typical themes in Celtic lore; they also appear in folklore worldwide, revealing deep insights into human nature and development towards maturity, through magical transpersonal psychology which far predates our modern theories. Such insights were eventually woven into the highly ethical and religious Grail legends in an attenuated but coherent and persistent set of expressions.

Peredur, the Blundering Hero, gains his arms and armour in a conflict with a being from the Underworld, and incidentally learns all about fighting techniques during the encounter. At that point we leave him, though in traditional legend he has many further adventures ahead of him. Our anonymous pupil, listening to the stirring teachings of his aged mentor, finally realises that there is more than one type of warrior and that the battle of the spirit is as essential to the land, and to its people, as the clash of swords and spears.

Many are the ballads and tales concerning Peredur son of Evrawg; during the long winter nights when snow presses on the roof thatch and ice drips from the smoke-hole, men and women are glad indeed to hear of his youthful exploits. But I heard of Peredur and his greatest adventure early one mid-summer morning just at sunrise, from old Father Melchior, in his tiny chapel of great stones and turf, roofed with withies and a golden net of flowers to the light.

First he praised God the Originator of the Worlds, crossing himself many times as he intoned the chant; next he drew aside the altar cloth of richly dyed wool, to reveal a mystery that I had not seen before. The altar was of dark oak, almost black, and carved in the semblance of a man sleeping in a little chamber bed or perhaps in his coffin. Many curious designs and solemn triangular faces surrounded this figure; here was the old earth-woman with her generous organ open for all, men on horses and carrying stout spears, three hooded ones staring out into the church, and a procession which wound around the border of the sleeper, filled with tiny men and women bearing a platter on which a severed head was displayed, and a lance that seemed to fountain drops of fluid upon the company. All of this I saw in an instant, interwoven with leaves, coils, serpents, and complex traceries and maze trails; then Father Melchior opened the breast of the sleeping figure, and, putting his hand within, drew out something covered in a pure white cloth embroidered with a cross and flying bird.

I knew that this object could not be the elements of the mass, for they were kept in a hollow in the thick stone block behind the altar, just below the ever-burning lamp with its coiled dragons in bronze and silver, said to have come from Rome, Imperial city. It was as if the father had reached into the sleeper's body and plucked out his heart, and for a foolish moment I expected the old holy man to turn with a bleeding fragment of flesh in his thin hands. The sight of the delicate embroidery calmed my strange imaginings; then Father Melchior deftly eased the cloth to reveal a golden platter holding an aged yellowing skull. I could hardly believe my eyes, and crossed myself several times invoking Saint Brigit with a silent prayer. Hardly had I completed this act when the skull was placed reverently upon the altar, still sitting upon its platter, staring sightlessly to the west and therefore directly toward me.

'This service', said the priest, his back straightening from the bow of age, his weak eyes shining with a sudden fire, 'has been undertaken here in the holy place since before our ancestors came sailing up out of the West. Here, child, is the mystery that may not be broken. . . .' With these words, he stood to one side and let the full light of the early morning strike upon the skull; it reflected in the polished golden dish, and for a moment I saw a great radiance surrounding a face of such unearthly beauty that tears sprang into my eyes. Then it was gone, and I blinked back the water where I had been dazzled by the reflected dawn-light upon the gold.

With slow careful movements, Father Melchior raised a small earthenware ewer, and gently sprinkled water from the holy well upon the skull. Three times did he sprinkle it in the names of the Trinity, three times again in the names of the kings, heroes and bards, and three times again in the names of the Virgin, her mother and her sister. After each sprinkling he carefully wiped the aged bone with a clean linen cloth, and crossed himself three times. Then he uttered the prayer of our Lord, kneeling and remaining in contemplation.

As he knelt I looked upon the skull, looking back at me, where it rested beneath the ornately jewelled and enamelled cross that bore a Wheel atop the Pillar of earth-to-sky. The Saviour had hung upon that Wheel, I knew, but who had once looked out of that skull and what had he known of God or gods or goddesses?

Without further ceremony, the priest turned almost without rising, and sat upon the worn stone altar steps built of three slim huge sarsens laid one upon the other when the chapel was first assembled. The fire in his eyes had dimmed, and he coughed formally. I knew this cough, it was the preliminary to a lesson; I wondered what it might be . . . Jesus and his love for Mary Magdalene, perhaps, or the story-telling contest between the druid and Saint Martinus or that favourite of Father Melchior's in which the love and forbearance of Joseph the Carpenter were extolled. But it was to be none of these, nor was it to be verses from the Gospel.

'So the kings, heroes and bards are tucked in between the Trinity and the Virgins for their safety, and we can begin our lesson without fear of interruption. Listen while I tell of the adventures of Peredur son of Evrawg, which may not be changed in the re-telling though a thousand times a thousand men summon them upon their tongues. This story holds the secrets of the Blessed Head, the Holy Vessel, and the Quest for Peace. Long before our Saviour came into the human world this tale was known to men who walked in darkness and sought the light; by the power of His angels and archangels is it made at one with His revelation. Long after our Saviour departed for the realms of Summer and left us longing for his return, has the tale been upheld and the service of the Blessed Head celebrated at dawn each midsummer. In the maze of time, shown outwardly upon the traceries of the Cross with its pillar supporting the Wheel, we uphold the promise that our Saviour will come again, Christ the only Druid, returning in beauty, in glory, and in victory, blessing all shadows and transforming them to light. Then, in that last day, and only then, will this service end; but until that day all who undertake it through the years of shadow will be known by the name of Melchior.'

I waited, almost thinking that he had forgotten about the story of Peredur in this ritual preamble; as I waited, I wondered why a tale known in every house and tavern and poorly heated steam-room or ruinous public bath across Britain should be given such a holy circumstance.

'Once there was a lad called Peredur son of Evrawg, seventh son of his noble father who was chieftain of the fortress North. But his war-wise father and lusty bloodstained brothers were killed in battle with the savages, and, thinking to save her last son, Peredur's mother withdrew with a company of women to her maternal estate. He was not trained in arms or riding, or even wrestling, though he was big and bonny and strong like the wind upon the hills or a hawk in the mountains. Instead of fostering him out as was proper, his mother had a house built in the forest, where she surrounded him with a veritable tribe of maidens and woman servants, as if this ploy could keep him from the evils of the world.' At the mention of a tribe of women, Father Melchior crossed himself absent-mindedly. I had heard this tale before, and found it hard to be attentive sitting upon the cold unyielding stone flags of the chapel floor.

'Now Peredur was flushed with youth and powerfully innocent; one morning while out leaping great leaps in the sun, he ran with the herd of goats from his mother's farm, bleating as they did, and prancing to and fro for joy. Soon he outran these fleet caprines and sped onwards into the golden green forest; there he met with three hinds which he mistook for goats without horns, and so he herded the deer, swiftest of the swift and wildest of the wild, back to the goat pen. His mother and her nine maidens were astonished at such speed and strength, while Peredur clapped his hands to see the deer leap over the goat-wall and run away once the truth was explained to him.

'Not long after this Peredur and his mother were sitting at the door of the hall, each before a doorpost, his mother before the red doorpost and Peredur before the gold. In the distance through the trees a flashing light caught their eyes, and as it flashed it drew closer and closer, bobbing up and down. Soon they could see that it was sunlight flashing and reflecting from helmets of gilded and enamelled steel atop the heads of three riders.

'Peredur sat with his jaw dropping like a gate to the Underworld, but his mother frowned and muttered. Each rider wore a fine kilt of supple tooled leather set with iron plates and gilded spiral-patterned studs. Each wore a red leather tunic woven with gold wire threads in the pattern of spiralling serpents, and across their broad chests were black belts fitted with silver and steel rings, bearing short flesh-biting swords sleeping in their engraved scabbards. Each bore two spears, long and short, with inlaid magical patterns upon the blood-drinking blades. As these wondrous riders drew close, Peredur could see that the leader bore a helmet on which a wide-winged bird seemed about to leap up into the blue heavens, so fine were the metal and enamel and flashing jewel eyes. The two riders following this hawk-crowned chieftain wore headgear without bird or beast upon it, but their helmets were brightly polished and worked with inlays and spirals and weavings that made Peredur cross his eyes with strain studying their intricate patterns.'

For a moment, Father Melchior paused and closed his eyes; he knew that he had caught my attention and deliberately waited for me to ask a question; but this teaching game was one that I was beginning to understand, and I restrained myself from asking why he had introduced warriors in their modern dress armour into an ancient bardic tale. With a slight cough of disappointment, he looked at me suddenly, as if to be quite sure that I did not sleep after all....

'"Mother, who are these men?" Peredur cried, in a loud penetrating voice such as youths always have. "They are not men," she muttered crossly, "they are... angels. Now be a good boy and run along and play with the pigs for a while, and don't tip the boar on his head again." Peredur knew better than to disobey his mother, and reluctantly left her sitting at the door to welcome the strangers.

'But as every boy knows, Peredur waited until the guests had been welcomed and feasted, until their horses had been fed and watered and rubbed down and re-saddled, and when the guests set off into the late afternoon sun he crept after them through the long tree-shadows. With his grace and speed he ran alongside the startled horses crying, "Greetings, oh angels, what are those long sticks that you carry and why does that hawk sit so still upon your chieftain's head?" And so he amazed the warriors with his speed, his stealth and his stupidity. They dismounted and told him patiently that they were *equites*, which is Roman for horsemen, from the warband of the young King Arthur. They had come upon a mission to bid his noble mother remarry and sulk no longer with her nine maidens in the woods, changing the colour of her dresses every day. But they had little success with such politics, for no man living has yet been able to dictate policy to a Celtic woman. Peredur asked a thousand boyish questions about weapons, horses, and the gathering at Arthur's fortress of Caerleon, and as he seemed a strapping likely lad, though perhaps wanting in wit, they answered patiently before sending him home.

'Thus did he learn about Arthur, his warriors, weaponry, horses, and the bold attempts to bring order to the conflict-torn land of Britain. And of course he ran off home and broke his mother's heart, for nothing would do but riding off to join the warbands just as his father and brothers had done before him. But she laid a *geas* on him that he would not find arms either on earth, under sky, or over water; and being a simple innocent youth he lumbered off to look for something else that might do instead. He took the tattered, haltered old nag used for hauling firewood, and laid a leather bucket, which he squashed flat, over her back as a saddle. He picked up two long-pronged meat-forks from the kitchen, and, as the cook threw an iron pot at him for the theft, stuck this upon his head as a helmet. Then surrounded by wailing women unable to stop him, he rode off after the angels to the gathering of the warriors of Arthur.'

Although I had heard the tale before in the kitchens, or in the high bardic language of the hall before chieftains, Father Melchior filled his telling with curious details, twists and turns, woven as tightly and as mysteriously as the twists and mazy patterns upon the Cross or around the edges of dress armour or a queen's royal robe. The midsummer sun rose high; through the wide-open chapel door the air curled in warm, slow, pollen-filled, gentle breaths. I had risen before dawn, and, with the shock of that strange early service, my two-day fast, and the priest's singsong bardic intonation, I became drowsy. Even as I half-slept I knew enough of the tale of Peredur to catch at the verses where he innocently defends a slandered queen, though Father Melchior cunningly made her into Arthur's own bride, as if the story had happened yesterday and not many lifetimes past. Just as the hero defeated an arrogant disrespectful bully by flipping his fork into the horseman's eye-socket right through his leather mask and on into the brain, I fell over, my forehead striking the moist stone floor. The shock of that tiny fall, and the cool touch of the aged sarsen, laid flat long ago from its upright stance in the druid sanctuary, brought me wide awake in an instant.

Father Melchior looked at me sternly, prepared to wait forever in silence while I suffered the reproach of his watery old eyes. It was certainly time for me to ask an intelligent question. . . .

'Father, why do you warn against women in this story? First the mother of the hero and her maidens, then the insulted queen and . . .'

'That, my child, is a typical error of one who sleeps when he should be awake, eats when he should fast, and daydreams when he should pay strict attention to his tutor. The teaching today is not against women, but against men who see only one aspect of woman. The robust loud-voiced Peredur saw his mother only as a mother; the degraded and insulting robber chief saw the young queen only as a maiden belonging to the king; if you pay close attention in the true mode of priest and poet rather than sleep and grunt like a Roman governor, you will understand certain mysteries. A woman has three aspects, not merely one role, just as the ancient goddesses of Rome and Gaul and Britain were once in triple form, but now are transcended by the Virgin, her Mother, and her Sister.'

Here he muttered a short prayer and crossed himself several times, while I turned my eyes heavenward to seek blessing, and bowed to the altar. On coming upright from my bow I saw the skull, and for a moment it seemed to smile at me in jocular friendly manner from its golden platter in the sunlight. I remembered the gospel story of the Druidess Salome and the mad seer Johannes; perhaps this skull once nodded on the shoulders of some frothing prophet bounding across the moorlands yelping like a wolf. At this wandering thought-ful image I smiled and almost laughed aloud, as if the skull had shared a joke with me, but Father Melchior looked so outraged that I crossed myself several times and sat down abruptly, looking intense and respectful.

'Now Peredur,' continued the priest, 'still wearing his iron cooking pot and carrying his forks bloodied in the service of Arthur Dragon Chief, refused to attend the assembly because of some imagined insult or other from the steward Kei. The two giant blockheads had insulted one another, and thinking to behave in a noble manner (which nowadays means a muddy mockery of both British and Roman civility) Peredur rode off on his stumbling nag, with the queen's favourite table napkin tied lovingly around his arm.

'So it was that he came to a great river, by the side of which lay a lame chieftain or king, grey with age, lined with wisdom. All about this lord were supporters and kinsmen by blood and by marriage, casting nets into the fast clear water and drawing in salmon which leapt high across the foam-flecked rocks. The chieftain reclined upon a rich red golden litter, hung with resplen-dent curtains of green and white fashioned with images of lilies and royal crowns. By his side were two handsome boys, one with red flame hair and yellow tunic, one with jet black lustrous hair and green tunic. These two played chess upon a marvellous board where the pieces moved of their own accord. The light squares of the board were of purest silver, while the dark squares were of exotic ebony blacker than peat; as for the chessmen, they were of jade inlaid with crystal. Each of the horsemen on the board had two tiny golden spears and bright helmets, but the white king was laid out in a litter while the dark king rode a champing black stallion frothing at a bronze bit and hung with tiny silver skulls about its trappings.

'As Peredur stood gazing in wonder at this assembly, servants ran up to him and begged him in soft pleasant voices to dismount and rest. They took his pot and forks, and stripped the bucket from the nag's back as lovingly as if these were arms made by the fabled Wayland Smith in Segontium. None, however, touched the queen's favour tied about his broad upper arm.

'Soon the lame king, for king he surely was, bade Peredur approach, asking him if he played the game of chess. "Alas," cried the youth in his loud penetrating voice, combined of piping treble and gruff bass in most unharmoni-ous mis-union, "I do not know the steps of this tiny dance at all, though perhaps I could learn. How do the little men and women cross from black to white and white to black squares of their own accord with no hand to guide them from above?" The two boys, green and yellow, looked at one another and smiled.

The Blundering Hero. Peredur rides through the forest towards his destiny, armed with cooking pot, forks, and an old bucket for a saddle.

'"I see from your mark of favour," said the king, changing the subject as civilised manners require when a guest displays folly, "that you have already fought honourably and victoriously for the blessing of a woman. Judging by the stains of gravy and honey and the quality of the woven linen, I would say that she must be a queen at least. It is our custom to welcome nobles such as yourself to a feast and to a night of rest in the hall wherein I rule, and all of my line have ruled since the Creator laid out the Four Beginnings beyond the summer stars."

'And without further glance or words, the king signalled to his company by striking a tiny silver gong. Immediately they drew in their nets, and evening came on; bearing the golden bed upon their shoulders his body servants stood upright and tall, while his runners and ghillies blew horns and shouted and hallooed shrilly; the two youths picked up the chessboard and marvellous game pieces and marched along boldly, while riding bards upon white horses plucked harps and sang, and pages bearing long silken banners marked with lilies and golden crowns strutted and stumbled behind, pausing to hitch up their kilts at every few steps. Thus they all processed by the broad shining river into a dark shadowy forest as night fell. As they passed beneath great oak trees, the last rays of the sun touched the branches, and it seemed to Peredur that he passed beneath a tree half of green leaves and half of living burning flame. Then they were on a shadowed forest path, winding through the ferns, with the runners singing softly to the muted harps of the bards, tuned to that evening scale beloved of all Britons.

'At length they came to a level meadow lit not by sun or moon but by the light streaming from the open doors of a great hall set upon pale silver grass. Each pillar of that door was seven times the height of a man, and carven like an ancient giant such as walked the world in former times. One giant bore a surly sneering snarling face, and the other a happy smiling jovial face. So vast was that hall that the runners and ghillies and horsemen and fishers and boys and pages with banners and bards with harps and lads with whips and hounds wearing bronze collars studded with green and blue glass all passed straight in without pause or confusion. In the porch, the company all dismounted and stable boys took the horses and hound masters took the great hounds and mastiffs, coaxing them with raw meat, and scullions rushed up from the kitchens below to snatch away the bag of salmon fresh from the river.

'Peredur looked around him, turning in a slow circle, his jaw hanging slack and his bright blue eyes goggling; the porch alone could have held Arthur's hall at Caerleon or the camp at Camelodunum, or both at once. Through the towering pillars that upheld the distant roof, each pillar shaped like a different kind of tree in its prime and glory, Peredur could see a variety of halls, rooms, passages, chambers, galleries, baths, vaults, stairs, columns, arches, and pleasant walkways filled with singing birds. Some were of rich carven wood, some of rough or hewn stone, others had walls of glowing crystal, while a few were of brightly burnished metal that looked fresh out of the furnace.

'The two boys of green and yellow tunics, red and jet black hair, led Peredur, entranced, taking him by either hand and drawing him gently towards an inner hall. Never had he been more self-conscious, never had he been so aware of his boorish lack of manners or courtly civilized style and grace; bemused and confused as he was, Peredur made a strong silent vow to follow the teachings of his wily old nurse, and to hold his tongue whatever he might chance to hear or see in that place.

'At the doorway to the inner hall, Peredur was met by the steward who gave him bread and salt, and a bowl of silver engraved with stags leaping and filled to the brim with clear water to bathe his filthy feet. Thus he became a sacred guest in that mysterious place, and all unknowing took bonds upon himself that no man may loose without great daring joy and terror.

'When he had washed, a most beautiful young maiden wearing a gown of spring green woven with bright yellow daffodils came up to Peredur, and lightly touching his arm said: "Chieftain, for such I take you to be by your great size and vigour, it is the custom of this hall that any guest shall be obliged to strike a blow at my request. Can you use a sword?"

"I could," answered Peredur as he blushed hotly at her touch, "if I had instruction, but I have had none. Besides, my mother laid this *geas* upon me that I shall not have arms or armour either on earth, under sky, or over water." At this the maiden frowned, and gazed earnestly into the youth's sweaty face. "Nevertheless," she murmured, "you can bear the sword that I request, for here you are neither on earth, under sky, nor are you over sea. But you will not be able to bear this sword when you leave me, and the lifting of a mother's curse must be done alone and unaided."

'Then she took Peredur by the hand, which made him tremble and think that the hall was too hot for the time of year, and led him to a huge stone column rising up in the middle of the place. Resting beneath the stone was a long black iron sword singing and humming to itself with power. "Take the sword," said the maiden, "and strike a blow at the stone."

'So Peredur picked up the sword, which moaned and writhed at his touch, and, striking a great blow at the stone, cut it into two parts; and the sword also shattered into two and stopped murmuring. But the maiden came and joined the stone together with a pass of her gentle hands, and likewise fused the sword as new by stroking it. A second time she bid him strike, and again he broke both sword and pillar. She gently joined the stone and revived the sword again, and bid him strike home with a will. And on this third stroke both sword and stone flew apart from one another and could not be joined together.

'"Well struck indeed," murmured the maiden. "And now I hear my father calling to bid us to the feast." At this the sound of a silver gong rang through every chamber and hall, and they passed into a place lit with great crystals and silver lamps in the shape of serpents. There was a feast laid out upon groaning oaken boards, and all men and women served one another equally of the abundant food and wine and none sat above the other or had precedence of gifts or rich couches.

'Peredur sat on one side of the king and the maiden upon the other; pleasant was the conversation in that hall, and they laughed and talked in high spirits for many hours. But as the feast drew to a close, the two lads of green and yellow entered from a long dark doorway in the shadows; they carried between them a huge spear so fierce that it seemed to draw them forward rather than be supported by their hands. From the sharp blade set in a stout socket there spurted three streams of blood running and flowing over the floor of the feasting hall. Peredur longed to know the meaning of this mystery, but held his tongue just as his nurse had taught him. The assembled company set up a wailing and crying and ululating such as would break a man's heart with grief and sorrow and longing, until Peredur, clutching his tongue with his right hand, could hardly bear to be in that place another moment.

'As the lamenting died away, there was a moment of deep silence, and two immaculate young girls appeared robed in purest white. They bore between them a large platter upon which was set the severed head of a man, gory with clots of blood and horrible with white upturned eyes and matted locks of dark hair. Again the company mourned aloud, and this time Peredur almost bit through his fingers.

'No one spoke a word after this procession had passed, and all seemed lost in a strange languorous trance. Presently a boy servant crept up to Peredur and signed silently that he should follow; thus did the warrior of pot and forks find his sleeping cubicle for that silent and portentous night.

'When Peredur awoke from his deep youthful sleep, a servant brought him warm scented water in which to dip his head and a cup of wine mixed with honey and mint. He stumbled out into the great hall, and found the lame king sitting upon a royal throne with the two youths wrestling at his feet. First one youth would seem to gain the upper hand, then the other, but neither the yellow nor the green could make a winning throw.

'"Which of these two combatants do you consider most strong?" asked the old king. "Perhaps . . . the green one?" Peredur answered uncertainly. "But in truth I cannot tell." "Then try to throw him upon the ground," the king replied gravely.

'Peredur lumbered up to the dark-haired youth in the green tunic, who smiled sweetly at him. After great effort and struggling Peredur overthrew this youth by the fall known as "Jacob's Angel" which he found quite by accident before the kingly throne. As the youth fell, the great hall shook and trembled and the flames in the lamps guttered and dimmed for an instant just as day broke in the land of Britain.

'When he rose from this uncouth sport, Peredur saw the lovely maiden coming towards him where he stood by her father's throne. Her golden and silver mantles shone like the sun and her face was like the light of many stars blessing the radiant moon. Greatly daring, Peredur ventured to greet her, but she would have none of such greetings.

'"Greeting I will not give you, not in the British manner or the Roman," she cried, "for though you are great of strength, you are lacking in wit. What manner of man are you that passes his first test, fails the second, yet passes the third? Because of your silence in the hall of feasting and sorrow, you shall get no welcome from me. But because of your lucky wrestling fall, you may look for me again when you have arms and armour and are freed from your mother's curse." And with these strange bitter words and hidden promise, she turned and strode off down one of the long glittering galleries of that place.

'Peredur was confused and ashamed; he turned to the old lame king, but he was nodding as if asleep; he turned to the two youths, but they were now deep into a game of chess and not to be disturbed. So he turned again to seek his way out of the hall and back to the court of Arthur where the rules of conduct were more direct and simple. As he turned, he wondered how he might find arms and armour and be free of his mother's *geas* . . . and if the maiden really would welcome him again upon such freedom.

'In the great porch, his heart heavy and his mind dull, his body aching from the wrestling match, Peredur waited while servants brought out his nag, neatly groomed, and his well-polished bucket, pot, and forks. As he mounted he heard a wild cackling sound of laughter from behind the doorpost. Leering out at him was a withered filthy old crone; she had a wrinkled warty face, cross-grown brown and black teeth, snarling loose lips, gum-seeping red rimmed eyes, and a hunched back. This hag wore a threadbare black robe stained with old blood and egg yolks and grey powdery scum; she clenched and unclenched her grimy brown hands, bulging with blue veins and sporting horn-yellow earth-filled nails that twisted into long spirals and hooks.

'"Oh my, what a thick-headed buffoon you are," she croaked, sidling crabwise towards him. "Your grandfather must have been a legionary man or tax collector . . . but for a small gift I will tell you where you can find arms and armour that will lift your mother's curse in an instant, but you'll have to jump for it, mark my words. Well, bonny boy, what do you say?"

'Peredur was shocked at this apparition and her candid domineering manner of speech, but he knew that the ancient British code of honour demanded total respect to all women, for this much had his mother and his old nurse taught him from the cradle onwards.

'"I would willingly give you a gift, granny," he replied courteously. "But I have nothing worth giving. My strength comes from God and my lineage and is not my own to give. I am lacking in all skills, save perhaps striking blows and wrestling, and am cursed to bear no leather tunic, arms or armour, which are the very substance of a warrior's life. And above all this I have foolishly offended my host and his daughter, simply by holding my tongue as my old nurse taught me to do so well."

'"Well spoken, lad," the crone cackled and croaked. "You are beginning to wake up at last. Well spoken indeed . . . how many men truly know what is and is not theirs to give? How many men know when they have spoken rightly or wrongly or failed to speak? You are doing well, and in return for your progress, I shall only ask you for a little kiss. Come down off that poor feeble horse, and give me a little kiss, right here upon the mouth." And she pointed with her grimy nailed finger to her livid twisting mottled lips where her crossed rotting teeth stuck out like fangs.

'Now Peredur had learned from his nurse and his mother and the nine maidens in his mother's house that a woman's request was usually a command. He knew which requests could be flouted, and which were to be obeyed no matter how lightly they were uttered. So although he would rather have kissed the daughter of the king, he approached the hag and embraced her gently, closing his eyes. She stank of rotting meat and stale beer; she felt like a bag of putrid bones slithering around in his arms. Her breath was rich with garlic, wormwood, feverfew, vervain and yeasty fungus, while her stomach rumbled like a river underground. As he kissed her, she gently stroked his hair for a moment, then suddenly grabbed it tight in her fist and jerked hard. "Listen to me, little hero, go as fast as you can out of this forest and seek the great mound that lies upon its border. Climb the mound and you will find a tree, and beneath the tree you will find a stone. Blow the horn that rests at the foot of that stone three times, and fight whoever appears for the possession of his arms and armour." Then she boxed his ears hard, pushed him and his nag out of the great porch to the king's hall, and slammed the huge bronze-plated iron-studded doors behind him. "And remember to jump . . ." she screamed as the doors ground clashing together.

'With aching ears and burning scalp, Peredur plodded off down the ferny path, leading his tired old horse. When he came to the border of the great forest, he espied a mound rearing up to the sky, right between tree shadows and meadow sunlight. It was just as the crone had said, for standing upon the summit of this mound was a little gnarled hawthorn tree, beneath which stood an ancient Druid stone. Peredur climbed the mound and picked up the plain hunting horn that lay by the stone. Capping his iron pot tightly over his head, gripping his two cooking forks firmly in his right hand, Peredur summoned up his courage and blew both loud and shrill.

'With the first blast, clouds scurried over the sun and grey sorrowful light filled the sky; with the second blast, hail and rain fell from above the mound in a stinging torrent that stripped the leaves from the hawthorn tree . . . a great scurrying and running and galloping of creatures could be heard all around, though nothing could Peredur see but a sheet of falling icy water. With the third blast, the earth heaved up, and out of the mound reared a huge black man with one eye and one arm and one leg, wearing ancient rusty armour and bearing a huge spear and sword and long triple shield. Shedding soil and rocks from his head and shoulders, he towered over Peredur and his single eye blazed bright green with battle frenzy.

'All that day they fought, and the fight was equal yet unequal, for Peredur had never been in a true battle before with anyone larger than himself and more skilled, yet he learned so quickly that he copied every move that the warrior made. Every jink and jump, twist and turn, thrust and parry, Peredur copied, and by sunset he had many slight wounds, but had learned all of the warrior's subtle art. Not once had he touched the black man with his fork, and not once had he closed in to wrestle him; nor had the giant struck a deadly blow upon Peredur, for always the youth leapt beyond the full strike of his sword, or ducked beneath the length of the spear.

'As darkness drew on, the warrior of the mound seemed to grow in size and move with greater speed; Peredur hurled both his forks with all his strength and saw them strike home, yet no harm came to his adversary. Just as the one-legged one-armed warrior raised his terrible flesh-cutting sword to strike, Peredur remembered the words of the old hag who had sent him to this place, and leapt high off the earth to land hard upon the black warrior's head. As he struck there was a great clap of thunder, and the tree was struck and the stone shattered. The warrior vanished and Peredur crashed hard to the ground.

'He awoke to find himself atop the mound at night, with summer stars shining brightly overhead. Both tree and stone stood whole, as if he had dreamed of their destruction; but by his side was a full set of black leather and iron armour, a sharp sword, and a crested helmet with no less than two eagles flying from its crown.'

At last Father Melchior paused, and I sat in astonishment, thrilled by this heroic ending, but bursting with questions.

'Father, why did the hero . . .', but he laid his hand upon my mouth in the ancient sign for silence used in holy places since the world was young.

'But the crone was . . .'. Again the priest made the sign upon my mouth, and even as I drew in breath, he made it a third time, which was utterly binding upon any man, even a king. I knew that I was meant to meditate upon the questions that I longed to ask and upon the many deep meanings hidden in the old tale and the changes that the father had made in his curious re-telling. How were the women in the tale connected? What were the questions that Peredur failed to ask? What was the meaning of the sword and stone, mysterious procession, and the wrestling bout? Who was the dark warrior in the mound upon the borderlands? One thing at least I knew; that battle had occurred on an ancient mound between the otherworld of the lame king and the human world of Arthur and his chieftains; thus could Peredur lift his mother's curse by leaping high in the air and being free of all bonds. But the rest was beyond my skill; never had I heard such hard riddles woven into a story.

Father Melchior stood and stretched a little, discreetly as befits a teacher before his pupil or a saint before his acolyte. Then he crossed himself several times uttering the formula of the Breastplate of Light, and, lifting the old skull upon its platter, covered it with the cloth. Bending slowly, showing fatigue after the long telling, the priest touched his lips lightly to the covered relic, and replaced it in the secret chamber within the carved sleeping figure's breast. Then he drew the altar cloth over the carving, and knelt to pray, his eyes uplifted to the Cross. He did not summon me to the altar, and I knew that he uttered some silent personal petition to Christ who had hung upon the Wheel and summoned our Ancestors to paradise when he walked across the worlds between the worlds.

As for me, at that moment I suddenly longed to be Peredur, or any brave warrior gaining his arms; I wished that I had a supple leather tunic and sharp bright sword, or scale armour of steel and gold rings woven together and long and short spears; I would ride off to pledge service to the young King Arthur who even now assembled the chieftains and the land owners together to push back the invading savages from the north and the east and the seaways around the land of Britain.

Now Father Melchior motioned that I join him in prayer before the altar. Together we recited the Hymn of the Dancer which the Saviour had taught his beloved company, and the Devotion of the Two Vessels by which faith is embodied, and the Prayer of our Lord which is always heard in every world no matter where the supplicant may be wandering. Finally we intoned the Keystone of the Arch of Heaven, and remained in silent contemplation of the marvellous promise that God has made to Man, signified even today by the mystery of the rainbow that comes and goes without foreknowledge on our part.

Long night shadows filled the ancient chapel; the little dragon lamp from Rome radiated a firm gentle light against the darkness that threatened the land. As I meditated, my imagination was filled with pictures of Peredur, his leaping,

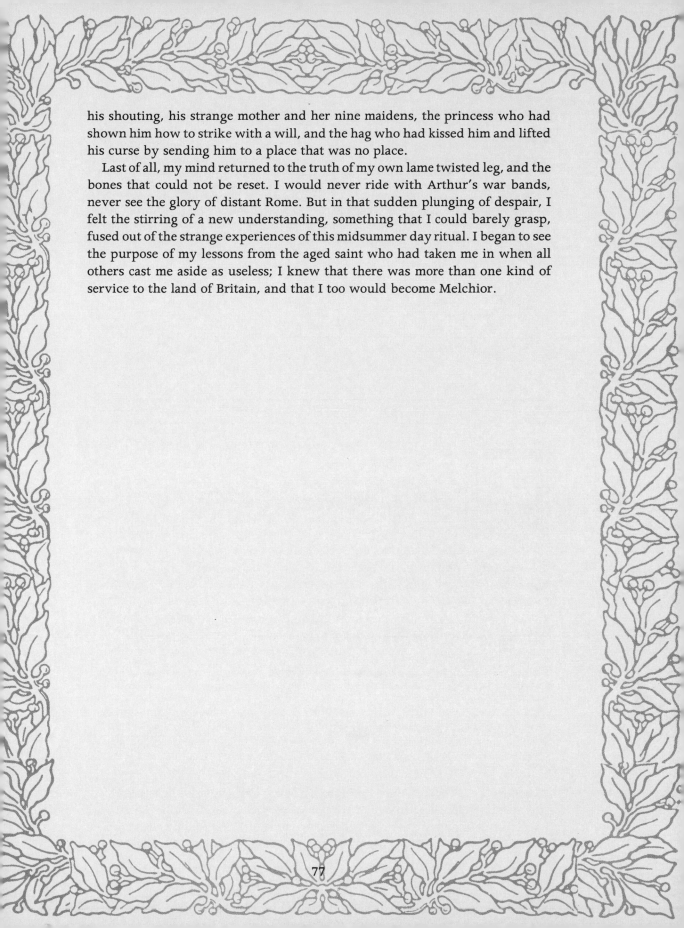

his shouting, his strange mother and her nine maidens, the princess who had shown him how to strike with a will, and the hag who had kissed him and lifted his curse by sending him to a place that was no place.

Last of all, my mind returned to the truth of my own lame twisted leg, and the bones that could not be reset. I would never ride with Arthur's war bands, never see the glory of distant Rome. But in that sudden plunging of despair, I felt the stirring of a new understanding, something that I could barely grasp, fused out of the strange experiences of this midsummer day ritual. I began to see the purpose of my lessons from the aged saint who had taken me in when all others cast me aside as useless; I knew that there was more than one kind of service to the land of Britain, and that I too would become Melchior.

3 · Warriors Male & Female

Tri Brenhinawl farchogion oedd yn Llys Arthur: nid amgen, Nafiens, mab Brenin Denmare; Medrod ab Llew ab Cynfarch; a Howel ab Emyr Llydaw, Brenin Bryttayn, ac nid oedd nag ammerawdyr, na Brenin, a ballei o'u neges i'r rhai hynny, o achos eu tecced, a'u doethineb, pan ddelynt mewn heddwech; a hefyd, nid oedd na milwr, na rhyfwr a allai eu baros pan ddelynt mewn rhyfel er daed vai eu harfau, ac am hynny i gelwid hwynt yn farchogion brehinawl.

Three Royal Knights were in Arthur's Court: *Nafiens*, fon of the King of Denmark; *Medrod*, the fon of *Llêw*, fon of *Cynfarch*, King of the Picts; and *Howel*, the fon of *Emyr*, King of Armorica. Their qualities were, that in time of peace, no King, nor Emperor in the world, could deny them what they demanded, for their extraordinary comelinefs, and wifdom: and in war, no foldier, nor champion, be his arms ever fo good, could withftand them; and therefore, they were called the Royal Knights.

THE CELTIC WARRIOR

HE EXTRAORDINARY vigour and bravery of the Celtic warrior has been acknowledged and celebrated from the earliest times. Roman histories abound in descriptions of wild, naked giants rushing furiously into battle, screaming their war cries, heedless of wounds, often overwhelming their better-armed foes by sheer personal physique and bearing. Taller by several inches than their Mediterranean adversaries, their blond or red-gold hair limed and combed into fantastic shapes; some tattooed, all wearing massive gold arm-rings and torques at neck and ankle, they must have presented a picture guaranteed to turn the blood to ice. 'The whole race is battle-mad,' wrote Strabo, 'high spirited and quick to fight,'; while Polibius, describing a battle at Talemon in 225 BC gives the following powerful description:

. . . the fine order and the noise of the Celtic host terrified the Romans; for there were countless trumpeters and horn-blowers and since the whole army was shouting its war cries at the same time there was such a confused sound that the noise seemed to come not only from the trumpeters and the soldiers but also from the countryside which was joining in the echo. No less terrifying were the appearance and gestures of the naked warriors in front, all of whom were in the prime of life and of excellent physique. . . . The Romans were particularly terrified by the sight of these men. . . .

The warriors in the front rank were the heroes or champions of the tribes; it was their task to offer single combat to their adversaries – something the Romans hardly understood and certainly scarcely ever responded to. Thus in a battle at Clastidum in Gaul in 222 BC when the Roman General Marcus Claudius Marcellus met an army of Gaulish warriors, their leader, Britomartus, having identified Marcellus from his badges of rank, rushed to offer him combat directly. He is said to have been clad in brilliant colours and to have been wearing golden and silver body armour (a variation from the usual description of the naked Celtic warrior). Marcellus coolly calculated the value of the gold and equally coolly dispatched his opponent − afterwards offering the armour to Jupiter as a thanks-offering for his subsequent victory.

In Arthur's time, as we have seen, the most important aspect of the warrior's fighting skills was his use of the horse. In the period we have been examining here, use of cavalry was still rare, and may even have been learned from the Romans. There is no doubt at all that the Celts were superb horsemen, and would thus have been a natural choice to form cavalry units once they were conscripted into the legions. At this point, warriors used to ride to battle, but would then dismount and fight on foot. However, Pausanius, describing a Celtic invasion of Greece, speaks of each nobleman being accompanied by two grooms, whose job it was to see that fresh horses were provided at all times, thus ensuring that a continuous number of armed men was maintained during the battle. We may not unreasonably suppose that similar tactics were employed by Arthur, who must have maintained large horse-runs for breeding and training horses to the demands of the fast hit-and-run assaults which so weakened the Saxon defences.

WARRIOR WOMEN

OWEVER, AMONGST the warrior class it was far from men only who fought against their supposedly more civilized foes. Women had an equally important part to play in battle as well as in their more traditional roles. Indeed the Roman Ammianus Marcellus observed that, while it was difficult enough to deal with the wild Celts, it could be far worse if they called on their women for help, since their blows were equal in force to that of a catapult!

The popular image of women in a heroic society, such as that of the early Celts or as late as the sixth century and Arthur, is that of a wilting sexual stereotype. This is far from the truth; such a misunderstanding derives from orthodox religious propaganda in which women are said to be a source of temptation, but it also arises from our failure to grasp the role of women in medieval legend and literature. The true role is a vital and effective one, with a surprising continuity through a long period of time.

Thus in 697, not so far distant from the Arthurian period in Britain, a gathering of clergy and laymen met at Tara in Ireland, and there established the *Cain Adamnan*, which forbade women and clerics from taking part in war. This is given as one of the benefits of Christianity, since it freed woman from the arduous necessity of attending military society − presupposing that beforehand this *was* a legal requirement.

GODDESSES

A NYONE WHO STUDIES the legendary Matter of Arthur will soon notice something curious about the childhood and training of the heroes: many of them are brought up, advised or educated by women. Thus Lancelot is fostered by the mysterious Lady of the Lake, who is undoubtedly a late manifestation of the Celtic otherworldly Goddess figures. Arthur himself receives his magical weapon, the sword Excalibur, from the same lady. Perceval, apart from being brought up solely among women, also learns most of his wisdom from Kundry, a hideous hag whose origin is clearly traceable to archetypes of Celtic mythology such as the fearsome Irish battle goddess known as the Morrigan.

The Morrigan was one of a trio of war goddesses who appear in Irish tradition, influencing the outcome of battle by magic and inspiring terror into the hearts of warriors. Possessing marked sexual characteristics, and appearing frequently in ornithomorphic or animal guise, this powerful group of goddesses reveals convincingly all the qualities and attributes suggested by the iconography and epigraphy. Appearing at one moment as terror-inspiring hags, at the next as beautiful young women, and yet again as beaked crows or ravens, these goddesses figure with impressive frequency throughout the earliest stratum of Irish mythological tradition. Their names vary, Morrigan seemingly being a collective term for the group as well as being one of the individual goddesses.

(Anne Ross, *Pagan Celtic Britain*)

While individual heroes were usually male in Celtic tradition, they were inspired, advised, trained and finally claimed by a female power. This theme remained active in tradition well into the medieval period, showing astonishing tenacity and endurance; but it was modified in two particular ways. Each of the modifications was an organic development in which one expression of the primal goddess (found in both classical and Celtic pantheons) took prominence. Before citing examples of female warriors from tradition, we should examine the two modifications of the goddess theme in literature and legend.

In *Courtly Love*, or in romantic chivalry in general, this aspect of the theme woman enacts in human terms the goddess Venus, or a similar nature power associated with love, sensuality and generous affectionate emotions. She may also be cruel and strict to gain her desired end, but this is in order to control the *emotions* of her proposed lover. In certain parts of Europe this pattern became virtually a cult in its own right, but the over all concepts permeated much medieval literature, legend and actual social behaviour among the upper class. The woman/goddess was the sole reason for a knight/lover's existence; his deeds, his valour, his gains in either battle or in music and poetry, were all attuned to the code of love. This superficially romantic behaviour masks an essentially pagan and ancient theme taken from collective tradition (the general beliefs handed down as stories and songs through the centuries) fused with literary developments and classical allusions. It is closely connected to the second variation of the same theme.

The woman warrior and her pupil. Young men were often sent to be trained by more experienced warriors. We know from several contemporary sources that these were often woman who were as hardy and fierce as their male counterparts.

The second variation is *personal* or *cultural maturity*, shown through a series of adventures in which a woman or an allegorical figure takes the role of Minerva, Athena, or a similar image associated with mental growth, experiential development, invention, skill, knowledge and wisdom. In some examples this involves not only personal or cultural maturity, but transpersonal levels of consciousness. The difference between variations is that our second interaction is non-erotic. Both involve sponsorship of a male hero by a female, either human, divine, or fusion of both divinity and mortal woman in one form.

MINERVA

 NE OF THE MOST highly-developed examples of the second variation is found in the *Vita Merlini* (1150) in which Merlin is brought to maturity out of madness through the enabling assistance of his sister Ganieda. She shows many skills in inspiring, educating and even manipulating men; but her relationship with Merlin is non-sexual. In the *Vita* the goddess Minerva is directly named as the inspiring agency behind bardic knowledge of the universe, and we find her name in other traditional associations with Celtic wisdom or magical teachings.

Meanwhile Taliesin had come to see Merlin the prophet who had sent for him to find out what wind or rainstorm was approaching, for both drew near together and the clouds were thickening. He drew the following illustrations under the guidance of Minerva his inspirer: "Out of nothing the Creator the world produced Four Elements as a prior cause and root material for all creation joined in harmony . . ."

(Geoffrey of Monmouth, *Vita Merlini*)

Bladud the son of Hudibras succeeded his father and ruled for twenty years [as king of Britain]. He built the town of Kaerbadum which is now called Bath, and constructed the hot baths there so well suited to the needs of mortals. He chose the goddess Minerva as the deity of these baths. In her temple he lit fires which never died or turned into ash, but as they declined became balls of stone . . .

(Geoffrey of Monmouth, *History of the British Kings*)

Geoffrey's chronicle account, drawing upon tradition and possibly upon that of Solinus in the third century, was vindicated by the discovery of the temple of Minerva in the nineteenth century.

As is frequently the case, the classical name 'Minerva' is used as a description of her function . . . it seems very likely that druidic lore was inspired by, among others, a goddess similar in many ways to Minerva. Julius Caesar states in his *Conquest of Gaul* that the Celts worshipped Minerva as the giver of handicrafts and industry . . . he also lists Mercury, Mars, Apollo, Jupiter. What Caesar is actually saying is that gods and goddess with similar functions to the classical deities were found when he invaded Gaul; clearly the independent culture of Celts which he began to subdue would not have been familiar with

A Celtic princess, from a bronze statuette at Vix in France.

Roman god-names. This *functional* use of classical deities persisted in various forms well into the eighteenth and nineteenth centuries when classical allusion was still employed in poetry and prose.

Minerva was the goddess of cultural development, invention, civilisation, and in Britain she was accepted as a variant form of a Celtic goddess with similar qualities . . . probably Brigit or Briggidda. We have a typical example of this fusion at Aquae Sulis (Bath) where a mysterious native goddess of healing, prophecy and the Underworld is fused with the Roman Minerva to make a pan-cultural deity Sul or Sulis Minerva. But Minerva, even in Roman tradition, masks an older figure, probably Etruscan. She sprang fully armed from the head of her father; she was a warrior goddess, deriving from a primal figure in which both life and death were invested.

Minerva also derives from her Greek counterpart, Athena. Both are virgin figures associated with wisdom and cultural development, and the tuition and support of certain chosen heroes. We may see the later more civilised or masked variants of the goddess as increasingly sophisticated symbols overlaying but never totally replacing the primal goddess.

83

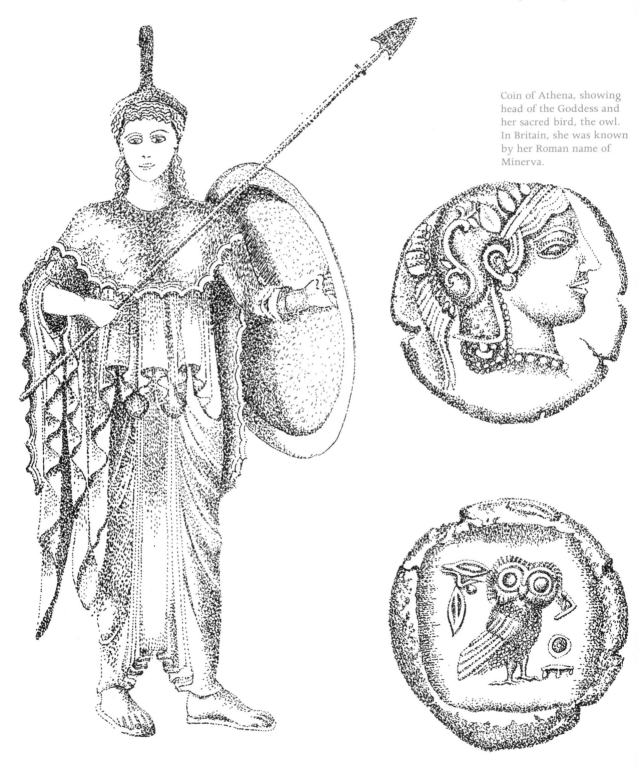

The warrior Athena, sixth-century, from the Temple of Aegina.

Coin of Athena, showing head of the Goddess and her sacred bird, the owl. In Britain, she was known by her Roman name of Minerva.

84

The Celtic goddess, known in Ireland as the Morrigan, took triple form. She was associated with death and battle, sexuality and procreation. She could appear as a screaming bloodthirsty hag or as a beautiful maiden; her totem bird was the crow. We must visualise not one goddess, but a fluid shape-changing collection of feminine beings with divine power. The name Morrigan may be a collective title as well as a specific name. It is in this savage Celtic goddess that we find the origins of the medieval courtly love and wisdom figures. Originally the Morrigan carried off the spirits of warriors slain upon the battlefield, and also supervised their rebirth. We know from Caesar and Posidonius that the Celts believed in reincarnation or something similar, as this was one of the druid teachings.

CELTIC GODS AND THE DRUIDS

The god they reverence most is [like] Mercury. They have very many images of him, regarding him as inventor of all arts, director of men upon journeys, and their most powerful divine helper in trade and obtaining money. Next to him they reverence Apollo, Mars, Jupiter, and Minerva about whom they have similar ideas to other nations . . . Apollo averts illness, Minerva teaches the principles of industry and handicrafts, Jupiter is king of all the gods, and Mars the ruler of war . . . A lesson which they [the Druids] take particular care to teach is that the soul does not perish, but passes after death from one body to another. They consider this the best incentive to courage, as it teaches men to disregard the terrors of death. They also hold long discussions about the heavenly bodies and their movement, the size of both the universe and the earth, the physical nature of the world, and the power and nature of the gods . . .

(Julius Caesar, *The Conquest of Gaul*)

By the medieval period the concept of reincarnation was, formally at any rate, rejected by the Church. The power of the goddess of death and life became symbolised and eventually replaced by the interaction between woman and lover or wise-woman and chosen male student. The interaction became personalised rather than metaphysical or overtly religious, but the transpersonal elements remained, for the hero was always transformed by his experiences. In classical mythology the rebirth is often upon a personal individual level; the hero is changed through his trials, adventures and experiences under the guidance of Minerva or Athena.

QUEEN BOUDICCA

 HIS ANCIENT THEME, therefore, manifested in Celtic culture as certain roles associated with women . . . roles which seem unusual to the modern reader. As mentioned above, women bore arms in the fifth to seventh centuries or later, and this was not regarded as an emergency measure but as part of their normal responsibility under certain circumstances. During the

first century we have the famous description by Tacitus of black-robed druidesses cursing the Roman soldiers who attacked Anglesey in AD 61. While the military under Suetonius Paulinus were thus engaged, the British queen Boudicca raised a revolt in the east of England, fired by violations of justice and rights. Tacitus states in his *Agricola* that the Celts thought it perfectly natural for a woman to lead armies, and made no difference between men and women in this role. Boudicca sacrificed prisoners to a savage goddess called Andraste ('Victory'), by impaling them upon stakes. It is this war-leading bloodthirsty type of woman that may be found at the roots of Arthurian legend, not a pale trembling maiden who faints at the very mention of battle:

Urged on by such encouragements the whole island [of Britain] rose under the leadership of Boudicca, a queen, for Britons make no distinction of sex in their appointment of commanders.
(Tacitus, *Agricola*)

THE HAG

 HE HAG-LIKE aspect of the Morrigan, or Kundry as she becomes in the Arthurian legends, reappears in the medieval romance *Gawain and Ragnall*, where Gawain, who was once known as the champion of the Goddess, is taught, by example, the meaning of chivalry and love. (He learns further lessons from the otherworldly wife of the Green Knight in the fourteenth-century poem which deals with the theme of the Beheading Game retold in this book.) Nor should we be surprised to find Gawain thus undergoing education at the hands of supernatural women; he has long been recognized as a later literary incarnation of the Irish hero Cu Chulainn, who also received his training in weaponry from a woman – though in a manner more direct and savage than that of his later self. This seems to be a reworking of the goddess theme from ancient Celtic culture, but may also have been based upon actual practice, as it is such a constant feature both here and in other stories of a similar kind. The adventures of Cu Chulainn contain a detailed example of this kind of training, in this instance received at the hands of Scathach-Buanand, daughter of Ard-Geimne in Letha. Her base was on the Island of Skye, which bears her name to this day, and she was an instructress of many youths in the skill of arms.

SCATHACH

Donall said that Cu Chulainn would not have perfect learning and knowledge of arms until he went to Scathach who lived to the east of Alba. . . . Cu Chulainn went on the road across the Plain of Ill Luck and through the Perilous Glen. This was the road that he took to the camp where the

Cadbury Camp, Somerset. From the topmost bastion of Cadbury Camp one may look out across the Somerset Levels towards the distant outline of Glastonbury Tor. Local tradition, as well as archaeological evidence, have long associated the figure of Arthur with this Iron Age fortress.

students of Scathach were. He asked where she herself might be found: 'In yonder island,' they replied.

'Which way must I take to reach her?'

'By the Bridge of the Cliff, which no man can across until he has achieved valour.' The nature of this bridge was that it had two low ends and a high middle, and whenever anyone leapt upon one end, the other end would lift itself up and throw him onto his back. A host of warriors from Erin were in that stronghold learning feats of arms from Scathach; Ferdiad son of Daman, Naisi son of Usnech, Loch Mor son of Egomas, Fiamain son of Forsa, and an innumerable host besides. Cu Chulainn tried three times to cross the bridge and could not do it. The warriors jeered at him. Then in a frenzy he made the hero's Salmon Leap right onto the head of the bridge, landing in the middle of it; the further end had not fully raised itself when he reached it and from there he threw himself onto the ground of Scathach's island. He went up to the stronghold and struck the door so hard with his spear that it went through it. 'Truly,' said Scathach, 'here is one who has achieved valour elsewhere. . . .'

To reach Scathach, Cu Chulainn had to travel over sea, and to leap across a perilous bridge. Eventually he found her in a great yew-tree, and forced her to consent to teach him skill in arms. She was also a prophetess, and foretold his future. In a later part of the legend, the hero fights a warrior maiden, Aife, and becomes her lover only through defeating her in battle. We shall encounter this

theme of male/female conflict again shortly, for it reappears in many legends and folktales in a slightly altered form.

Romano-British soldiery, from a fifth-century manuscript of Prudentius.

Scathach was at that time carrying out war against other tribes, ruled by the Princess Aife. . . . Aife was the hardest warrior woman in the world. Cu Chulainn went up against Aife as champion of Scathach. Before going to battle he asked what it might be that Aife loved most. Scathach answered, 'Her two horses, her chariot, and her charioteer.' Cu Chulainn and Aife went on the path of feats and began combat. She shattered his sword, breaking it off at the hilt. Then he cried out, 'Ah, the charioteer of Aife, her two horses and her chariot have fallen down the glen and have all perished!' At this cry Aife glanced up. Then Cu Chulainn sprang towards her, seized her under her two breasts, took her on his back like a shoulder load, and carried her off to his own army. Then he threw her to the ground and held a naked sword over her.

'Life for life, Cu Chulainn,' cried Aife.

'My three demands to me!' he replied.

'You shall have them as you breathe them forth,' she said.

'These are my demands . . . that you give hostages to Scathach, nor ever afterwards oppose her, that you remain here and lie with me this night, and that you bear me a son.'

'I promise all this to you,' she replied.

(*Ancient Irish Tales*; *The Wooing of Emer*, trans. T.P. Cross and C.H. Slover)

It is significant that Cu Chulainn cannot defeat Aife by strength of arms alone; she has him at her mercy, and he has to resort to a trick to gain the upper hand.

In Welsh tradition from the *Mabinogion*, we find the Nine Hags of Gloucester,

Arthur carries the image of the Virgin. In a famous early description King Arthur is said to have carried the image of the Virgin upon his shield or upon his shoulder. Such an image would have been acceptable to both pagan and Christian warriors, for She is the Goddess in all aspects.

who are fearsome warriors and in some legends teach the skills of arms. This is clearly the same tradition as that of Cu Chulainn, but appearing in traditional Celtic tales written out as late as the thirteenth century.

Towards dawn Peredur heard screaming; he rose quickly and went out in his shirt and trousers, with his sword about his neck, and saw a sorceress attack one of the watch . . . he struck her upon the head with his sword so that he flattened her hemlet and her headpiece like a dish upon her head. 'Thy mercy good Peredur son of Evrawc and the mercy of Heaven.' 'How knowest thou, hag, that I am Peredur?' 'By destiny and the foreknowledge that I should suffer harm from thee. And thou shalt take horse and armour of me, and with me thou shalt go and learn chivalry and the use of arms,' . . . and Peredur set forth to the palace of the [nine] sorceresses, where he remained for three weeks and chose a horse and arms.

(*Peredur, Son of Evrawc*, trans. Lady Charlotte Guest)

Elsewhere in the *Mabinogion*, the tale of 'Math, Son of Mathonwy' relates how the giving of arms was held by right by a woman, Arianrhod, whose charactor seems only a thin disguise for a Celtic goddess. She lays a *geas* or prohibition upon her son that he shall never receive arms unless they be from her own hands – something she further swears she will never do. In the end, through trickery and by means of a series of magical illusions, she awards her warrior son the arms he requires to take his place in the world.

This is of course parallel to the giving of Excalibur to Arthur by the Lady of the Lake. In Celtic religion from the earliest times lakes, wells and springs were associated with the Underworld and with female divinity. We find this connection diffused in the various accounts of wells and springs with their otherworld attendents in medieval legend, as well as in the gaining of arms by knights who defend a woman's honour or protect her estate. By this stage, the theme is beginning to lose its more overt paganism, and to become refined into the more familiar guise of romantic chivalry. As late as the sixteenth century, writing during his residence in Ireland, Edmund Spenser included a warrior maiden called Britomart (curiously similar to the name of the Celtic chieftain named by Marcellus) in his astonishing work *The Faerie Queene*.

RIDDLES

IN LATER VARIANTS of the theme, a simple sexual rationalisation begins to appear, but it always masks certain deeper magical symbols. Many traditional tales include riddle-battles between men and women; if the hero answers the riddles correctly, they sleep together. It may be significant that the riddles from oral tradition are basic magical questions found in all mystery teachings:

What is higher than a tree?
What is deeper than the sea?
What is greener than the grass?
What is worse than woman ever was?

Far from being mere jests, these are fundamental questions about material and mystical reality. The hero is once again being taught by a woman.

The role of women in the medieval Arthurian legends is derived from earlier Celtic mythology in which many of the female personae were aspects of a primal goddess. But this appeared in Celtic culture as a direct use of arms by women, at least as late as the seventh century. We may assume, without any certain historical evidence, that women would have borne arms at the time of the historical Arthur. There is no historical account that suggests that women took place in the great battles, or that they were trained in militaristic roles, but every suggestive piece of evidence from classical and Celtic sources implies that women had a tradition of bearing and teaching arms, and that it certainly would not have been regarded as unusual for women to wield swords and spears along with men.

We may also add to all of the foregoing evidence that the Arthurian culture was in many ways a besieged culture, constantly running a number of risks. While organised troops were fighting major battles, the home areas were still at risk from marauding pirates or raiders from the sea; we may assume that every household held arms for domestic defence. Furthermore we should not assume the stereotyped role of women waiting patiently or nervously at home while men are out fighting; a Saxon or Irish raider would have been likely to face a sword-swinging Briton of either sex during an attack upon a settlement.

Apart from the examples which are cited above, the Arthurian woman is not shown as fighting so much as being *defended*. This is not due only to the medieval code of chivalry which demanded the shielding of the weak and innocent. One of the primal understandings of Celtic and post-Celtic times was that the land represented the Goddess herself − the archetypal woman. The warrior did not fight only for his possessions or for his lord, but for the land itself which nourished and sustained him. The British Isles is still understood as a motherland, and has been symbolised by such figures as Brigantia, Britannia or Britomart − the warrior aspect of Elizabeth I. Whether Arthur bore the image of the Virgin upon his shoulder or his shield hardly matters: the fact that the chroniclers place the image of the Mother and Protectress of the land in such close connection with the supreme protector of Britain, is evidence enough that the King and the Land were joined in a mystical bond so mighty that no foe could stand against them.

The Abduction & Rescue of Gwenhwyfar the Queen

One of the most famous and well-known stories in the Arthurian cycle deals with the kidnapping and rescue of Arthur's queen. Chrétien de Troyes made of it his first great foray into the world of Camelot in his *Knight of the Cart*, where it is Lancelot who has the task of rescuing his lady from the evil Meleagraunce. The same story is told, in short form, by Malory. But it is to an earlier version than either of these, which is to be found in the *Life of Gildas*, written by Caradoc of Lancarven in 1150, that we turn for inspiration in our version.

Here, as seems more likely, Arthur is the hero, ranged against a wily, slightly sinister adversary. In Caradoc's tale it is the Saint himself who intervenes to bring about the release of the Queen, but for the purposes of this story Arthur himself must recover his wife unaided – though in the end it is Guinevere (Gwenhwyfar) who solves the impasse with a ploy borrowed from the Welsh story of Trystan and Essyllt (Isolt).

By placing Arthur at centre stage, we realize just how far things changed between the original events of the sixth century and the fanciful stories of the Middle Ages. There Arthur is little more than a figurehead, the central point about which the legends and fables constellate.

So, too, in pushing the whole story further back in time, we find some interesting things happening to the other protagonists in the tale. Sir Kay, for example, the braggart and buffoon of the later stories, becomes again Kei, a redoubtable hero who stands close to Arthur himself; and Melwas, the arch-villain, becomes again Melwas of the Summer Country, an ancient name for the Otherworld as understood by the Celtic people.

The story itself, of the abduction and rescue of the Queen, also dates back many millennia before the time of Arthur. It is indeed a form of a well-known folk-loric motif known as the 'Abduction of the Flower-Bride'. Guinevere herself, like Blodeuwedd in the Mabinogi of *Math, Son of Mathonwy*, can be clearly identified with an otherworldly figure created by magical means.

This may account for the rather unfavourable light in which Arthur's queen appears to be held in many of the stories. She should, given the times, have stood for the figure of *amour courtoise*. Instead we find a rather unsympathetic tone to many of her biographies – probably because many were written by clerics, who could hardly come out in favour of adultery.

Malory's portrait is, as ever, the most psychologically interesting, but the most one can say about the final impression of Guinevere's character is to quote the famous schoolgirl's answer to a question about Arthur's queen, that she was 'a lady much given to being run off with'.

It is said that the wife of the warrior Arthur, she that was named Gwenhwyfar, was the daughter of a giant and that Arthur won her only after terrible slaughter and on the death of her father. As to that – well, I do not know if it is true or not, but I have also heard that he met with a lady in the deep wood and that he bedded her on the grassy floor. Thereafter he brought her with him back to his stronghold at Camulodunum and made her his wife. And it is whispered – though none speak it openly – that she was of the Elvish kind and not of mortal stock, but that when Arthur married her he married the land, for she was the outward sign of the sovereignty of the realm, and brought with her the gift of the apple-tree that never dies and always bears fruit.

But be that as it may, the tale I would tell you now concerns another time, when Arthur was older – though years seemed not to have marked his queen – when the land was for the most part at peace. Then there came to Camulodunum a hero named Melwas, who named himself King of the Summer Country (though all who heard him speak thus made the sign of the horns against ill luck). But he seemed no more than a man for all that, and it is said that the women he bedded found no fault with him in that way. And so he came to be accepted among the war-band and men soon forgot that he had claimed a title beyond their understanding, and took him for one no different from themselves.

But all the while, he cast looks of longing and desire towards the Lady Gwenhwyfar, and when she would not return them he grew bold and maddened, so that one day it was found that the Queen was missing (though none knew how she had been spirited away) and after that it was found that Melwas was also gone – from which it did not take long to surmise who the two riders leaving Camulodunum strangely muffled in cloak and hood had been who had been seen before daylight, heading west towards the Summer Country.

At once Arthur mustered the war-band and set forth in pursuit, though many muttered that such a course could lead to no good and that the way ahead would soon leave this world behind. Only Gwalchmai and Lugh (who were said to love the Lady Gwenhwyfar equally) refrained from questioning their Lord, and because of this Cei and Bedwyr, Cador and Ydol also kept silence and hastened to keep pace with their grim lord who drove his mount hard from the anger that raged within him.

And for a while the way was easy and the trail not hard to follow, but in a while the character of the land changed, and there were less places that men knew from hunting there, and soon these were gone also, and the war-band

The Rescue of Gwenhwyfar. Arthur fights the Otherworld champion to rescue his queen.

rode through a dim world which seemed scarcely there at all, at which many were seen to cast looks of apprehension over their right shoulders, while others kept their faces between their horses' ears and looked neither right nor left.

Now whether they rode into the Otherworld I cannot say, but after they had followed that road for no longer than it would take to cover eight leagues from Camulodunum, they were in a place unfamiliar to any one among them. Where there should have been trees on either hand there were fields of standing corn, and though it seemed past the mid-point of the day, yet the sun stood still in the sky and burned down upon the warriors until they began to tire and their mounts to stumble beneath them. And then at last Arthur called a halt, and looking at them grimly said that he required none to follow him that were afraid of that place, but that he would go forward alone if need be while they waited his return. There were those who felt mindful to remain there, but when they fell to thinking of how it would be to be lost in that place without their leader they all pressed to be allowed to go where Arthur went. And without a word he lead the way onward, seeming to know where he should go.

And sure enough, before long there was the gleam of sunlight on water, and the war-band came to a place of creeks and narrow water-ways surrounded by great reed-beds that seemed alive with birds of many kinds; and there in the centre of that strange, shifting landscape, was a hall of wood, ornately carved, with a ring of sharpened stakes set round it and a gate firmly barred. And Arthur rode up to it, with Lugh and Gwalchmai, Bedwyr and Cei at his back, and set up a cry that made all the birds on the margins of the water-ways rise into the air on sudden wings. And the cry was to Melwas to come forth.

Soon enough the head of the Lord of the Summer Country appeared above the row of sharp spikes and looked down upon the warriors of Arthur, and laughed aloud to see them there.

'Melwas, you have my wife,' said Arthur with iron in his voice. 'Give her up or pay the price with your life.'

'I think not, Arthur,' Melwas answered. 'You have no power here unless I give you leave; only thus have you come so far,' and he raised a hand and spoke words of command whereat one half of the war-band found themselves unable to move either hand or foot, and then all knew for certain (if any still doubted it) that Melwas was no ordinary man. But Arthur did not cease from looking at Melwas, eye to eye, and he said, 'This quarrel is between you and I, Melwas of the Summer Country. Let you come forth and we will settle it man to man.'

But Melwas only laughed and said, 'Since I am not a man, that would be no contest; but if you, or one among you will offer to meet my champion, then it shall be decided thus which one of us will keep your queen.'

Lugh and Gwalchmai would both have spoken then, but Arthur held up his hand and said, 'I alone shall answer this challenge,' and he got down from his grey steed and drew the sword Caledfwlch, that men say was given to him by the goddess of the lake, and set himself ready to meet whatever might come.

Presently the gate of Melwas' stronghold opened and there came forth a fierce and terrible warrior, a span taller than any there. He was tattooed all over with spiral patterns, and carried a great axe in his hands; and many there were who deemed him kin to the Green Gnome with whom Gwalchmai played the Beheading Game and won; and even Lugh of the Strong Arm drew back a pace when he saw the size of the warrior. But Arthur merely smiled and said: 'This one has need of cutting down to size,' and he went forward unafraid.

Of that combat men tell many tales that are even longer in the telling than this whole adventure; therefore I will say only that it lasted throughout all the long hours of the afternoon and at the end of it the grass was stained red with blood and the breaths of the two warriors came harsh and heavy. But neither might find advantage over the other; for while Melwas' champion had the strength of ten men and the swiftness of the Otherworld about his movements, Arthur was guarded by the power of his sword. And so at last Melwas himself appeared in the gateway and bade them stop, and then he summoned his followers within to bring forth the Lady Gwenhwyfar, and said that she might settle this dispute between them, for no other way was there that the matter could end, unless it be in bloody battle or dark enchantment.

And Gwenhwyfar, whom none might look upon without loving her for the beauty and gentleness of her appearance, took thought how best to mend this sorry matter. And at the end she spoke thus (and let it be known that those who say these words were spoken of the woman Iseult and her lover Drystan, that they are liars):

'Let this be the judgement between Arthur and Melwas; that I shall be with one while the leaves are upon the trees and with the other while they are not, and to this both must agree.'

Then Arthur and Melwas looked long at each other and Gwenhwyfar, and so it was agreed between them both; and Melwas spoke first and said that he would have her while there were no leaves on the trees (for he deemed that then the nights would be longest). And Arthur laughed and said: 'Holly and ivy and yew keep their leaves until death; you have lost, Melwas, my queen is restored to me.'

And for that his given word was binding, Melwas gave up the Lady Gwenhwyfar, though he did so with ill grace; and the war-band found that movement was restored to them, and so they left that place and returned to Camulodunum, which seemed but a short ride after all from the Summer Country. But it is said that, afterwards, Lugh of the Strong Arm returned there and slew Melwas – but there are many tales told of Arthur's greatest warrior and I am unable to say which are true and which are not.

4 · Battle on Land & Sea

Tri châd Farchawg oedd yn Llys Arthur: Cadwr, Iarll Cernyw; Llawnfelot dy Lac; ac Owain ab Urien Reget: Cynneddfau y rhain oedd, ni chilynt nag er Gwayw, nac er Saeth, nac er Cleddyf, ac ni chafas Arthur gywilydd mewn brwydyr dydd i caffai ef weled eu hwynebeu, ac am hynny i gelwit hwynt Câdvarchogion.

Three Battle Knights, (or Generals of Horfe) were in King Arthur's Court: *Câdwr*, Earl of Cornwall; *Lancelot du Lac*; and *Owen*, the fon of *Urien*, Prince of Reged. They had this quality, they never gave way for fear of a fpear, fword, or arrow; nor was Arthur ever put to fhame in battle, if he faw their faces that day in the field; and therefore, they were called the Knights of Battle.

NENNIUS AND THE BATTLES

HE NAME OF Arthur has been at the centre of controversy almost from the moment when he stepped from the shadows to become one of the great figures of history and legend. Nor has this controversial aspect ceased today, when scholars still argue hotly over dates, places and people associated with Arthurian Britain. Indeed, as we have seen, there are still those who deny the very existence of Arthur; while few can agree as to when or where he lived.

Almost no aspect of Arthur's life and times has received as much attention as the twelve famous battles in which he drove back invading Picts, Scots and Saxons and successfully ended their encroachments into mainland Britain for some thirty to forty years. Nennius lists these victories in a famous passage of his *Historia Brittonum* as follows:

The first battle was at the mouth of the river called Glein. The second, the third, the fourth and the fifth were on another river, called Dubglass, which is in the country of Linnuis. The sixth battle was on the river called Bassas. The seventh battle was in Cellydon Forest, that is, the Battle of Cat Coit Celidon. The eighth battle was in Caer Guinnion, and in it Arthur carried the image of the Holy Mary, the everlasting Virgin, on his shield, and the heathen were put to flight that day, and there was a great slaughter upon them, through the power of Our Lord Jesus Christ and the power of the Holy Virgin Mary his mother. The ninth battle was fought in the City of the Legion. The tenth battle was fought on the bank of the river called Tribruit. The eleventh battle was on the hill called Agned. The twelfth battle was on Badon Hill and in it nine hundred and sixty men fell in one day, from a single charge of Arthur's, and no one laid them low save he alone; and he was victorious in all his campaigns.

(Nennius, Ch.56, trans. J. Morris)   Map of Arthurian Britain.

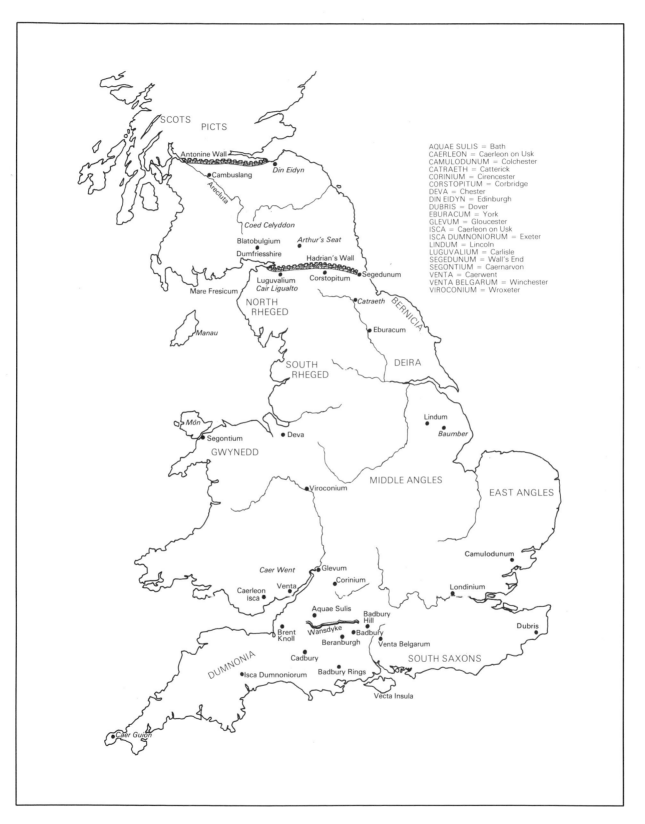

SCOTS

PICTS

Antonine Wall

●Cambuslang

Din Eidyn

Arecluta

Coed Celyddon

Blatobulgium
Dumfriesshire

Arthur's Seat

Hadrian's Wall

Luguvalium
Cair Ligualto

Corstopitum

●Segedunum

Mare Fresicum

NORTH
RHEGED

Catraeth

BERNICIA

Manau

SOUTH
RHEGED

Eburacum

DEIRA

Môn

●Segontium

GWYNEDD

●Deva

Lindum

●Baumber

MIDDLE ANGLES

EAST ANGLES

●Viroconium

AQUAE SULIS = Bath
CAERLEON = Caerleon on Usk
CAMULODUNUM = Colchester
CATRAETH = Catterick
CORINIUM = Cirencester
CORSTOPITUM = Corbridge
DEVA = Chester
DIN EIDYN = Edinburgh
DUBRIS = Dover
EBURACUM = York
GLEVUM = Gloucester
ISCA = Caerleon on Usk
ISCA DUMNONIORUM = Exeter
LINDUM = Lincoln
LUGUVALIUM = Carlisle
SEGEDUNUM = Wall's End
SEGONTIUM = Caernarvon
VENTA = Caerwent
VENTA BELGARUM = Winchester
VIROCONIUM = Wroxeter

Caer Went

●Glevum

Camulodunum

Caerleon
Isca

Venta

●Corinium

Londinium

Aquae Sulis

Badbury
Hill

Wansdyke

●Badbury

Dubris

Brent
Knoll

Beranburgh

Venta Belgarum

DUMNONIA

Cadbury

●Isca Dumnoniorum

Badbury Rings

SOUTH SAXONS

Vecta Insula

Caer Guion

Third-century graffito of a Roman cataphract.

So much ink has been spilled over the proposed sites and dating of these battles that the subject has become one of great complexity. New theories and restatements appear every year, with resulting confusion for those who are not specialists. In fact, it is unlikely that we shall ever know the truth. On existing evidence, even with the full weight of contemporary scholarship, Nennius' list bears little resemblance to identifiable place names. Nor is one helped by those who have suggested that the old chronicler made up the list, compiling it from various sources and attributing battles of other leaders to Arthur. However, the very difficulty of most of the names point to a degree of authenticity, since Nennius would have been more likely to choose well-known sites (at least in his own day) for any such fabricated list.

R.G. Collingwood, whose masterly *Roman Britain and the English Settlements* stood as a standard reference work on Arthur and his times for many years, was among the first seriously to examine the question of the battles. He poured scorn on Nennius because, of the twelve battles, eight seem to be in the north of Britain, and the remainder in Wales or the west. None of these areas, as Collingwood points out, ever seem to have been either threatened or occupied by the Saxons – though, in fact, as we shall see, more than half of Arthur's campaigns were probably against other enemies. Ignoring the fact that the reason for the non-appearance of Saxon remains in the western part of the country may be because Arthur was active there, Collingwood goes on to

Bosphoran warrior from Tanais near the mouth of the Don.

relocate the battles in the south – chiefly in the area of what is now Sussex. Thus the great forest of Cat Coit Caledon (battle number seven) becomes part of the Sussex Weald, while Guinnion (battle number eight) is interpreted as variously Caer Wen, Caer Gwent, Caer Silurium, Venta Belgarum or Winchester. Drawing on known Saxon settlements and the lack of battle burials to support his evidence, Collingwood is unwilling to concede that the Saxons – even as an advance army – ever penetrated as far as Bath or Badbury Rings, where others have placed Arthur's greatest battle of Badon.

Another expert in the field, O.G.S. Crawford, observes that most annals rarely give more than one battle per year and that Nennius' list could have been fought over twenty years or so. He therefore concludes that it is unlikely they could all have been associated with Arthur. However, he acknowledges that not all the battles need have been against the Saxons, but that in all probability they included both Picts and Irish. We must also not forget that Nennius states that Octa and Ebissa, Hengist's son and nephew, were 'given land in those regions

101

which are in the North next to the wall . . . ' and that they sailed from there to ravage Orkney. This gives credence to at least some of Arthur's campaigns having taken place in the north.

Crawford's image of Arthur as a petty chieftain, in military command of tribal Celts against raiders or invaders, seems to fall short of the truth, as does his theory that Nennius' list preserves battles fought by the tribes against such invaders and recorded subsequently in bardic sources as part of a supposed Celtic resistance.

Various other writers have suggested other solutions to the problem of the sites. P.K. Johnstone, on very tenuous evidence found in the biography of the sixth century St Finnian of Clonard, declares that Badon was on the lower Severn, and that the Saxons were camped there in force and that Arthur defeated them totally. In reply D.P. Dobson suggested Brent Knoll as a contender for Badon. Roman and Romano-British finds have been made there, including a Roman cuirass, and there are indeed traditions that Brent Knoll was given to the monks of Glastonbury by Arthur, while the Rev. Armitage Robinson, in his history of Glastonbury, says that Arthur took the warrior Ider

Sir Galahad by Edward Burne-Jones.

Mounted warrior from the Antonine wall.

102

to fight against three giants at Brent Knoll. However, none of this really adds up to a positive identification – although it must be admitted that the positioning of Brent Knoll, close to Badbury Rings, on the coast at a place where the Saxons would have been likely to land, make it unwise to rule out this identification totally, and, as we shall see, recent opinion has suggested that it may be identified with another of the battle sites.

Amongst the more recent attempts to identify the twelve sites, that of Nikolai Tolstoy, demands close attention. Tolstoy's findings are summarised here as the most likely and up-to-date results of accumulated scholarship.

The Battle of Glein, Tolstoy thinks, was probably fought against a recent settlement of Frisians, perhaps under Octa. He dates it as around 496 and places it at the River Glen in Northumberland.

Battles two, three, four and five – according to Nennius all fought on the river called Dubglas in the Country of Lindsay – were probably fought against Scots from Dalriadian Ulster. The present River Douglas is only three miles from the area of Lennox (which may be Linnius in Latin) and there are tribal genealogies claiming descent from Arthur ic Uibar among the Campbells of that region.

The sixth battle, on the River Bassus, is identified as Cambuslang, marked as the burial-place of the Pictish chieftain named Caw. According to various genealogies (page 143) Gildas was Caw's son, while his sister, Cwyllog, was married to Medrawd, Arthur's nephew/son and his greatest enemy. The story is told that Arthur slew Caw in battle and that this was the reason why there is no mention of him in Gildas' history of the period. Another son, Hueil, kept up a feud or *galanas* with Arthur until he also fell to the Dux's sword. The River Bassus or Bas cannot be traced, but Ca*mbus*lang is derived from 'camus long' – the bight of ships – so it is not unreasonable to suppose that this battle might have been a sea-going engagement, perhaps even against Hueil, who is often referred to as a pirate.

The seventh battle at Cat Coit Caledon has long been identified as taking place in the area of the ancient Caledonian Forest. Tolstoy further narrows it down to a point on the Roman road where it crosses the mountains where the three areas of Peebles, Lanark and Dumfries meet. This is near to Arthur's Seat, and south of Hart Fell where Tolstoy's recent researches have placed the area once frequented by Merlin. If the adversaries here were not Hueil's Pictish pirates they could have been a colony of Saxons from Dumfriesshire, near the Solway Firth. It is worth noting (again with Tolstoy) that the Picts were probably expelled from the Lowlands sometime between 450 and 550, and that the Kingdom of Rheged, the primary British establishment of power in the North, was probably established at this time – perhaps with Arthur's help. Certainly, if this is so, it would have formed a permanent bastion against raids from the further north (Orkney or the Highlands). This in turn matches well with the records of Arthur's association with Urien, King of Rheged, and his son Owein.

Battle number eight, Guinnion, is tentatively identified as Caerguidn (Land's End) fought against a Saxon leader with the oddly British name of Cerdic in about 500.

The ninth battle, at the City of the Legions, has given much trouble, since

The Battle of Badon. Here Arthur with his force of mounted warriors inflicted a crushing defeat upon the invading Saxons. After this they made no further incursions for many years.

there are several places which bore this title in Arthur's day. Chester was a strong contender for a number of years, but Tolstoy's suggestion is Exeter, Isca Dumnoniorum, called by the Britons *Cair Wisc*. A Welsh poem from the thirteenth-century *Black Book of Carmarthen* describes a battle against the Saxons in which Arthur is commander and Geraint ap Erbin his general. In the *Triads* Geraint is described as 'one of the three fleet-owners of the Isle of Britain', and the poem establishes his harbour at Llongborth (which means ship-harbour). Geraint was prince of Dyvnaint (Devon) and Exmouth Haven seems a likely spot for his harbour. Tolstoy suggests that Cerdic, defeated at Land's End, turned and gave battle at Exeter, where Geraint was killed.

We shall examine evidence for battle at sea shortly; meanwhile, the tenth battle occurred at or on the River Tribuit or Tryfrwyd and the eleventh on Mount Agned, and it is here that Tolstoy makes the identification of the hill with Brent Knoll, and has the battle take place on the area of sands surrounding it – the Serts Flats and the Berrow Flats.

The twelfth battle, that of Badon, or *Mons Badonicus*, is the final conclusive victory against the Saxons. It established peace in Britain for the remainder of Arthur's lifetime, and like all the rest it has been the subject of much argument over the years. Geoffrey of Monmouth placed it at Bath in Somerset (now Avon), and Tolstoy agrees with him, setting it at Bathampton Down, just outside the present city, dating it at 501 – though we would suggest a slightly later date of 515. The statement in Nennius that Arthur slew hundreds of men single-handed has caused many commentators to believe that the whole matter is simply another fabrication, even allowing for the Celtic love of exaggeration. In fact, it

Sarmatian warrior from Chester.

seems clear that the reference is simply to the daring and strength of Arthur's picked band of warriors, whose prowess so impressed their fellows that legends began to grow from that moment.

Wherever we believe the twelve battles were fought, there is no avoiding the outcome, which is attested to by historical and archaeological evidence of a virtually irrefutable nature. The Saxons *were* repulsed, for long enough to take on the nature of settlers rather than invaders. If, as Tolstoy suggests, Arthur established and manned a series of forts, possibly *baddan-byrigs*, a chain of 'Badons' stretching from Badbury Rings in Dorset to Baumber in Lincolnshire, this is in line with archaeological evidence already provided by John Morris in his *The Age of Arthur* as to the distribution of finds indicating Saxon presence in the south-east.

CONFLICT AT SEA: ARTHUR AND NAVAL WARFARE

UCH EMPHASIS has been placed upon Arthur's land campaign and the battles specifically noted by early chroniclers; we have already discussed the two major theories held by modern historians and scholars, in which Arthur's battles are either located in the north or in the south west of Britain. With a chronicled list of obscure sites to be compared to actual locations, there is little wonder that the true placement of Badon

A mounted Saxon warrior from Hornhausen, Germany,

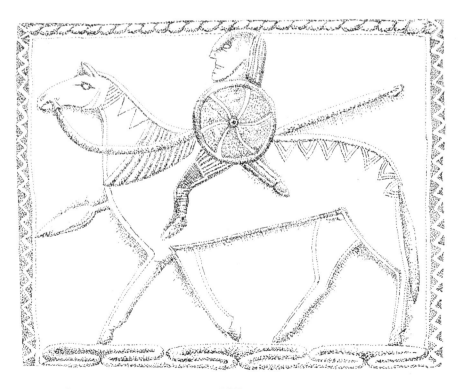

or Camlan and the rest has occupied so much attention and provoked so much dispute through the years.

Britain is a small island; maritime commerce, fishing and general mobility are fundamental aspects of British culture. Indeed, until the recent development of air transport, they were essential to survival. Maritime activity, freedom of the sea, is therefore a major issue in the context of Arthur's war against the Saxons and other invaders. No specific sea battles are listed in any Arthurian record (though as we have seen one at least may be so described), but there is evidence of sea-fighting traditions among the Celts, particularly those of the south-west and of Brittany which held close ties to both Wales and south-west England and Cornwall during the fifth and sixth centuries.

The main enemies of the Britons were the invading Irish and Saxons; both came, inevitably, by sea. During the late Roman years of occupation, sea forts were built against invasion; but by Arthur's time inroads had already been made in the east by Saxons, and the concept of static defence gave way to that of mobile units. Use of cavalry later led to medieval legends of knighthood associated with the period in romantic retellings of early chronicles. We can be sure, however, that there was no Arthurian navy in the modern sense, nor even in the style developed by King Alfred (849–901) who is often wrongly cited as the founder of the British navy. A true state navy did not begin to appear until the seventeenth century under the organisational talents of Samuel Pepys; it was this quite late systematic development of the navy that led to a vast Empire dominated by British sea-power, in the eighteenth and nineteenth centuries.

Nor should we assume that any sixth-century British maritime organisation was modelled upon that of the Roman navy; organisation and manpower for such a development simply were not present in the post-Roman period of invasion and conflict. Furthermore, the new wave of Celtic independent consciousness precluded Roman-style organisation upon a large scale.

If we imagine an Arthurian 'navy' at all, it must be as a motley collection of vessels ranging from swift lightweight scout ships to occasional fighting vessels of a larger size built specifically for warfare or converted from merchant ships. Such larger vessels may have been employed to move troops, and would also have been part of any concerted campaign within reach of inlets and rivers where supplies of arms and fodder could be landed or taken on board.

Geoffrey of Monmouth states in his *History* that Arthur built or assembled a fleet of ships to invade Europe; in this statement he seems to be echoing the earlier and historically-proven invasion of Maximus in 383, an ill-fated claimant to the Imperial purple who invaded from Britain and enjoyed considerable success for a short period. To make his invasion and following troop movements successful Maximus needed ships; it is likely that he drew upon a similar motley collection of native and Roman-style vessels to that which would have been available to Arthur in the following century. When we consider that there are still wooden ships of the eighteenth and nineteenth centuries afloat and in some cases restored and sailing today, it is not unreasonable to assume that the Britons may have drawn upon shipping built during the occupation as well as contemporary craft.

Apart from Geoffrey's statement suggestive of Maximus rather than Arthur, but nevertheless connected to an oral or chronicle tradition, there are a number of other useful references which help us to build a picture of the maritime capabilities of the Britons and Celts against invaders during the fifth and sixth centuries.

Battle at sea. British scouts in hide boats attack an invading Saxon ship.

Our first important source is an early one describing the cultural background and naval skills of the Celts in Brittany. Julius Caesar, writing in 52 BC, gives a graphic description of powerful fighting vessels. Although this war fleet would have been destroyed or absorbed by the Romans, Caesar's description gives us some indication of shipbuilding skills and maritime warfare among the Celts of an earlier period . . . traditions of which may have survived in both practical and patriotic or legendary terms into the post-Roman period.

The ships of the Gauls were built and rigged in a different manner from ours. They were made with much flatter bottoms to help them ride shallow water caused by shoals or ebb tides. Very high bows and sterns fitted them for use in heavy seas and violent gales, and the hulls were made entirely of oak to enable them to withstand shocks and rough usage. The cross-timbers were beams a foot wide fastened with iron bolts as thick as a man's thumb. Anchors were secured with iron chains rather than ropes, and sails were made of raw hides or thin leather, either because they were ignorant of flax, or more probably because ordinary sails would not stand the violent storms and squalls of the Atlantic, and were not suitable for such heavy vessels. In meeting them the only advantage our ships possessed was that they were faster being propelled by oars; in other respects the enemy ships were better adapted for sailing in treacherous and stormy waters. We could not injure them by ramming as they were so solidly built, and their height made it difficult to hit them with missiles or use grappling irons to board. Furthermore, when it began to blow hard they ran before the wind and could weather storms more easily; they could bring to in shallow water with greater safety, and when left aground by the tide had nothing to fear from reefs or pointed rocks . . . whereas to our ships all these risks were formidable.

(Caesar, *De Bello Gallico*)

Caesar is describing warships admirably suited for the seas and weather of the Atlantic; such sea conditions do not change with the coming and going of empires, and shipping employed during the centuries following would have been equally well adapted. In contrast we have evidence that Saxon ships may, in some cases, have been unwieldy; and while we cannot compare Caesar's early description directly with remains of Saxon vessels built five hundred years later, we may infer that the ship-building skills and traditions of the Gauls and Britains were more advanced than those of the Saxons.

In the Nydam bog one of the [Saxon] boats has been preserved. Low amidships it is 77 feet long by 11 feet, and clinker built . . . the rowlocks for the fourteen oars a side were also tied to the gunwale and each oar went through another rope . . . As a result the rowers could only row in one direction; the ship was steered by a large back-paddle. And there was scantly manoeuvring power; the buoyant frame could take neither mast nor sail, and needed much ballast. Some forty persons could probably have crushed in for a chancy sea voyage.

(Jack Lindsay, *Arthur and His Times*)

In contrast to this clumsy vessel, we have a contemporary description from the poet Sidonius:

The Armorican March awaited the Saxon pirates who think it sport to plough the British sea with hides and cleave blue waters in stitched boats.

It seems likely from the above that both Celts and Saxons used hide vessels; such light and mobile craft were still used in Ireland well into the twentieth century, particularly for fishing. Numerous theories and experiments have been made with the use of hide vessels for larger long-distance sailing, and they have been found to be successful. Thus the contrast between the efficient strong oaken ships described by Caesar, and the later clumsy Saxon oarship summarised by Lindsay represent two extremes within which it is risky to suggest any definite comparisons.

Britain was famous for certain trade goods, including corn, lead, gold to a lesser extent, hunting dogs, slaves, wool, carpets, and woven cloth or actual garments. Such movement, either in the form of imperial tribute or free trade, implies an active fleet of ships and sailors; after the so-called Roman withdrawal (which was actually a slow decline of authority) trade persisted between Britain and Gaul. Despite diminishing Imperial influence and continual barbarian inroads the link between Britain and Gaul remained strong; we may visualise a situation in which armed merchant ships sailed across the channel ready and able to defend themselves against piracy. Such traders would form the foundation of any sea force organised by Arthur.

The coastal defence system in the south-east of England was built towards the close of the third century; a sea-commander, Carausius, was based in Britain possibly upon the Humber. He crossed into Gaul and declared himself Emperor for a short period of time until assassinated in 293. Once again we find this early historical source affecting later chronicles; Carausius is mentioned in Nennius who in turn was a source for Geoffrey of Monmouth who has Arthur assembling fleets and invading various European countries. Thus Celtic tradition which mentions both Carausius and Maximus tends to fuse their achievements together in the figure of Arthur, though this does not suggest that there were no Arthurian achievements! The pattern of rising kings is repetitive, and dictated by geography as much as politics; hence the use of ships by earlier commanders gives us some insight into that of Arthur. Carausius commanded a formalised fleet which patrolled the seas between Gaul and Britain, perhaps the last such fleet to be based officially in Britain.

A century after Carausius we find Maximus transporting his soldiers to Europe, though there is no suggestion of a formalised fighting fleet. Little more than a century after Maximus, we find Ambrosius as Roman style *dux bellorum* . . . in Geoffrey and other traditional histories Ambrosius arrives with a fleet from Brittany to challenge the traitor Vortigern who had invited Saxons into the land. Next we have the figure of Arthur fighting a series of land battles against invaders and containing the Saxons within specific areas.

As the Saxons held areas to the east of England, it seems likely that Arthur's maritime activity, both trade and war, would have been mainly confined to the south-west. The connections between western England, Wales and Brittany were enduring, and it is the seaways between these regions that would have been policed.

We have some general evidence for shipping and maritime practices around this period; vessels were made of both skins and of clinker-built wooden

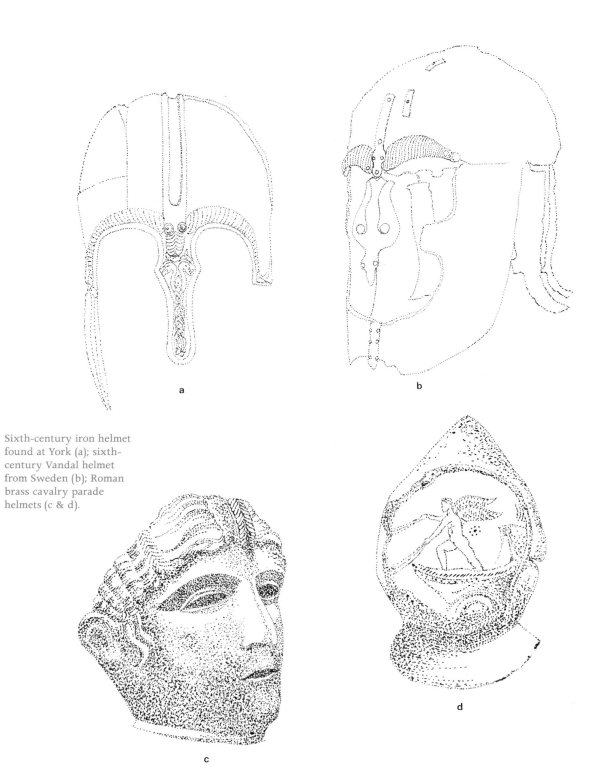

Sixth-century iron helmet
found at York (a); sixth-
century Vandal helmet
from Sweden (b); Roman
brass cavalry parade
helmets (c & d).

113

construction. In Vegetius' *De Rei Militari* the practice of camouflaging scout-ships is mentioned.

Thus we can imagine a maritime tradition of considerable strength, with continual trade and regular crossings between Britain and Gaul; with increasing piracy and barbarian activity, mariners would arm themselves, and possibly trading groups or fleets would employ defensive and scout ships. The capacity to assemble fleets was not lost with the gradual diminution of Roman authority, but we must see these fleets as being collections of fishing boats, scoutships, traders and possibly old troop carriers or fighting vessels, impressed or volunteered or bought for service as the moment required.

Action at sea would have been mainly that of small conflicts; boarding and hand to hand fighting, the use of bows and arrows perhaps, or slings. Large galleys of the type still used in the Mediterranean during the fifth and sixth centuries would not have been found, and techniques associated with galley warfare such as ramming and the use of catapults seem unlikely.

It is worth stating that no major sea battle has been recorded, and that if a large conflict between organised fleets had occurred it would surely have found its way into the chronicles as did the land battles. In other words, neither Britons or Saxons (or Irish and Picts) generated war fleets in the Roman sense, where the fleet itself is the fighting weapon. In the uncertain movements of boundaries and territories of the period, this seems obvious; the Britons were not able to maintain a standing fleet, though they had the skills, and the Saxons did not have the skills or, at first, any potential base ports. The general report of invaders in early histories is that they arrived in small groups, occasionally in fleets, and fought on land. Vessels such as the Saxon oarship described above would hardly have been suited to conflict at sea, and while skin-covered frameships make good lightweight scouting vessels, they too could not pose a serious threat as war vessels.

We may reasonably conclude, therefore, that Arthur fought no great sea battles, but maintained a constant link with areas of Gaul, particularly Brittany, and that such links demanded armed vessels and the native skills of a maritime community.

CAMLAN, THE LAST BATTLE

ROM ALL OF THE foregoing it looks as though Arthur spent his youth learning how to fight on campaigns in the north, probably against the Picts and Irish raiders. Here he came to the attention of Ambrosius, Roman Britain's last general, and from there proceeded to the south, where his strength was needed against the encroaching West Saxons. Here he first made use of mounted warriors, clad in light mail and carrying round shields, long swords and spears. These men, the core of Arthur's warrior elite, struck again and again at the heart of the Saxon settlements, weakening them until the moment came

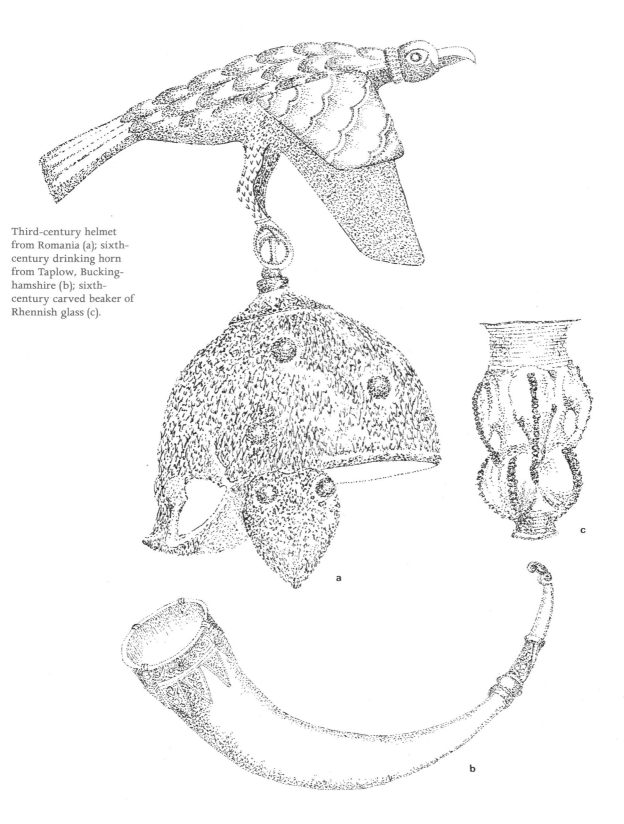

Third-century helmet from Romania (a); sixth-century drinking horn from Taplow, Buckinghamshire (b); sixth-century carved beaker of Rhennish glass (c).

when, gathering the forces of Ambrosius' Roman-British army and the wild tribesmen of the north, the new Duke of Britain (or the Emperor Arthur if one accepts the appellation contained in several Welsh documents) crushed the Saxon shield-wall at Badon.

But there still remains one further battle, not listed by Nennius but appearing in more than one chronicle of the time. This is the ill-fated battle of Camlan, where according to the *Annales Cambriae* 'Arthur and Medraut fell, and there was plague in Britain and Ireland'. This is dated as 537, although a better dating would be 557, and nothing more is known of it in historical documents. Tradition makes Medraut Arthur's nephew, or even his son, and makes this last battle the one in which Arthur died, perhaps at the hand of Medraut – although the chronicle entry does not say this, merely that both men fell there.

There are no surviving elegies for Arthur, no death-song written by one of the bards attached to his court – but he may never have been a member of the class of nobles who warranted such a threnody. It is left to later times to celebrate him, declaring that though such-and-such a man fought well 'he was no Arthur'. In less than 50 short years Arthur and his warriors made such a mark on history that they have never been forgotten; where they fought and how seem of little importance in the face of the great weight of legend and myth which has gathered about them through the centuries since they died. Yet these battles are themselves the stuff of an heroic age, which has perhaps never seen its like again in these islands. It is justly celebrated then, as are its heroes, whose struggles we record here.

A later Welsh poet celebrated Badon, Arthur's greatest battle, thus:

The action of the Battle of Badon was shown in the day of the victorious dragon's anger; a track of shield-cleaving and shattering, a path of hewing-down with red blades.

(Cynddelw)

Arthur, the Victorious Dragon, was here to stay!

Kei & the Giant

This tale, deliberately short for reasons revealed by the story-teller himself, encompasses a number of themes that run through Celtic and Arthurian legends in their more primitive or primal variants. Kei is a magical warrior in the oldest versions of his adventures; by the medieval period he begins to be rationalised as the steward or even the butler of Arthur's court. This gradual change does not, however, totally disguise his magical nature:

> So Kei went to the kitchen and the mead cellar and returned with a jug of mead and a golden cup, and his hands held skewers full of chopped meat. They took the chops and drank the mead, and then Kei said 'Let me have my story as you promised . . .'
>
> (*The Countess of the Fountain*, The Mabinogion)

Stewardship has a significance which modern readers often miss, especially when Kei or Kay is shown giving out food and drink as in the quote above. In fact he is a guardian figure; a steward is one who oversees the operation of the king's household and therefore the smooth running of the land itself. In his most ancient forms he is an aspect of a god-form, known to the Romans as Janus, the guardian of gateways; in Arthurian tales Kei often has the keeping of the gate to Arthur's court and may refuse or admit as he wills. The significance of stewardship is shown by the historical fact that the Stuart kings of Scotland and then Britain were originally *stewards* to the royal house . . . they eventually became kings in their own right when the earlier Scottish line died out in 1371, and Robert the seventh high steward became King Robert II, first of the Steward or Stewart dynasty. The importance of this office is reflected in the medieval description of Kei riding into battle, where, like the historical high stewards of Scotland, his place within the army is second only to that of the king himself:

> . . . the men at the edge of the host were running to the centre and the men at the centre were running to the edge. A rider arrived armed in mail with rings as white as lilies and rivets as red as the reddest blood, and this rider careered through the host . . . 'the rider you see is Kei, the most handsome man in Arthur's kingdom. The men at the edge of the host are rushing to the centre to see Kei riding, while the men at the centre are fleeing to the edge to avoid being trampled by his horse.'
>
> (*The Dream of Rhonabwy*, The Mabinogion)

Clearly, even in this late description, Kei is a man of great power. Nor is this description mere flattery, for it reveals the ancient power of polarity, or attraction and repulsion, inherent in the guardian figure. The Arthurian host seethes about Kei the steward, moving in and out around his central power.

But this is the most sophisticated expression of Kei as a magical warrior, tied to the medieval role of high stewardship. The primal guardian is a being of prodigious strength; he can grow to giant size and generate heat; but he is not sinister or anti-human, no matter how violent he may become at times. He is an echo of an Otherworld being or hero, but in the service of kingship and the land.

If he is my son he will be stubborn, whenever he carries a burden great or small it will be visible neither from before or behind; no one will brave fire or water as well as he, nor will there be any steward or officer like him...

(Kynyr Elegant Beard speaks of Kei in *Culhwch and Olwen*, The Mabinogion)

He had this talent; nine days and nights he could hold his breath under water, nine days and nights he could go without sleep. No doctor could cure a wound from his sword...he could be as tall as the tallest tree in the forest, and his hands generated heat for the kindling of fires.

(Description of Kei in *Culhwch and Olwen*)

Kei is found in the following tale in this early or primal form; he is a giant who changes shape and challenges the titanic powers of nature, the world, even the stars. He is also a humorous character, and this is very important indeed. The beneficial giant/heroes are often subjects of humour or ridicule, even at the height of their great adventures which confer benefit upon all of humankind.

The contest of giants is an enduring mythological theme found worldwide; Kei is the giant warrior who links the human world or tribal world to the Otherworld, while his adversary is a giant of a quite different type who spans the starry heavens.

As so many elements of the primal Kei character suggest a myth, it seems fitting that he should fight the battle that reflects the relationship between humans and environment, seasonal patterns, weather lore, and ultimately the pattern of the cosmos. His adversary is the giant Orion, the most terrifying hunter ever known. This constellation, with that of the Pleiades, played an important role in seasonal and astronomical/religious calenders in the ancient world. On the most simple level, sailing seasons were defined by these constellations, as were the turning points of the agricultural year; Kei therefore becomes a hero standing at the centre of the world (shown by Arthur's court) and perceiving the mysteries of the seasons and the four cardinal directions.

Thus Kei, the guardian of Arthur's court, has a battle of prodigious nature...or as it turns out is willing to enter into such a battle, but his adversary is so vast that he is almost beyond reach. Kei also unwittingly maps out the world by his grumbling comments upon weather; ordered patterns of 'world-making' were important to Celtic culture, mystical cosmologies were shown forth as actual geography and social relationships. We know from historical literary sources that Irish kingdoms were divided according to geographical/

cosmological plans with highly defined social castes and roles allocated to certain areas or directions.

A fourfold pattern, connected to the Four Elements and the Seasons, was central to both religion and philosophy in the ancient world, and certainly had prominence in the sixth century in Britain, as both poetry and archaeological remains show. This pattern was perpetuated right through the Middle Ages and on into the eighteenth and even nineteenth centuries; it still persists today as the foundation for modern magical arts and astrology. The origins of this worldview are rooted in observation of the weather and of the stars, and in various ancient and enduring practices of meditation and religion.

So a silly tale about a ludicrous giant who clubs oxen to death with his bare fists and boorishly challenges the stars themselves to battle can lead us, as with so many Arthurian themes, into the most elemental mysteries. Kei's adventure on the roof of Arthur's hall (which is of course the centre of the world!) stops short just as he is about to reach into the star-world above. Such visions persisted in medieval texts such as the *Prophecies* and *Life of Merlin* in which Celtic, Greek, and encyclopedic knowledge were fused together under the unifying figure of the British prophet. If the reader wishes to know what Kei might have seen in the stars, the answer is found in those two books.

It is well known, at least among civilised people, that King Arthur's steward Kei was big. But you must understand that the size of Kei was changeable; at one time as tall as an oak tree, at another merely the height of the rooftop but broad as a wine butt. This too is an understanding that comes to people of culture rather than to barbarians.

On the subject of Size, and the essential brother of Size who is of course Strength, we must pause and reflect. It is frequently given out in songs and tales that Kei grew, or shrank; sometimes roaring like a full angry river in spate, sometimes merely rumbling like a millstone grinding on a quiet summer evening... heard for miles around but not threatening in tone. There are certain judgements upon this matter of Size and Strength, civilised comparisons that may be made, for a savage sees such forces in a very different way to a man of culture, tradition and wisdom.

Without further preamble or ado, therefore, we must be aware that Kei was no bigger (most of the time) than any healthy champion. His appetite for beef was no greater than that of any hero; his capacity for wine no more cavernous than any truly civilised person remote from barbarism. But there are certain facts worthy of your attention; firstly men are smaller nowadays than were their ancestors. The mighty men of old were indeed of a stature greater than the weaklings of today; secondly all measures of height, breadth, depth, or of bread, meat, wine, weapons and the like, have not diminished in proportion to the size of men. Thus a six-foot sword is still a six-foot sword and a gallon of mead still a gallon; but the man that swings the blade after drinking the gallon is more likely to cut his own head off than to think of it as light exercise after a refreshing tipple.

Thirdly, and most important of all, barbarians are, or were, inevitably smaller than civilised men. This diminution of the savage was due to his poor diet, his wearing of restrictive uniform clothing, his collective habit of marching up and down in tight clumps of regular numbers, and his housing within stone boxes devoid of air and healthy rainfall. In short, if you will excuse my pun, the Romans were squat and weak while our ancestors were tall and strong. Indeed, there are weak-minded sycophants who will argue to the contrary; would-be inheritors of land ownership or exotic detractors from simple ancestral values, but the historical facts speak loudly for themselves.

A proof? You want proof; very well. If anyone doubts my words, let him go to the remains of Caerleon or Chester or Aquae Sulis, and examine in details the remains of the buildings and the content of the inscriptions upon the stones. He will find from the inscriptions that the men stationed in these places or visiting the temples to worship were all members of ancestral Celtic tribes, or even distant cousins from far Sarmatia or Russia; their own names and messages still visible today confirm this fact. Then let the doubting researcher measure accurately the size of the buildings that remain or the breadth of the foundations of the ruins; he will soon realise just how tall those ancestors of ours really were, and why the dwarfish meagre degenerate Romans enlisted them to strengthen the enervated Legions of the Empire. Then let our diligent scholar travel if he will to Rome itself, or what is left of it, and discover that the Celtic soldiers of the mad Emperors were of such a height that vast colonnades, circuses, roadways and tall overleaning buildings were constructed to accommodate them.

The size of Kei undoubtedly was of ancestral order; normal to his civilised fellow warriors, but enormous to squat, flour-fed, leather-wrapped, hob-nail-sandalled Romans.

Ah . . . what about the Giant? The Giant, I hear you mutter; Kei and the Giant? Well, that is not hard to answer: it goes thus.

One New Year's Day, by the true Celtic Church calendar, and not that of the Roman Church which is merely an unruly offshoot, Kei was butchering an ox

Kei and the Giant. The steward Kei looks out upon the Four Directions of the World, seeking for the mysterious thief who stole his ox.

for supper. First he killed the ox by thumping it upon the head with his fist, then he plucked out the tongue by the roots; next he squeezed out its eyes and ripped . . . what? Ah, indeed, the Giant. I was coming to that shortly.

Well, as Kei hung the freshly butchered ox over the fire to roast, he tripped upon the rim of the great iron pot that stood by the side of the fire-pit. In so tripping he fell full-length, landing with his face in the warm porridge left over from that morning's breakfast . . . Such a splash did he make that this porridge still falls as frozen flakes each winter; and that was how the first snow fell in Britain, for before that there was only healthy rain and wind.

But with his head under the washing turbulent waves of lukewarm porridge, Kei did not see a long well-muscled silver arm reach down through the smokehole of the roof and snatch away the still quivering barely seared ox. When Kei finally stood up, lifting the pot from off his head and licking the porridge from his beard, no ox could he find. He looked into the flames and sang this song:

> Little flea, little flea
> you hopped in my coat,
> you were not a cat or a dog
> or a goat,
> You fit not a spoon nor a shoe
> nor a box,
> But you fit in my glove
> the size of an . . .

But of course he did not sing the last word as this would reach the ears of the thief who would then know that he was being sung against and hunted. This is the origin of the expression 'a flea in your ear' and of course the phrase 'to box his ears'.

All the women who worked around King Arthur's house and hall very much admired the song that Kei had made, and began to sing out 'Little flea, little flea . . . ' until everyone in the region knew it so well that they mimicked the creatures in the song, sitting like cats in a spoon, barking like dogs in a shoe, and being stubborn as a goat who will not go into her box at night. And this was the first theatre show in all of Britain, though not the last.

Now Kei was angry at the loss of the flea; his shoulders flexed and his neck stretched, he drew in a great deep breath filled with smoke and song and falling porridge, and he thrust his head right up through the smoke-hole of the roof. The cooking fire was ground out by his feet and the glowing sparks flew up to singe his knees; his great broad shoulders fitted snugly into the roofbeams and his wide throbbing neck filled the central hole to bursting point; the four great winds of the world blew into his gaping nostrils and flung his hair writhing in all directions. Kei looked about him, and this is what he saw.

Looking down, he saw the reed thatching spread out in a great circle below him like the radiating spokes of a giant wheel. This circular roof was coloured rich brown and yellow and green with little grasses and growing flowers. And this was how the Wheel of the World was first known, from what Kei saw sticking his head up through the roof of King Arthur's house.

Looking east, Kei saw a red sphere rising over a distant flat line at the very rim of reality; this was tomorrow's sunrise, so far could he see from that roof that he saw it coming before today's sun had set. And Kei muttered into his beard, saying 'seeing tomorrow's sun doesn't find my flea . . .' and this was the first prophecy uttered in the land of Britain, though not the last.

Next Kei looked west; he saw a great roaring purple sea with deep green waves crested by white frothing creamy foam; he saw fish leaping and spouting and sporting, and many islands floating to and fro yet never crashing into one another. He saw pluming fountains of water rising into the cloudfilled skies and circling back to fall as rain through vast wheeling flocks of birds that called and cried in many different tones and voices. In the depths he saw glimpses of a beast so large that even he had difficulty measuring its size. 'The world is wider than the land of Britain', Kei muttered into his salt-encrusted beard; and this was the first definition of geography ever made in Arthur's realm. Shaking the blown sea-weed and a goggling haddock from his hair, Kei turned to look south.

Southwards were the vast territories of the corrupt Empire of Rome, peopled by hot sweating midgets toiling under whip and lash to build houses tall enough for the incoming civilised soldiery who would soon take that Empire for their own, again and again and again. In the southern sky the great Invincible Sun roared and spread his wings in joy; he breathed out and blasted his worshippers with insufferable light and heat. Kei shook the drops of sweat from his forehead and gasped 'Rain is the healthiest of weather', and thus were the sciences of medicine, meteorology, psychology, and political economy created.

Kei made progress around the circle of the roof by turning and observing the spokes of radiating reed thatch that stretched out from the collar around his neck, which had once been a smoke-hole, to the very edge of the roof itself. Below this edge nothing could be seen, but he knew that the land of Britain lay somewhere beneath it; he counted the numbers of spokes as he turned east, west, and south, and thus by calculation he knew when he was facing north. So were mathematics and geometry defined for the first time.

As Kei looked north, he could hear faint sounds floating up from within the hall below the encircling roof; it was the company of Arthur, led by the King himself, clashing their golden wine cups together and singing, 'A flea, a flea . . .'. But these jovial noises were lost when Kei looked into the mirror of

Night, where the stars live and move to ecstatic music in their spiral dance. So deep was the north that Kei opened both his eyes wide; he saw the shapes of Bear and Spindle, Dog and Weaver, but largest of all was the image of a Giant brandishing a club made from the shin-bone of an ox.

'Aha,' roared Kei, 'so it is you that stole my little flea!'

But the Star Hunter merely tightened up his belt, and took a step across eternity.

'Oho,' roared Kei, 'so it is Orion who stole Arthur's supper . . . I will have some satisfaction from you for this!'

But the Giant's shoulders soon filled the northern sky; storms sprang up across the Irish Sea, and the Atlantic heaved and tumbled until the song of 'Little flea' all up and down the length of Britain was utterly drowned out by the howling wind and lashing rain of winter.

Kei, barely able to breathe in the first onslaught of this terrible star Giant, finally looked upwards. His eyes narrowed as his vision sped towards the central pivot of all worlds; the roof-wheel fell away below him and the land of Britain seemed to shrink and tumble until it was a green speck in the purple ocean. Up he rose above the ever-breathing clouds and up until the world itself seemed little more than a smear of blue upon star-mirror . . .

But what Kei saw next is for another day, and in another story. Three things, then, to remember: never trust a short barbarian, never fall into the porridge, and never eat all of an ox or tell all of a tall tale at one sitting.

5 · Magical Weapons & Warriors

Tri Chynghoriad farchawg oedd yn Llys Arthur: nid amgen, Cynan ab Clydno Eiddun; ac Aron ab Cynfarch, ab Meirchion Gul; a Llywarch hên ab Elidir Llydanwyn: a'r tri Marchawg hynny a oeddynt gynghorwyr i Arthur, pa ryw ryfel bynnag, pa bygwth a vai arno, hwynt a'u cyngherynt hyd na chai neb y gorvod ar Arthur, ac am hynny i gorfu ef ar bôb cenedloedd drwy dri pheth a oedd yn ei ġanlyn, nid amgen, gobaith da, ac arfau cyfegredig, y rhai a ddanfones Iefu Grift iddaw ar hinwedd ei filwyr; ac am hynny i gwifgodd ef ddeuddeg Coron am ei ben, ac i bu ef Amberawdyr yn Rhufain.

There were Three famous Counfellor-Knights in King Arthur's Court: that is, *Cynon*, the fon of *Clydno Eiddyn*, (or Edinburgh;) *Aron*, the fon of *Cynvarch*; and *Llywarch hên*, the fon of *Elidyr Llydanwyn*: and thefe Three were Arthur's Counfellors, to advife him in whatever difficulty happened; fo that nobody was able to overcome him; and thus, Arthur maftered all men in every exploit, and in all nations, through the power of the ftrong fpirit, and the faith and hope which were in his heart, and the confecrated arms which *God* had given him; and by the virtue, and fuccefs of his warriors. On that account, he wore twelve Crowns; and he was confidered as Emperor in Rome.

LEGEND AND ARCHAEOLOGY

HILE WE ARE attempting to draw a picture of a historical Arthur and his warriors, it should not be forgotten that their enduring fascination lies in traditional or legendary elements. Arthur, a fifth–sixth century warlord or king, and his soldiers who inherited both British and Roman cultural and military patterns, act as timeless focal points for accumulated traditions. Paradoxically, it is the traditions which illuminate the historical picture, and not vice-versa.

Not all historians share this viewpoint, however, and as early as 1190 William of Newburgh wrote in critical dismissal of Geoffrey of Monmouth's *History of the British Kings*: 'It is quite clear that everything this man wrote about Arthur or his successors, or indeed about his predecessors, was made up partly by himself and partly by others, either from an inordinate love of lying or for the sake of pleasing the Britons.'

Modern research and revised opinion has shown that the Newburgh school of thought, which persists even today and caused Arthur to be written out of chronicles and histories from the twelfth to the early twentieth centuries, is far from being truth. To gain a clear picture of Arthur we cannot rely solely upon literary history; a problem of such reliance was already puzzling chroniclers by the twelfth century, when they found that British traditions, especially those amplified by Geoffrey, simply did not square with literary history such as that of the Roman Empire:

This Arthur of whom the Britons go out of their way to tell idle tales ... For if Arthur had won

125

thirty kingdoms as Geoffrey tells us, and made the King of France subject to himself, if he had slain Lucius in Italy, the procurator of the Republic, why is he not spoken of by the Roman, French, and Saxon writers, since they speak so much of other lesser men?

(Higden's *Polychronicon*, early fourteenth century)

While Arthur is challenged, the same chronicles abound with legendary beasts, talking trees, weapon-breaking stones, and other curious folklore and misrepresentation of classical mythology. In short, the argument against Arthur may have been biased politically, and was certainly biased against Geoffrey, who claimed to have drawn his *History* from an ancient book in the British tongue (which would have been Welsh or Breton).

Modern archaeology plays a very significant role in the reassessment of Arthur, for it enables us to compare hard evidence with tradition, a comparison that simply was not available to earlier writers. The amount of scientific evidence assembled by archaeology, combined with a radical reassessment of early Welsh or British sources and traditions, shows Geoffrey in a rather more sympathetic light, even in quite obscure matters which were previously thought to be mere fancy or decoration. Some of these, such as Arthur's personal armour, are dealt with later in this chapter.

CELTIC TRADITIONS

ARLY BRITISH traditions (Celtic traditions) are found not only in Geoffrey of Monmouth, but in certain earlier chroniclers, and various Welsh, Irish, Scottish and Breton texts such as genealogies, hero-tales, and later collections of legends such as the famous *Mabinogion* containing a number of important references to Arthur and his warriors. Yet another source of genuine tradition, but difficult to prove, is the embroidery and embellishment of later chronicles amplifying the tales of Arthur or of the knights, or the prophet Merlin. Despite the quite inaccurate medieval dressing that has been applied, many literary versions of Arthurian legend retain remarkably ancient lore. In all cases, however, discretion must be supported by the various streams of evidence available.

Before moving on to deal in detail with both weapons and warriors, from tradition and archaeology, we should consider the special relationship between man and weapon which is clearly stated in Arthurian legend, a relationship which derives from an ancient and enduring heroic pagan worldview. It is quite different to the modern attitude that weapons are hardware and nothing else, and gives us several remarkable insights into the historical Arthur.

There is a difficult and dangerous borderline between the magic and poetry of weapons clearly stated in Celtic tradition, and the spurious nonsense of nationalist propaganda regarding death, glory, war and honour. Much of the Arthurian legend has become corrupted by false politics; relying on concepts

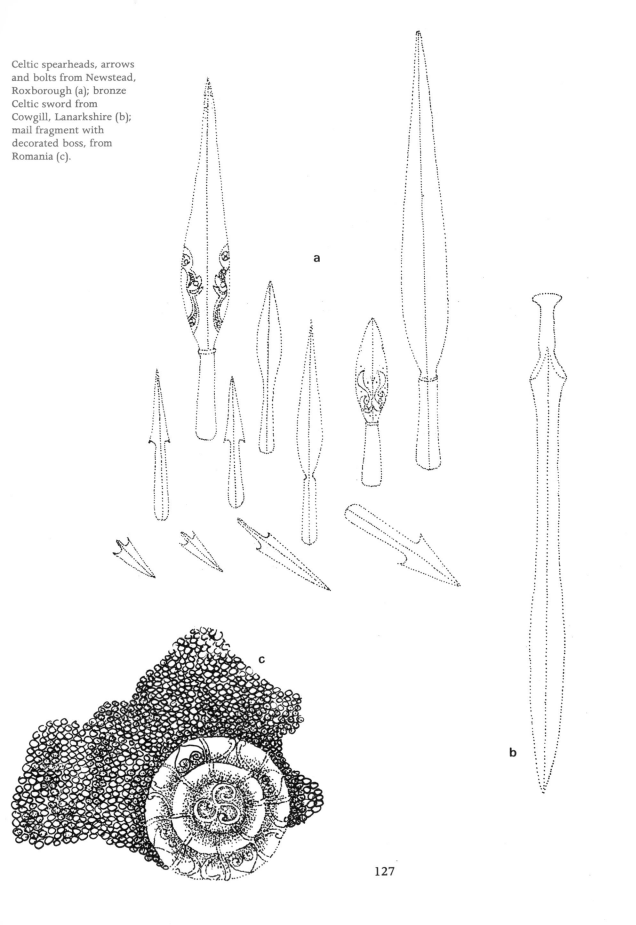

Celtic spearheads, arrows
and bolts from Newstead,
Roxborough (a); bronze
Celtic sword from
Cowgill, Lanarkshire (b);
mail fragment with
decorated boss, from
Romania (c).

127

which may have been alien to the historical Arthur and his people. In Celtic tradition, and many other heroic traditions worldwide, the king, his warriors and their weapons take on a magical poetical aura; this is not merely a romantic quirk of imaginative historians or propagandist chroniclers, it is central to the type of culture to which Arthur belonged.

The relationship between a weapon and a hero, for all of Arthur's legendary warriors were heroes, no matter how they behaved in history, is essentially a magical matter. Examples of this magic are now world-famous; only Arthur the true king could pull the sword from the stone, and, although this theme has been used repeatedly in fiction, it has a root in fact, as we shall shortly demonstrate. It also has a deeper root in primal myth, extending far beyond mere militaristic totemism.

In many ancient cultures the king was not merely the toughest bandit or biggest property owner, as is often assumed by materialist historians, though the theory is frequently borne out by historical fact. The land over which this king ruled was held in trust for the people, a system perpetuated by the Irish kings well into historical times. This ancient system has strong echoes in the Arthurian legends, yet on the surface does not seem to apply to the historical image of Arthur as a Romano-British warlord. Nevertheless, we must always fuse tradition and factual history when we consider Arthur, and it is very likely that the symbolic elements of kingship were, if not active, lying dormant near to the surface of the British consciousness so increasingly independent after the Roman withdrawal of the early fifth century.

KINGSHIP

O DEMONSTRATE THAT this relationship of chieftainship or kingship and the land was of enduring nature, we need only turn to eighteenth-century Scotland. Clan chieftains or lairds enclosed vast tracts of land to which they held English-style title (based on Roman laws of property). Yet their Gaelic-speaking illiterate clansmen, to whom the chieftain was a father figure, had always assumed that the land was held in common trust. They discovered in the hardest possible way, by losing their homes and all rights to remain upon the land, that their ancient traditional concept which dated perhaps to a pre-Christian Celtic culture, was no longer valid. Some modern historians have made the mistake of equating this ancient family/land relationship with communism or even Marxism, by deliberately ignoring the blatantly magical traditional elements which hold it together. We find precisely these elements in the figure of Arthur, and they appear even in some of the earliest sources, or in later sources such as the *Mabinogion* which draw upon early themes and ancient oral traditions.

The weapons and attributes of the king are reflected in a lesser and more spe-cialised manner by the individual heroes; these also have a curious relationship

Items of military equip-
ment from an early manu-
script of the *Notitia
Dignitatum*.

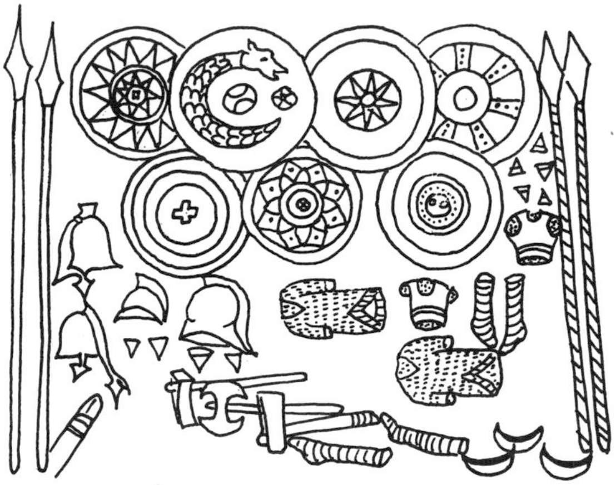

Romano-British saddle
(reconstruction based on
that of Dr W. Groenman
van Waateringe), and
Roman-type spurs.

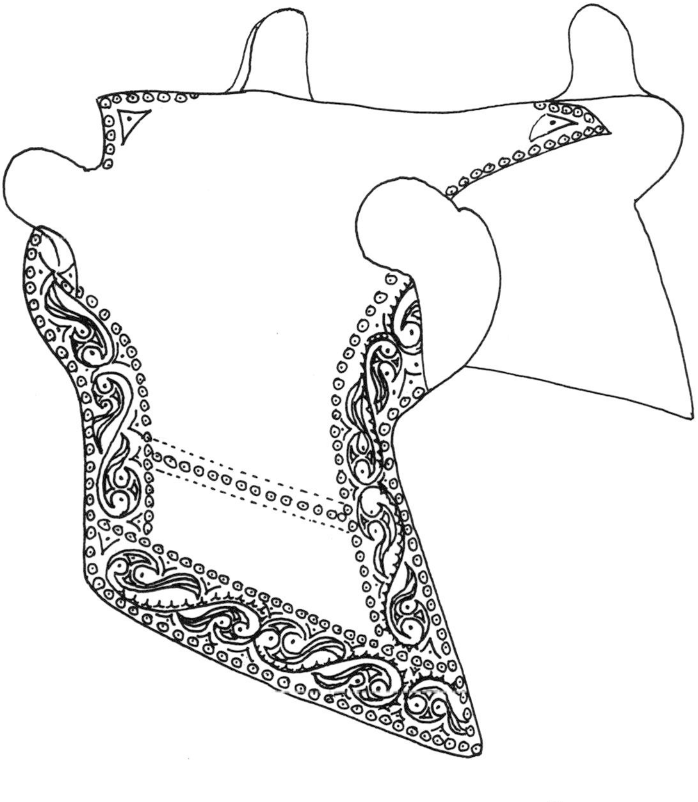

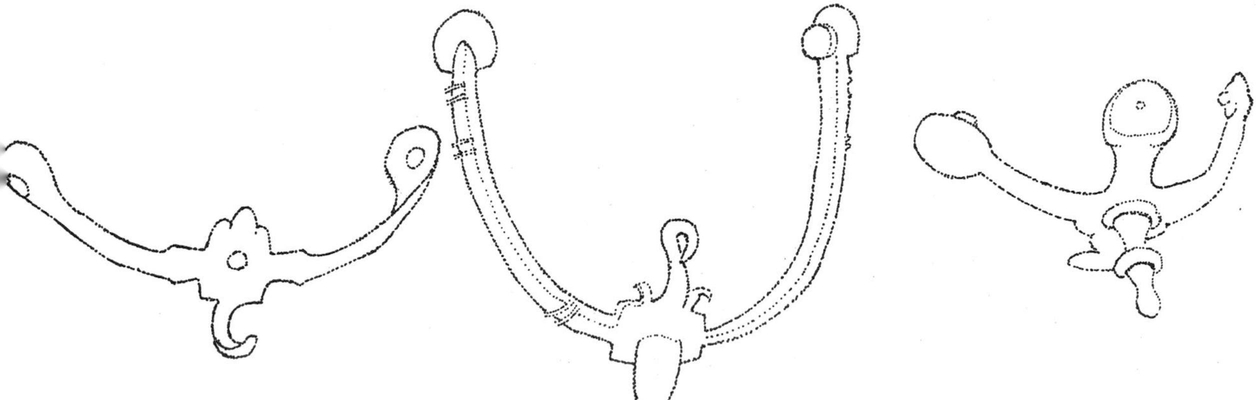

to environmental matters and in some cases clearly show magical attributes of the most ancient type, or become involved in mythical stories such as *Gawain and the Green Knight*, retold in this book as *The Beheading Game*. It is clear that no matter what we discover about the historical Arthur and his warriors, they have absorbed images, tales, symbols and mythical potency from traditions which may predate their historical appearance. The question is not one of proof of Arthur, for this surely exists sufficiently, but of the reasons for this mythical magical accumulation.

As a post-Roman war leader the historical Arthur would have been familiar with Roman-style culture in Britain; he followed directly from Ambrosius, who in history presents as an altogether more 'Romanised' figure. Celtic traditions and early texts from Wales, Scotland, Brittany or Cornwall have numerous references to Arthur; these are the *source* references from which later medieval accumulations derived. Ambrosius does not command this traditional respect or repeated reference, perhaps because he was personally identified with Rome or Roman-style culture, while Arthur was the spear-head of the British resurgence of independence. Traditions from a heroic early culture which had to a great extent been suppressed, though not destroyed, by the Roman invasion and colonisation over several centuries could be attached to Arthur, but not to his predecessor Ambrosius. The more one considers Arthur's relationship to Rome or Roman culture, often proposed by modern historians, the less likely it seems. Undoubtedly the troops picked up various items from a Roman style military, either copied independently or retained within families for generations, but this does not suggest that Arthur followed a Roman-style military or social system.

Arthur's warriors in tradition are not merely muscle-bound hackers and cutters, or the remnant of a Roman cavalry unit; they have accumulated magical weapons and mythical attributes. The lists and descriptions shown in this chapter derive from some very early sources, and leave no doubt as to the quite un-Roman nature of Arthur and his men in the popular imagination and oral tradition. Curiously, this magical accumulation is not found in connection with other important persons around the Arthurian period; the hated Vortigern who invited Saxons into Britain (called 'Vortigern of the Repulsive Lips' by early Welsh chroniclers), and the Roman-style war leader Ambrosius, do not merit legendary powers or traditional development. As immediate predecessors of Arthur, with traditional associations with Merlin the prophet, we might expect these characters also to be infused with mythical elements, but this is not so. We may also add that quite significant early figures in British history, such as Julius Caesar or Claudius, are hardly mentioned by tradition, let alone gifted with powers of shape-changing or magical weaponry.

Arthur and his warriors may have been identified at a very early stage in their organisation with national mythical tales from heroic culture far predating the fifth and sixth centuries. Why should this be so? Because the historical Arthur was the first truly 'British' war lord after the Roman collapse, and the ancient identification of king and land, far deeper than superficial modern political nationalism, was reinstated in his figure.

The Hunting of Twrch Trwyth. Arthur and his warriors hunt the semi-mythical boar, the Twrch Trwyth. Their dress and weapons reflect what is known of the huntsmen of the time.

130

The prevalence of legendary matter in Arthurian lore has tended to convince historians, particularly pro-English chroniclers from the twelfth to the twentieth centuries, that all or much of the Arthurian story is fanciful. Conversely, we must be cautious enough not to take the opposite extreme and value tradition over factual history; in the following pages we examine some of the relationships between archaeology, tradition, and history which reveal Arthur and his warriors.

WEAPONS AND MOBILITY

ESPITE THE SEMI-BREAKDOWN in government in Britain enough contact was maintained with the Roman forces in Gaul for the Romano-Britons to be aware of the latest developments in warfare and tactics. They had sufficient craftsmen and armourers to be able to produce excellent chain-mail, swords and helmets. They also knew that a mobile force was essential (even as early as the fourth century, the ratio of cavalry to footsoldiery was six regiments of horse to three of foot). All of these factors together helped create the conditions which produced the Arthurian battle-force – a lightly-mounted, armoured band who could move and strike swiftly in almost any part of the country and be away to defend other places before the enemy knew what was happening. Small wonder if the name of Arthur began to strike terror into the hearts of the Saxons invaders, or that his name remained for so long in the roll of honour which accounts for all such great national heroes.

If we examine specific accounts of the arming of Arthurian warriors, and compare them with what we know of the actual conditions of military equipment in sixth-century Britain, a picture of the kind of armour and arms of Arthur's men begins to emerge. To begin at the anachronistic end of the spectrum we see that in the work of Chrétien de Troyes – in particular *Erec and Enide* (c. 1170) – and in the English *Sir Gawain and the Green Knight* (c. 1400), we find there very precise descriptions of the type of armour worn by the twelfth- and fourteenth-century knight. Both are accurate as to detail and all show the precise order in which a knight was armed: from the feet upward, to prevent tiring the warrior before battle (the average weight of a fully armed Knight at this date was approximately 240 lb.

There is no such account available from the period of the historical Arthur. However we can go some way towards showing the kind of arms he would have worn. We are helped in this by a number of sources, which although none dates from the sixth century, all contain clues to the historical image. The first of these is our old friend Geoffrey of Monmouth, who describes the arming of the King before the battle of Badon. Interestingly, however, he does not equip Arthur in twelfth-century armour but in gear close enough to what we know to have been the norm to pass for an accurate description.

Arthur . . . put on a leather jerkin [lorica] worthy of so great a king. On his head he placed a golden helmet with a crest carved in the shape of a dragon; and across his shoulders a circular shield called Pridwen, on which there was painted a likeness of the Blessed Mary, Mother of God, which forced him to be thinking perpetually of her. He girded his peerless sword, called Caliburn, which was forged on the isle of Avalon. A Spear called Ron graced his right hand; long, broad in the blade and thirsty for slaughter.

(Trans. Thorp, Bk.ix,4)

Several authorities have pointed out the similarities between this catalogue of weapons and the arms discovered in the Sutton Hoo ship burial. Although this is in fact a Saxon grave, there is evidence from the nature of the goods discovered (see page 148) that a good deal of it consisted of booty captured from Romano-Celtic adversaries. The Saxons themselves had little or no body armour, other than that looted (or bought) from the Roman armies. So that, interestingly enough, the two forces must have resembled each other to a considerable degree when armed for battle. For this reason there may well have been some kind of personal insignia worn by either side by way of identification. There are references in several ancient texts to warriors who went into battle wearing a sprig of greenery (heather or broom) tucked into helmet or shield rim. We do not know what the Saxons wore, but some kind of identification would have prevented the kind of disaster which took place at the Battle of Barnet, (1471), where the streaming star of the Lancastrian Earl of Oxford was mistaken for the sun in splendour of the Yorkist King Edward IV, with tragic results for the Lancastrian contingent.

Arthur's men would, in all probability, have been generally better organized and equipped than their foes. Armour left behind by the departing legions – or indeed, as suggested by Geoffrey of Monmouth, copied by British armourers – would have been sufficient to equip at least a small force, so that one may believe that the Britons looked, at least superficially, Romanized, while still varying in details such as helmets (more elaborate among the higher dignitaries), swords (of varying lengths and styles) and footwear.

Of one matter we can be sure: armour, of whatever style or kind, was extremely valuable. It would never have been deliberately discarded or abandoned, as long as there was a solid link or plate or buckle which could be utilized to patch another set of gear.

Thus, we may imagine that Arthur's warriors (at least the less wealthy or high-born) would have worn rather a patchwork of armour, reflecting more than one style or period. (As late as the Civil War of 1642–46 soldiers were fighting with 'heirlooms' – pikes and helmets dating from the Wars of the Roses, nearly 200 years earlier.)

The basic military equipment among the warrior-class, irrespective of such additional items as splendidly ornamented weapons specially named or possessing particular attributes, were:

a) a helmet (*cassis or galea*);
b) a short-sleeved mailshirt (*lorica hamata*);
c) a shield (*scutum*);
d) a sword (*gladius*).

133

To this may be added the non-obligatory items:

e) shaped body armour (*cuirasse*);
f) light throwing spear (in the case of lightly-mailed warriors);
g) a heavier cavalry lance.

Apart from the warriors who fought on foot, there is ample evidence for the use of mailed cavalry (*cataphracti*). These would have worn heavier, possibly scaled body armour, covering them to below the knees, carried light, round shields strengthened with bronze or iron round the rim and the boss, and wielded long, double-bladed swords, heavier than those carried by the foot-soldiers and able to deal out a terrific blow with the weight of the armoured rider behind them. They would also have carried long lances with heavy warheads able to pierce most body armour.

The *Notitia Dignitatum*, the muster-roll of the Roman Legions, shows that there was an unusually high concentration of cavalry stationed in Britain, chiefly at Binchester (Vinovia), Ribchester (Brenetennacum) and Housesteads on Hadrian's Wall. Helmut Nickel, Curator of Arms and Armour at the New York Metropolitan Museum, has pointed out the similarity between the Arthurian mounted knight (*miles*) and the *cataphract* of the Roman cavalry wing. He has drawn attention also to some curious similarities between the culture of the Sarmatians, who made up the greater part of these cavalry units in Britain, and the later Arthurian heroes. Among other points are their worship of a naked sword stuck upright in the ground or on a platform; their use of a wind-sock type standard (see page 106) in the likeness of a dragon – and perhaps not least that their most famous commander during the third century was named Lucius Artorius Castus!

The historian I.A. Richards has pointed out that the description of Brene-tennacum (Ribchester) as a veteran station may mean that the contingent of Sarmatian cavalry who had worked out their service, were permitted to settle in the area where they had previously served. There were some fifteen and a half thousand of these tribesmen – whose origins are vaguely placed on the eastern Steppe – stationed in Britain, so that it would be surprising if they did not leave some trace of their presence behind, even assuming an almost total absorption by the native population.

These factors make Dr Nickel's theory – that over the years the name Artorius had become a title rather than a personal name, and that this, together with the use of cavalry, the sword-in-the-stone motif, and the dragon standard, may have given rise to certain aspects of the Arthurian mythos – far from improbable, though we must await Dr Nickel's forthcoming book for a detailed appraisal of all the evidence.

A striking version of the description of Arthur's war gear in the *Historia* is to be found in the verse-retelling by the Saxon poet Layamon:

> He put on his byrny fashioned of steel
> An elvish smith made it well and was hight Wygar

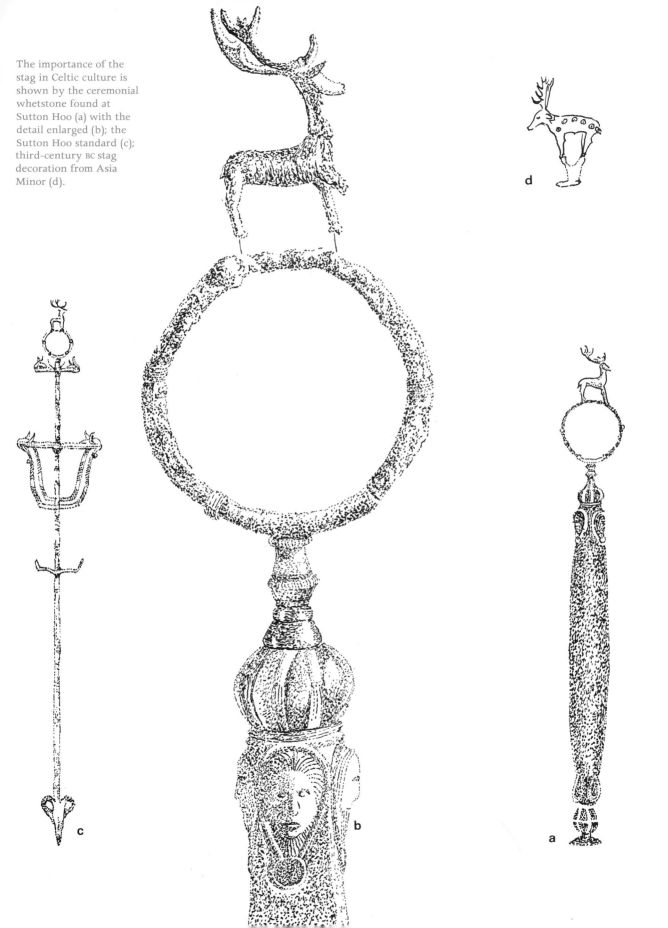

The importance of the stag in Celtic culture is shown by the ceremonial whetstone found at Sutton Hoo (a) with the detail enlarged (b); the Sutton Hoo standard (c); third-century BC stag decoration from Asia Minor (d).

A witty smith. And his legs he covered
With hose of steel. Caliburn his sword
Hung by his side, that was wrought in Avalon
With craft that was magic. Helm he set on head
Of steel very high, and many gemstones on it
All set in gold. It had been Uther's
That noblest of kings. He hung on his neck
A precious shield. Its name was in English
Called Pridwen. Thereon was graven
With red gold tracing a very fair image
Of the Mother of God. His spear he took then.

(Trans. E.J.B. Kirtlan)

In the thirteenth-century story of *Rhonabwy's Dream* from the Mabinogion, further and more elaborate details of Arthur's war-gear and possessions are offered. Although it was not written down until the thirteenth century this text contains matter from a far earlier period. Here Arthur's goods include several with magical properties, including his Ring, which has the property:

to enable thee to remember that thou seest tonight, and hadst thou not seen the stone, thou wouldst never have been able to remember aught thereof.

(*Mabinogion*: Guest, p. 152)

Arthur's Sword is here described as having 'the similitude of two serpents' upon it in gold:

And when the Sword was drawn from its scabbard, it seemed as if two flames of fire burst forth from the jaws of the serpents, and then so wonderful was the Sword, that it was hard for anyone to look upon it.

(*Ibid.*, p. 155)

Another description deals with Arthur's chair, a throne which, it must be admitted, is fit for any king! It is brought by a large red youth, who takes it from his pack, along with a carpet on which to place it:

And he spread the carpet before Arthur, and there was an apple of red gold at each corner thereof, and he placed the chair upon the carpet. And so large was the chair that three armed warriors might have sat therein. Gwenn was the name of the carpet, and it was one of its properties that whoever was upon it no one could see him, and he could see everyone.

(*Ibid.*, p. 155)

Clearly the youth and his pack are both magical, and the operations of the ring and the carpet are to aid the memory and the vision of their owner. And if we look at the ancient Welsh *Triads*, and in particular at the list of the 'Thirteen Treasures of the Island of Britain' we find there, amongst the magic cauldrons and wondrous steeds:

The Mantle of Arthur in Cornwall: whoever was under it could not be seen, and he could see everyone.

(*Welsh Triads*, trans. Bromwich)

Here there has been a confusion between the Carpet and the Mantle, which other sources describe as being named Gwen.

Elsewhere in the *Mabinogion*, in the story of Culhwch and Olwen, Arthur lists his prized possessions as including:

my ship; and my mantle; and Caledvwlch, my sword; and Rhongomyant, my lance; and Wynebgwythucher, my shield; and Carnwenhau, my knife . . .

(*Mabinogion*: Guest, p. 106)

Lady Guest translates these names as 'Hard-Breaker', for the sword; 'Night-Gainsayer' for the shield; and 'White-Haft' for the knife. Later translators have added 'Cutting-Spear' for the lance, but have not disagreed substantially with Lady Guest.

From the foregoing it will be seen that in common with most great heroes 'the Warrior Arthur' is equipped with a set of possessions which are archetypical of the gear owned by 'lesser' men. Arthur's sword, spear and shield, his ship, his mantle and his ring, are special, magical items which serve to protect and enhance his personal abilities or attributes.

THE HEROES

 E MIGHT VERY easily have called this book 'The Age of Heroes', which is in any case a far more appropriate name for the Arthurian period than, say, 'The Dark Ages'. Arthur's men were all heroes, and we possess remarkably detailed lists of them and their special skills. Rather like the characters in modern 'role-playing' games, each one has certain attributes which mark him out as unique. In *Culhwch and Olwen*, Kei (the Sir Kay of later Arthurian stories) is said to be able to hold his breath for nine days and nights under water, and to be able to go without sleep for as long; he could also be as tall as the tallest tree and generate such heat that even when it rained no one who stood near him would get wet. Before we dismiss such characteristics as merely fictitious or mythical, let us not forget that it is only a step from having keen sight, or being able to run swiftly, to being able to see things happening miles away or to run faster than the wind itself. Behind such attributes lie hidden the bravery, courage and resourcefulness which characterise the men who followed Arthur — and who gave us, ultimately, the legendary world of Camelot with its magnificent Chivalry and its own gallery of heroic denizens.

On the following pages will be found a list, numbering some 200 names, drawn from early Welsh genealogical tracts, warrior lists in such literary works as *Culhwch and Olwen*, *Rhonabwy's Dream*, and a remarkable fifteenth-century Welsh document known as *The Twenty-Four Knights of Arthur's Court*, quotations from which have provided us with chapter headings throughout this

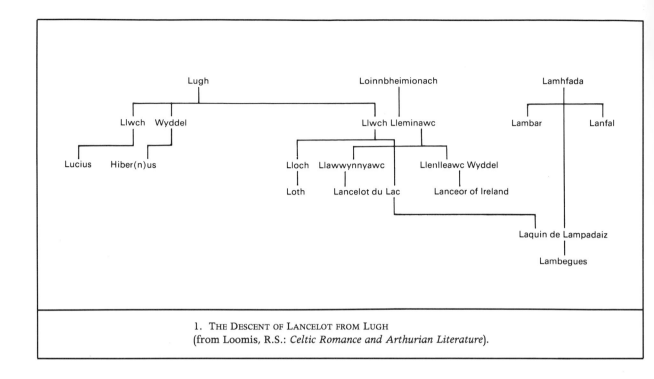

1. THE DESCENT OF LANCELOT FROM LUGH
(from Loomis, R.S.: *Celtic Romance and Arthurian Literature*).

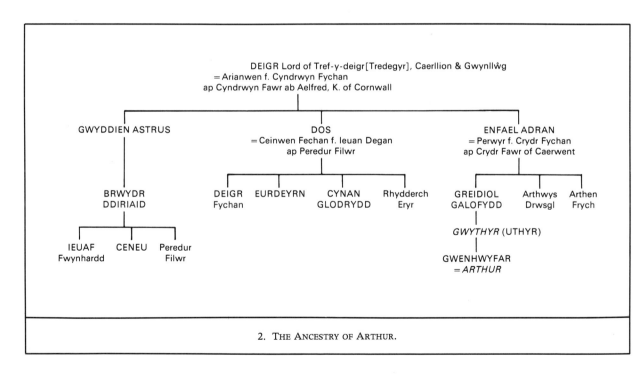

2. THE ANCESTRY OF ARTHUR.

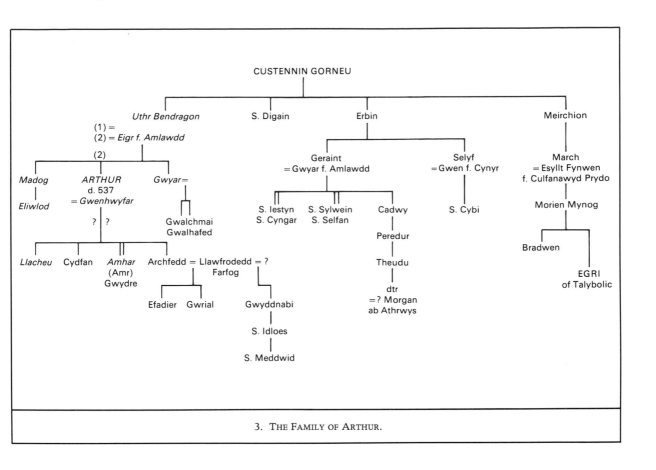

3. THE FAMILY OF ARTHUR.

book. Although this is of late provenance in the versions which have survived, it contains material of an earlier date, and as its most recent editor, Dr Rachel Bromwich, has pointed out, where one would expect, in a work of this period, to find a substantial number of French names (derived from the later Arthurian romances) there is an almost totally Celtic flavour to the work.

We have also included a selection of genealogies which refer to the period of Arthur's life. All are authentic (as far as such things can be after so lengthy a span of time) and many of considerable antiquity. Many of the names from the warrior-lists will be found side by side with other historical figures — a fact which demonstrates the high degree of cross-fertilization which exists between the areas of history and myth.

For the genealogies included in these few pages we are indebted to the magisterial work of Dr Peter C. Bartrum, whose *Welsh Geneologies AD 300–1400* provides a seemingly bottomless quarry for all concerned with the matter of Arthur and his times. We have simplified and sometimes adapted Dr Bartrum's edition according to the needs of the present work. Names in italic type are of particular relevance.

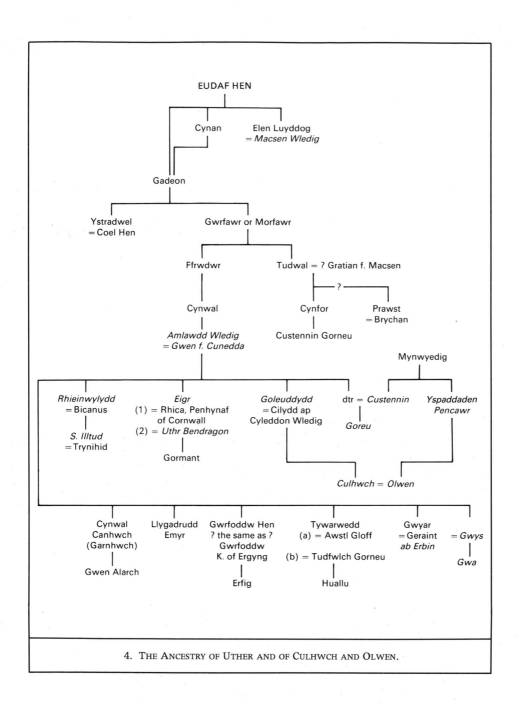

4. THE ANCESTRY OF UTHER AND OF CULHWCH AND OLWEN.

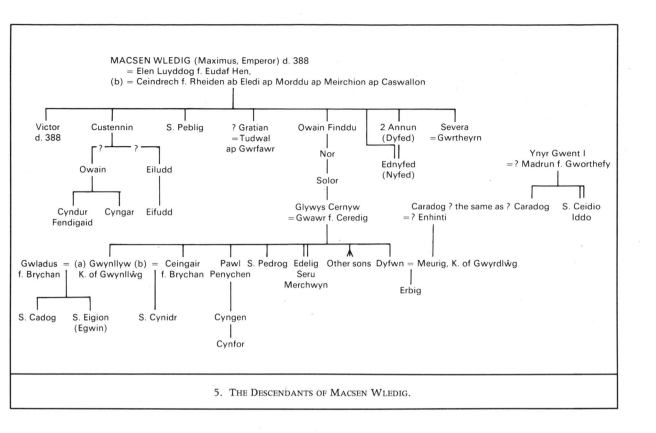

The diagram shows:

MACSEN WLEDIG (Maximus, Emperor) d. 388
= Elen Luyddog f. Eudaf Hen,
(b) = Ceindrech f. Rheiden ab Eledi ap Morddu ap Meirchion ap Caswallon

Victor d. 388 — Custennin — S. Peblig — ? Gratian = Tudwal ap Gwrfawr — Owain Finddu — 2 Annun (Dyfed) — Severa = Gwrtheyrn

Custennin: ? — ? → Owain, Eiludd

Owain → Cyndur Fendigaid, Cyngar
Eiludd → Eifudd

Owain Finddu → Nor → Solor → Glywys Cernyw = Gwawr f. Ceredig

2 Annun → Ednyfed (Nyfed)

Severa = Gwrtheyrn

Ynyr Gwent I = ? Madrun f. Gworthefy → Caradog ? the same as ? Caradog = ? Enhinti, S. Ceidio Iddo

Glywys Cernyw = Gwawr f. Ceredig → Gwladus f. Brychan = (a) Gwynllyw (b) = Ceingair f. Brychan, Pawl Penychen, S. Pedrog, Edelig Seru Merchwyn, Other sons, Dyfwn = Meurig, K. of Gwyrdlŵg

K. of Gwynllŵg

Gwladus = (a) Gwynllyw (b) = Ceingair f. Brychan → S. Cadog, S. Eigion (Egwin), S. Cynidr

Pawl Penychen → Cyngen → Cynfor

Dyfwn = Meurig, K. of Gwyrdlŵg → Erbig

5. THE DESCENDANTS OF MACSEN WLEDIG.

THE ORIGINAL KNIGHTS OF ARTHUR

HE CELTS LOVED lists, and have left sufficient of them to enable us to identify many of the characters who moved in the Arthurian sphere of action, or who were, at the very least, active at the time. Just as we can turn to the crew-lists in Homer, or to the genealogies and *dindschencas* of Ireland, so can we find, amid the compilations of names, places, islands, cities and marvels, the names and styles and sometimes even the ancestry of the Arthurian warriors.

Tradition — some of it ancient, though dating in written form from medieval times or later — assigns twenty-four knights to Arthur's court. These are listed in several texts and referred to throughout Welsh literary sources. In *Culhwch and Olwen* this list becomes expanded to the number of 250, often duplicating itself in order to do so. Examination of the MSS of works like these demonstrates how names were sometimes added to fill in lacunae between the bottom of one column and the top of another. Once these have been deleted, along with others of suspect provenance (names of gods, for example, or names deriving from later Continental sources which have been Celticised) together with obviously folkloric elements, it is possible to arrive at a list which may, with reasonable

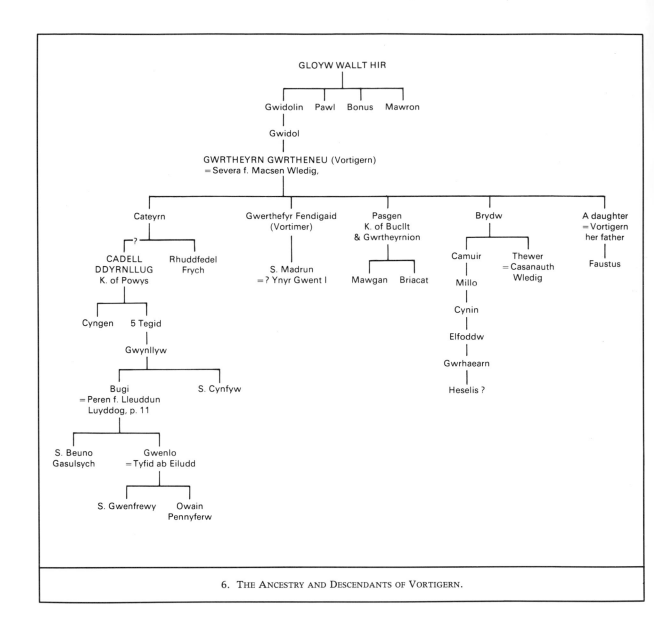

GLOYW WALLT HIR

Gwidolin Pawl Bonus Mawron

Gwidol

GWRTHEYRN GWRTHENEU (Vortigern)
= Severa f. Macsen Wledig,

Cateyrn | Gwerthefyr Fendigaid (Vortimer) | Pasgen K. of Bucllt & Gwrtheyrnion | Brydw | A daughter = Vortigern her father

CADELL DDYRNLLUG K. of Powys | Rhuddfedel Frych

S. Madrun = ? Ynyr Gwent I

Mawgan Briacat

Camuir | Thewer = Casanauth Wledig

Faustus

Cyngen 5 Tegid

Millo

Gwynllyw

Cynin

Bugi = Peren f. Lleuddun Luyddog, p. 11 | S. Cynfyw

Elfoddw

Gwrhaearn

S. Beuno Gasulsych | Gwenlo = Tyfid ab Eiludd

Heselis ?

S. Gwenfrewy Owain Pennyferw

6. THE ANCESTRY AND DESCENDANTS OF VORTIGERN.

certainty, be said to constitute the warriors who rode with Arthur. While these must not be taken to be 'true' in any obvious sense, there is, we maintain, an element of reality to be glimpsed behind the typical Celtic hyperbole present in all such heroic lists.

That this is by no means solely the provenance of ancient times, we have only to look at Geoffrey of Monmouth's *Historia Regum Brittaniae*, where the list of guests in attendance at the coronation of Arthur and Guinevere, which, seemingly nonsensical, when examined reveals some surprising details. After listing the various Kings and dignitaries who attend, Geoffrey adds:

142

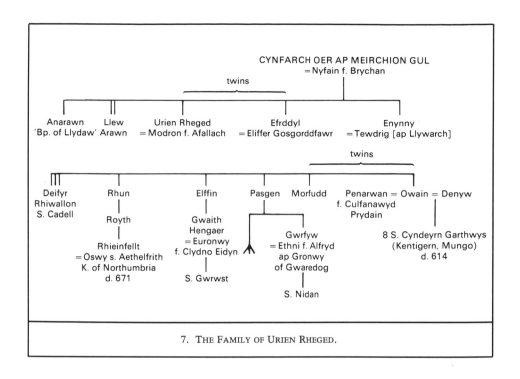

7. THE FAMILY OF URIEN RHEGED.

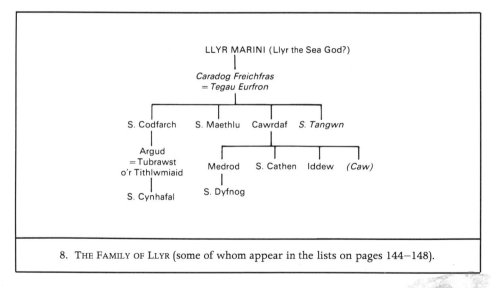

8. THE FAMILY OF LLYR (some of whom appear in the lists on pages 144–148).

In addition to these great leaders there came other famous men of equal importance: Donaut. Mappapo. Cheneus. Mapcoil. Peredur. Maperidur. Grifud. Mapnogord. Regin. Mapclaut. Eddeliui. Mapoledauc. Kyncar. Mabbangan. Kynmaroc. Gorbonian. Masgoit. Worloit. Runmapneton. Kymbelin. Edelnauth. Maptrunat. Cathlus. Mapkathel. Kynlit. Maptieton and many others whose names it is too tedious to tell.

(*Historia*, Bk.ix, Ch.12)

One has only to look at this for a few moments to see that Geoffrey has taken an already extant King list or similar compilation of ancient Celtic names, and run them together to make an almost meaningless jumble. It is the matter of a few moments to untangle them to read as follows:

Celtic warrior from a first-century coin.

> *Dunaut map Pappo map Ceneu map Coylhen. Peredur map Eriddur. Griffudd map Nogoidd. Regin map Claut. Eddellu map Leddauc. Cynan map Bangan. Cynmaroc. Corbonian map Coit. Gorloitt. Rhun map Neithon. Cymbelin. Eddelnaudd map Trunaudd. Cathlus map Catleau. Cynlidd map Neithon.*

Certain names, such as Peredur (Perceval) and Gorloitt (Gorlois?) are already familiar; others may have been simply taken over from a totally non-Arthurian king-list. The importance of its appearence in Geoffrey's text is that it shows that such lists were still current, and that a compilation of the members of Arthur's court was considered to be not unusual as late as twelfth-century European literary tradition.

War chariot from a first-century coin.

A point which we must not neglect is precisely the high preponderance of Celtic names amongst the lists quoted. This may signify that the majority of Arthur's supporters were of Celtic national stock; or it may simply mean that originally Romanised names have been Celticised by subsequent writers. Either way, we are not saying that this is an exact roster of Arthur's warriors, merely that within the sphere of Romano-British, heroic warrior class, this kind of figure would have been present at the time and place under review. Some we know to have had historical existence, and these are indicated in the lists. Much still remains to be done which is outside the scope of the present work before a more accurate and precise list of the people of sixth-century Britain is fully revealed.

THE WARRIORS OF ARTHUR

(A list compiled from original sources, including *Culhwch and Olwen*, *The Dream of Rhonabwy*, *The Twenty-Four Knights of Arthur's Court*, *The Welsh Triads*, and *Welsh Genealogical Tracts*.)

Names indicated with an asterisk (*) are known historical personages. Where these are known, the meaning of names or epithets are given in brackets after the name. The term 'ap' means 'son of'.

1 · Cei; 2 · Bedwyr; 3 · Greidawl Gallddofydd (Tamer of Enemies); 4 · Gwythyr ap Greidawl; 5 · Greid ap Eri; 6 · Cynddylig Cyfarwydd (The Guide); 7 · Tathal Twyll Golau (The Deceitful); 8 · Maelwys ap Baeddan; 9 · Cynchwr ap Nes; 10 · Cubert ap Daere (The Irishman – possibly Curoi mac Daire?); 11 · Fercos ap Roch (Fergus mac Roth?); 12 · Lluber Beuthach; 13 · Corfil Berfach; 14 · Gwyn ap Esni; 15 · Gwyn ap Nwyfre; 16 · Edern ap Nudd; 17 · Cadwy ap Geraint*;

Pomparles Bridge, Glastonbury, Somerset. Local tradition tells that it was at this spot that Bedwyr, Arthur's last surviving warrior, threw the magical sword, Excalibur, back into the water whence it had come.

18 · Fflewdur Flam Wledig (Blazing Lord); 19 · Rhuawn Bebyr ap Dorath; 20 · Bradwen ap Moren Mynawg; 21 · Moren Mynawg; 22 · Dallaf ap Cimin ap Alun Dyfed ap Saidi ap Gwrion; 23 · Uchdryd Ardwyad Cad (Protector in Battle); 24 · Cynwas Cwryfagyl (the Clumsy); 25 · Gwrhyr Gwarthegfras (Rich in Cattle); 26 · Isberyr Ewingath (Cat Claws); 27 · Galloch Gofyniad (The Hewer); 28 · Duach ap Gwawrddur (Hunchback); 29 · Brath ap Gwawrddur; 30 · Nerthach ap Gwawrddur; 31 · Cilydd Canastyr (100 Grips); 32 · Canastyr Canllaw (100 Hands); 33 · Cors Cant Ewin (100 Claws); 34 · Esgeir Gulhwch Gefyncawn (Reed-cutter); 35 · Dwrst Dwnhaeadn (Iron-Fist); 36 · Glewlwyd Gafae lfawr (Mighty-Grasp); 37 · Llwch Llenlleawg (Mighty-Hand); 38 · Anwas Adeiniawg (The Winged); 39 · Sinnoch ap Seitfed ap Bedyn; 40 · Wadu ap Seitfed ap Bedyn; 41 · Naw ap Seitfed ap Bedyn; 42 · Gwenwynwyn ap Seitfed ap Bedyn; 43 · Mael ap Roycol; 44 · Garwyli ap Gwythawg Gwyr; 45 · Gwythawg Gwyr; 46 · Gormant ap Ricca; 47 · Selyf ap Sinoid; 48 · Gusg ap Achen; 49 · Drudwas ap Tryffin; 50 · Twyrch ap Peryf; 51 · Twyrch ap Anwas; 52 · Sel ap Selgi; 53 · Teregud ap Iaen of Caer Dathal; 54 · Sulien ap Iaen of Caer Dathal; 55 · Siawn ap Iaen of Caer Dathal; 56 · Cradawg ap Iaen of Caer Dathal; 57 · Mabsan ap Caw; 58 · Angawddm Gofan; 59 · Gwynad ap Caw; 60 · Llwybyr Coch; 61 · Cynwal ap Caw*; 62 · Gildas ap Caw*; 63 · Calchaf ap Caw*; 64 · Hueil ap Caw*; 65 · Samson Finsych (Dry Lips); 66 · Llary ap Easnar Wledig; 67 · Sarannon ap Glythfur;

68 · Anynnawg ap Menw ap Teirgwaedd; 69 · Fflan ap Nwyfre; 70 · Geraint ap Erbin*; 71 · Ermid ap Erbin; 72 · Dywel ap Erbin; 73 · Llawr ap Ermid; 74 · Cyndrwyn ap Ermid; 75 · Hafaidd Unllen (One Mantle); 76 · Eiddon Fawrfrydig (The Magnanimous); 77 · Rheiddon Arwy; 78 · Llawrodded Farfawg (the Bearded); 79 · Noddawl farf Trwch (Boar's Beard); 80 · Berth ap Cado; 81 · Rheiddwn ap Banon; 82 · Isgofan Hael (The Generous); 83 · Isgawyn ap Banon; 84 · Morfran ap Tegid (The Ugly); 85 · Sandaff Pryd Angel (Bright Angel); 86 · Sglit Uohdryd (Lightfoot); 87 · Henwas Adeiniawg ap Erim; 88 · Carnedyr ap Gofynion Hen (The Aged); 89 · Gwenwynwyn ap Naw (Arthur's Champion in Culhwch); 90 · Culfanawyd ap Gwrion; 91 · Dyfnwal Moel (the Bald); 92 · Terynon Twrf Liant; 93 · Gwrddyal ap Efrei; 94 · Morgant Hael (the Generous); 95 · Gwystl ap Nwython; 96 · Rhun ap Nwython; 97 · Llwydel ap Nwython; 98 · Gwydre ap Llwydeu; 99 · Eidoel ap Ner; 100 · Cynyr Ceinfarfalig (Fair Beard); 101 · Berwyn ap Cyrenyr; 102 · Gwyddawg ap Menestyr; 103 · Garanwen ap Cei; 104 · Llwyd ap Cil Coed; 105 · Huabwy ap Gwryon; 106 · Gwyn Eddyfron; 107 · Gweir ap Galellin Tal Ariant (Silver Brow); 108 · Gweir Gwryhyd Enwir (Malicious in Battle); 109 · Gweir Gwyn Paladr (Bright Spear); 110 · Cas ap Saidi; 111 · Gwrfan Arfwyn (Wild Hair); 112 · Garselit the Irishman; 113 · Penawr Penbagad (Leader of the Host); 114 · Atlandor ap Naw; 115 · Gwyn Hywar (Steward of Cornwall); 116 · Gilla Goeshydd (Stag-Shank); 117 · Huarwar ap Halwn (The Unsmiling); 118 · Gwarae Gwallt Eurin (Golden Hair); 119 · Gwelfyl ap Gwastad; 120 · Uchdryd (Cross Beard); 121 · Elidyr Cyfarwydd (the Guide); 122 · Brys ap Brysethach; 123 · Gruddlwyn Gor (The Dwarf); 124 · Eheubryd ap Cyfwlch; 125 · Gorasgwrn ap Nerth; 126 · Gwaeddan ap Cynfeln; 127 · Dwn Diysig Unben (Valorous Chieftain); 128 · Eilader ap Pen Llarcan; 129 · Cynedyr Wyllt (The Wild); 130 · Sawyl pen Uched (The Overlord); 131 · Gwalchmai ap Gwyar (Arthur's Nephew); 132 · Gwalhafad ap Gwyar; 133 · Gwrhyr Gwastrad Ieithoedd (Interpreter of Tongues); 134 · Iddawc Cordd Prydain (Churn of Britain); 135 · Eliwod ap Madoc ap Uthyr; 136 · Gwarthegyd ap Caw*; 137 · Ephin ap Gwyddno*; 138 · Afaon ap Taliesin; 139 · Caradawg Freichfras (Strong Arm); 140 · March ap Meirchyawn* (First Cousin of Arthur); 141 · Cadwr* (Earl of Cornwall); 142 · Urien ap Kynfarch*; 143 · Owein ap Urien*; 144 · Selyn ap Cynan Garwyn (White Shank); 145 · Gwgawn Greddyrudd* (Red Sword); 146 · Gwres ap Rheged (The Standard Bearer); 147 · Blathaon ap Mwrheth; 148 · Gwenloynwyri ap Naw; 149 · Daned ap Ath; 150 · Goreu ap Custennin (Constantine); 151 · Peredur Paladyr Hir (Long Spear); 152 · Nerth ap Cadarn; 153 · Gweir ap Gwestyl; 154 · Gadwy ap Geraint; 155 · Trystan ap Talwch*; 156 · Moryen Menawc (the Noble); 157 · Granwen ap Llyr; 158 · Llacheu ap Arthur (Son of Arthur); 159 · Amr ap Arthur (Son of Arthur); 160 · Cydfan ap Arthur (Son of Arthur); 161 · Archfedd ap Arthur (Son of Arthur); 162 · Llawfrodedd Farfawc (The Bearded); 163 · Rhyawd ap Morgant; 164 · Dyfyr ap Alun Dyfed; 165 · Llara ap Casnir Wleddig (The Mighty); 166 · Pasgen ap Urien*; 167 · Gilbert ap Cadgyffro (Battle-tumult); 168 · Menw ap Teirgwaedd; 169 · Gwrthmwl Wledig; 170 · Cawrdaf ap Caradawg Freitchfras; 171 · Cadynaith ap Saidi; 172 · Rhun ap Maelgwyn Gwynedd;

Reconstruction of a lorica segementato from Newstead.

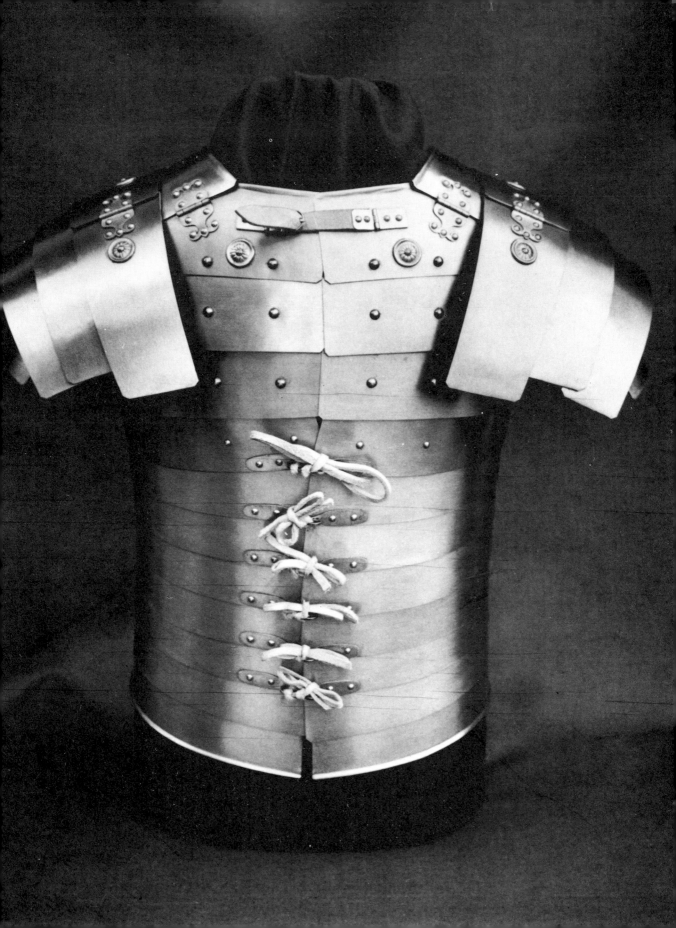

173 · Dawweir Dallben (the Blind); 174 · Taliesin pen Berydd (Chief Poet); 175 · Teithi Hen (the Old) ap Gwynnan; 176 · Gwrfoddw Hen (the Old) (Arthur's Uncle in Culhwch); 177 · Tegfan Gloff (the Lame); 178 · Tegyr Talgellawg (Cup Bearer); 179 · Gwewlyuddyn Saer (the builder who made Arthur's Hall Ehangwen 'Fair and Roomy'); 180 · Amren ap Bedwyr (Arthur's Huntsman); 181 · Rhun Rhuddwern (Red Alder) (Arthur's Huntsman); 182 · Eli (Arthur's

It is believed that this helmet from the Sutton Hoo ship burial is actually Celtic, looted from a dead warrior and buried with his Saxon opponent. It is thus possible that this kind of helmet was still being worn by the warriors of Arthur's time.

Huntsman); 183 · Myr (Arthur's Huntsman); 184 · Rheu Thwydd Dyrys (Fast and Cunning) (Arthur's Huntsman); 185 · Trachmyr (Arthur's Huntsman); 186 · Gweir Dathar Gweinidog (Arthur's Servant); 187 · Eirynwych Amheibyn (the Splendid) (Arthur's Servant); 188 · Cacamwri (the Thresher) (Arthur's Servant); 189 · Bedwini (the Bishop); 190 · Cethrwm (the Priest);

THE WOMEN OF THE COURT

191 · Gwenhwyfar (the Queen); 192 · Gwenhwyach (her Sister); 193 · Rathyen ferch Clemenyl; 194 · Celemon ferch Cei; 195 · Tangwen ferch Gweir Dathar Gweinidog; 196 · Gwen Alarch (Swan White); 197 · Eurneid ferch Clydno Eidin; 198 · Eneuawg ferch Bedwr; 199 · Enrhydred ferch Tuduathar; 200 · Gwenwledyr ferch Gwaredur Cyrfach; 201 · Erdudfyl ferch Tryffin; 202 · Eurolwyn ferch Gwdolyn Gor; 203 · Teleri ferch Peul; 204 · Indeg ferch Garwy Hir; 205 · Morfudd ferch Urien Rheged*; 206 · Gwelliant the Fair; 207 · Creiddylad ferch Llud Llaw Ereint; 208 · Ellylw ferch Noel Cyncroc; 209 · Essyllt Fynwen (White Neck); 210 · Esseyllt Fyngul (Slender Neck)

('ferch' means daughter.)

Reading through this extraordinary list, several things become apparent. One is the extreme normality of many of the epithets – 'the clumsy', 'the generous', 'rich in cattle', 'the deceitful', 'the unsmiling', 'boar's beard'. These are recognizable characteristics of real people. Others, like 'reed-cutter', 'cup bearer', 'Servant' give us a picture of the status and position held by many of these people. Another example is the fact that whole families (that of Iaen of Caer Dalben, for example) and sometimes several generations fought alongside Arthur, demonstrating the duration of his leadership and the strong ties of loyalty he inspired. All this and much more can be learned from a careful study of the names of Arthur's warriors.

MERLIN AND THE DRUIDS

 NE NAME IS SIGNIFICANTLY absent from the list of Arthur's followers and supporters, perhaps because this particular figure is not a warrior — although he does serve as an advisor in military matters throughout several Arthurian campaigns. Yet, despite extensive connections in fiction between the magician Merlin and the legendary King Arthur, from the romances of the Middle Ages right up to the modern film *Excalibur* directed by John Boorman, the earliest sources, such as the warrior lists, do not connect the two best-known characters; Merlin comes before Arthur in Geoffrey of Monmouth's *Historia* – a fact which may add support to the idea that he is also Ambrosius Aurelianus (see Chapter 2) – and though he helps in Arthur's begetting, he does not act as a court advisor or mentor. But the image of the sage or magician guiding the development of the young king is so enduring and potent that it deserves examination in the light of our knowledge of Celtic culture. There were well-defined relationships between kings and Druids, which are echoed in the legends accumulated around the historical Arthur and the historical Merlin.

We know from classical sources such as Diodorus Siculus and Julius Caesar that druids were the highest order of priesthood in Celtic society. Three basic orders of druid were known, and although this division changed after the Roman invasions, and was further altered with the advent of Christianity, it was retained as late as the sixth century in Wales, and much later in Ireland. The three orders were: *Druids*, knowers or judges; *Vates*, seers and prophets; *Bards*, singers of praise. The vates were also associated with battle frenzy and the inspiration of warriors, a tradition which is curiously inverted in the legends of Merlin being driven wild with grief and horror at a great battle on the Scottish borders.

This triple system, with certain minor alterations, persisted into medieval times in Ireland, and the term bard was retained for many centuries in Wales, absorbing the other two functions to a certain extent. During the fifth and sixth century, there was apparently an upsurge of bardic poetry in Wales, at exactly the time when the historical Arthur flourished. During the Roman period, however, druids were forbidden by the Empire as disruptive nationalist priests (something very unusual in the atmosphere of Imperial religious tolerance; this oppression and attempted destruction of Druidism was equalled only by the destruction of the Temple at Jerusalem). An expedition was led by Suetonius Paulinus against the druid college or sanctuary on the island of Anglesey (North Wales) as late as AD 61.

In the context of the traditions of Arthur and Merlin we have to consider the post-Roman revival of a barely suppressed system in which wisdom, prophecy and poetry, originally associated with pagan religion, are related to the government of the land. In short, the role of the druid was to advise the king, and originally to mediate between divine powers and mortals. The druidic association with the land of Britain is strong; Caesar stated (*De Bello Gallico*) that it was the original and primal home of Druidism. The system of dissemination of wisdom (druids), knowledge or fore-knowledge (vates), and music and verse (bards), was disrupted by the Roman Empire, and virtually obliterated in Gaul and the east of England. Yet it remained in fragmented and underground form in the west, the north, and of course as a whole system in Ireland which was never invaded by the Romans.

By the fifth or sixth centuries, Welsh poets called bards were beginning to write down traditional oral verses, to create new praise poems, laments, and to define genealogies. Some of these historical literary sources are still available to us as proof of the bardic system at this time. The most famous names in this bardic revival, or first phase of literate bardism emerging from oral tradition,

Arthur takes strange advice. Before giving final instructions, King Arthur takes advice from his wise man or druid. A bard observes the battle ground, ready to inspire warriors with song and to remember the deeds that will be done for future generations.

are Taliesin, to whom a number of poems and legends or tales are attached, and Merlin, in two possible forms or historical personae.

Three views of a tentative reconstruction of a late third- to fourth-century Roman cavalry trooper's iron helmet, based on fragments found at Burgh Castle, near Great Yarmouth. Helmets of Arthur's time were probably derived from such sources.

ORIGIN OF THE NAME 'MERLIN'

GEOFFREY OF MONMOUTH, writing in the middle of the twelfth century, seems to have combined a legendary Myrddin Emrys with a historical Myrddin ap Morfryn or Merlin Celidonius, to whom some extant poems are attributed, and who seems to have been a contemporary of Arthur.

Geoffrey combined traditions of both Myrddins, changing the name to *Merlinus* for his Norman audience, possibly to avoid ridicule at the similarity between the Welsh name and the word *merde*, which means excrement. Although Merlin Emrys is a purely magical character, he is associated with King Vortigern, the usurper who ruled shortly before Ambrosius, Uther, and Arthur. Merlin Celidonius, the wild poet, seems to have been contemporary with Arthur, but there is no proof of any connection between the two.

Thus we have basic proof that bards and poetic chroniclers were active in the sixth century or earlier, both as singers of praises and laments, and with overtones of magic and prophecy. This proof comes not merely from later statements of tradition, but from actual literature composed by such bards.

The traditional *Prophecies of Merlin* re-stated by Geoffrey of Monmouth and attributed by him to Merlin Emrys prophesying before Vortigern, are far more than a mere fantastical concoction. They represent a development of the *vaticinal* arts among Celtic people. Such tradition persisted well into the eighteenth century in many regions, both as oral verse and as the more diffuse phenomenon of the Second Sight.

It is very likely that 'Myrddin' was a title or descriptive name, always associated with prophecy and other magical arts, though the use of 'magic' in the popular sense is curiously absent from the early sources that described Merlin.

The developed figure of the medieval wizard associated with Arthur has little foundation in the source material up to the twelfth century, but after Geoffrey of Monmouth's expansion of the character in his *Prophecies* and *Life of Merlin* a considerable body of literature developed creating or re-stating traditions of Merlin advising the ruling Arthur. Originally, Merlin prophesied the entire future history of Britain, was mysteriously connected with the assembly of Stonehenge, and helped Uther Pendragon to beget Arthur upon Ygraine, wife of Gorlois of Cornwall. In Geoffrey's *History* Merlin subsequently disappears, though a detailed magical psychology and cosmology revolving around Merlin, Taliesin and Merlin's sister Ganieda forms the basis of Geoffrey's last book, the *Life of Merlin*. In other words, the popular image of Merlin guiding the court of Arthur and therefore British culture in times of darkness, has no basis in early

sources; but this does not imply that it has no basis whatsoever, as we shall soon discover.

Merlin, regardless of his division into more than one possible character, appears as both vates and druid, first he is revealed as the wild prophet of the land uttering mysterious truths and previsions; in later developments he becomes a wise guiding elder who assists the king in the fight against barbaric enemies. It is this clearly druidical role attached to Merlin that suggests that tales of his connection to Arthur are not mere fancy; they are derived from traditions reflecting the solid truth of druids in Celtic culture and their courtly judicial educational function. In various ways, all tales of Arthur and Merlin partake of the two functions described, but the role of bard or praise-singer is never attached to Merlin.

To put this picture into a possible historical context, we may reasonably assume that post-Roman but essentially 'druidic' practices had some place in the tribal assembly of Arthur and his warriors. All leaders, chieftains, kings, even emperors, relied heavily upon vaticinal or predictive and magical arts, ranging from astrology to divination to formal ritual . . . both pagan and Christian. Such practices eventually devolved into mere superstition, such as the mass popular astrology or divination known today, but in early cultures they were a very serious matter indeed, drawn from the most profound philosophies of the pagan Celtic and pagan classical religions; furthermore early Christianity did not restrict practices such as astrology and divination which were only frowned upon and eventually banned in later centuries.

MAGICIANS, PRIESTS AND SPIES

THE HISTORICAL Arthur may have been a Celtic Christian, as traditional descriptions of his armour suggest, but he also inherited the mantle of the long line of pagan kings linked to the health of the land. Seership, prophecy, traditional practices of blessing and cursing (which were held in great respect and awe) are likely to have formed essential elements in his civil and campaigning apparatus. To put this into perspective we must remember that late-Roman gentry in Britain still decorated their villas with pagan images, even when combined with early Christian signs or symbols such as the chi-rho or cross, and that pagan classical poetry, practices and philosophy were by no means annihilated by the fact that the Empire had taken up a branch of Christianity as its political cult. Thus in Italy, for example, we find one of the earliest representations of Arthur, where he is shown riding a goat and surrounded by images of the Zodiac.

To this pan-cultural, pan-religious background, we must add the Celtic resurgence after the Roman decline in Britain; a culture in which prophecy, poetry, music, song and mystical or fervent inspiration were the very fabric of life . . . no king would have been adequate or secure without a druid, seer or bard.

Thus far we have summarised the possible existence of Merlin or Merlins, and the connection of such a person to Celtic traditions of druidism and the important relationship between king and land. Of equal importance is the role of Merlin as wise man or even scientist; this occurs repeatedly in legendary sources, and requires some attention in its own right. Any competent war leader or king needs continual and up-to-date advice on weapons, engineering, tactics and above all a regular flow of intelligence or espionage, carrying information about invading troops, overseas developments, terrain, fodder and of course weather. While some of the more mundane details may be attended to by military specialists, the far-seeing and strategic or scientific matters require specialist advice and operation.

The boundary between *intelligencer* and *magician* in the service of a royal court or war leader was thin indeed; as late as the reign of Elizabeth I, the magus Dr Dee combined his scientific, magical and cryptographical skills in the service of the Crown and state. Even Samuel Pepys in the reign of Charles II prepared a study of far-sight among both Spanish and Scottish people, on the royal assumption that it might be used as a potential weapon of war. The traditions of Merlin associated with the Arthurian period are connected to this role of the magus, king and state, just as they are to the prophet, king and land.

Finally we may touch upon the most mysterious weapon of all in Arthur's armoury . . . the spirit of the land of Britain. In early records Britain is sometimes called 'Clas Myrddin' or Merlin's Enclosure; here we find a faint echo that not only was 'Merlin' a title for a seer, prophet or priest, but that he may have been connected to a tutelary deity of the land. When we consider that Merlin as a youth predicts the whole future history of Britain, inspired by two dragons who live deep within the earth, we find a poetical connection between the seer and the land . . . Merlin was someone through whom the power of the land made itself known to the king. Little wonder, therefore, that there was an enduring theme in which Merlin guided and aided Arthur; Merlin was the mediating magical factor or overview of wisdom, while Arthur was the active dynamic factor of change, purification, resistance to invasion.

The Age of Arthur was indeed an heroic one, where so-called imaginary figures rode into battle shoulder to shoulder with actual sixth-century warriors. It is no longer possible perhaps to separate the two, but, though few now remember the men who fought and died alongside their leader, in the epic myth-haunted stories of King Arthur and his knights of the Round Table, of Merlin and Lancelot and Guinevere, their memory is enshrined for all time.

The Beheading Game

The main tale in this sequence is primitive; it is found in Irish in its most direct variants, and as the remarkable legend of Gawain and the Green Knight in medieval developments. The features most important to Arthurian lore are those of honour, courage and typically a magical battle between life and death or summer and winter. This ancient battle occupied the imagination of Arthur's culture; if we could eavesdrop upon a sixth-century story-telling, we would undoubtedly hear a version of 'The Beheading Game'.

To give us some insight into the history of the period immediately preceding Arthur, and the role of bards and intelligencers in the complex political and military changes of the time, the tale is told by a British ambassador to the Emperor of the West. That there were networks of spies and informers, both Imperial and otherwise, is certain. The fact that our story-teller is given the title of 'Myrddin', which later became Merlin, is speculation based upon evidence. In other words, there was more than one Merlin, for the name was actually a title or description given to a particular type of druid, seer or bard.

Towards the close of the story, the teller utters a curious prophecy about Bears and Boars, and speculates upon how tradition will tell of the descendants of Ambrosius, the war duke. We know, of course, that Arthur followed shortly after the period in which this sequence is set, and that, as late as the twelfth century, prophecies about bears, boars, giants, dragons and other marvels were associated with Merlin and the history of Britain. It seems likely, though unproven, that the mysterious verses set out in Latin by Geoffrey of Monmouth are derived from a genuine Welsh or Breton sequence in an oral tradition stemming from at least as early as the fifth century. Thus a little poetic or perhaps prophetic licence has put bears and boars into the mouth of the bardic spy who entertains the Last Emperor of the West.

The Emperor of the West sat in his palace at Ravenna and thought long gloomy Imperial thoughts. He had much to trouble him; his head ached, his stomach burned, and the tramp of marching Germans training in the surrounding courtyards did not help at all. But mainly it was this other Emperor in the East who upset him, who had a better claim, who had not been set up by a German general. Yet Emperor of the West he was, even though he woke at nights sweating and feeling like a man of straw. Perhaps he was after all a false Emperor, and the other one in the east was true. How simple it had all been in the earlier days when there was only one Emperor, and he only had little things to concern himself with: poison, daggers of assassination, exotic diseases brought on by debauchery, madness, and the revenge of pagan gods and goddesses. The Emperor of the West did not have such clear-cut problems; he had Germans (well he was mainly German himself), bishops, invading savages who were really cousins, territorial claims, and many other complex matters. He gazed gloomily at the inlaid floor of his private chamber, brooding on the vast wealth of distant lands that was rightfully his but would never be realised. The Empire was no longer centred on Rome . . . it was not centred anywhere.

In the corner his Greek physician stood ready with a compress of euphoric herbs; a masseur sat behind a discreet curtain, guarded by a stout Germanic warrior in fancy gilded uniform (masseurs were all suspect); three delightful young females sat at the opposite end of the chamber under the stern eye of their matron and procuress who had nodded greetings to the departing bishop as her scented party entered. From the passage to the kitchens, a silent procession of servants carried in sugared cakes, honeyed meats, sweet wine, spiced fish livers, whole tiny pigs' heads. All of these delicacies were rejected by a flick of the eyebrows from the Emperor's house-master, who was solely responsible for domestic matters in the private chamber. He considered none of these items new, thrilling, colourful or demanding enough for his master's present mood.

In short, the Emperor of the West was quite alone and very private at this time; he felt the fear of solitary rule (while wishing that he was the solitary and only Emperor) and dreaded a lonely death by boredom. The boots tramped on, the spears clashed, a constant reminder of where the power lay in Ravenna.

At length the Emperor lifted his little finger, left hand, very slightly. Immediately his favourite guard captain lumbered up to him and grunted. This communicative sound proved how concerned the chamber attendants were for their Emperor; normally the guards refused to speak to him at all unless directly ordered to do so.

'Bring me that story-teller from the land of Britain,' said the Emperor to the air in front of him, refusing to look at the soldier, 'the one that your men call Walu something or other. Make sure that he knows that I'm bored and in need of inspiration. I want to hear about battles . . . no, a combat . . . something where the best one wins, the one who is really himself and not someone pretending to be something that he is not or should not be. There has to be a glorious struggle in which the best man wins, and people sing about it for years to come or write scrolls, and no churchmen to criticise. He must have something like that tucked away in his head; if he does not, beat one out of him.'

The Beheading Game. The burning powerful warrior from the Otherworld breaks into the boastful hall of heroes with an unanswerable challenge.

The guard grunted again and stamped off across the chamber, causing the girls to pretend to flinch, and scraping the delicate tiles with his nailed boots. His long blond hair had been carefully powdered and brushed for this duty, and floated over his gilded leather cuirass. He hoped that the Walu shaman was in a jovial mood, as no one would dare to lift a finger against such a magician, no matter what the silly little Emperor said. Life was so complex; he really had preferred living on a mound and clubbing his neighbours for pleasure; once a man acquired power and possessions such as boots, he was on the road to effete degradation. But the wine was good, and there was plenty of opportunity to develop skill in arms that could be turned against anyone . . . even a puppet Emperor.

As soon as the guard had left the chamber, the Emperor of the West felt unhappy concerning his request. This Walu Mertanus or whatever his ridiculous name was had come from Britain, of all places, two months ago. His presence had aroused considerable dispute among the Christian priests, though he too claimed to be Christian. What was worse, he claimed to represent one Ambrosius, a *dux bellorum* who was supposedly setting the abandoned province in order. The Emperor of the West had immediate visions of a rival . . . perhaps he would soon be known as the Emperor of the Middle, or the Emperor Between, or even the Previous Emperor. But far from uttering grandiose claims to power, this curious ambassador respectfully requested trading terms and a treaty of assistance and support; the Britons wanted heavy armour, modern weapons, larger horses. In return they would ship corn, wine and of course the old traditional commodity of hunting dogs, plus promised gifts of gold. None of this seemed remotely likely to the Emperor, who was not altogether stupid, and he kept the ambassador waiting in order to amuse himself. Perhaps if he waited long enough the *dux bellorum* might collapse under the weight of his pretentious title.

More immediate was the embarrassing fact that the Briton spoke immaculate antique Latin, in a high musical voice, with no uncouth German inflexions or bastard words. There was no question of him ever grunting '*Ych hyght Mertinus, Imperator*' or some such gibberish; he even used courtly phrases normally found only in Latin literature. He seemed more patrician than an old family from Rome itself, and this made the Emperor of the West feel slightly inferior.

So the Emperor had resorted to one of the most ancient ploys known to monarchs; he commanded Walu Mertinus to tell him stories; was the ambassador from Britain not after all a *bard*? The Emperor had innumerable spies, though he was uncertain who else they worked for; they advised him that the Briton had been growing restless and might be ready to depart, with or without Imperial permission. Only that evening a bishop had been blustering about heresy and pollution in connection with the Walu, and had demanded that he be banished. All the more reason, therefore, to keep him on a little longer. Let them all suffer even as their Emperor suffered, and the tale for tonight had better be a good one, or by the phantom of Julius Caesar someone would suffer even more! As soon as he had made this inward oath, the Emperor looked around him suspiciously . . . the great Julius had been cruelly murdered, and perhaps his phantom did not enjoy being invoked trivially by someone who, after all, represented everything that Julius had sought to keep out of the realms of Rome.

As the Emperor rested his head upon his fist to brood, there was heard a discreet, barely audible, coughing sound from a corner of the chamber. Looking up, he saw his favourite guard looming over him, and felt again that sudden terror of assassination; but having caught the Emperor's attention, the guard merely stepped aside to reveal the Walu. Being alone, thought the Emperor, has the advantage of no trumpets or proclamations or pedigrees, but it also means that people can sneak up and take you by surprise. Once again he looked with discomfort upon the British ambassador.

The Walu was tall; he wore a simple white woollen robe of the type sported by philosophers, astrologers, and similar mountebanks. With a graceful movement, he glided towards the Imperial dais. His hair was swept back and tied in a long horse-tail with silver wire; his beard had been neatly cut and trimmed. The long nose and firm mouth of the Walu seemed stern and critical, and the Emperor of the West barely managed to restrain himself from the urge to feel his own beard and moustaches. After the most minimal of prostrations, which caused many raised eyebrows and fluttering hands to mouths around the private chamber, the British bard stood waiting for the Emperor to speak, as was the custom.

'As my men will have informed you, I shall give further attention to your requests if you are able to entertain me. I require tonight a story that I have never heard before; it must have honour, terror, falsehood and the discovery of falsehood, a hero who wins against tremendous odds, and a general theme that persons must not imitate that which they are not, even if they truly think that they are whatever it may . . . do you understand?' These last words were uttered slowly in the time-honoured manner of an emperor to a barbarian.

'Your request is immaculately phrased, great Imperial Warrior,' murmured the Walu in his perfect singsong Latin. He paused and closed his eyes for a moment, then continued: 'I have at my command the learned works of many authors; Homer, Horace, Virgilius, Socrates, Hecataeus, Solinus, or perhaps one of the modern poets . . . several of these have recounted tales similar to that which you seek.'

The Emperor of the West had not heard of some of the names mentioned, and

loathed modern poets. He knew that the Briton was demonstrating his legendary bardic powers of memory to impress not only the ruler of the Empire (in
the West) but everyone else who was with him while he sat alone in his private
chamber. He tried to look bored, while thinking furiously of some source of
tales that would flummox this self-satisfied savage from a forgotten colony.
Suddenly, an extremely cunning thought came to him:

'No, nothing Greek, or Roman, or modern; nothing political, or geographical
or doctrinal; I've heard it all before and find it dull. Do you not have a repertoire
from . . .' and here he paused, ready to devastate Walu Mertinus with a request
that even a bard would find hard to accommodate, 'your native land?' There, he
had said it. Everyone knew that Britain, though rich in corn and farmland, had
no writing or literature of its own; everything had been borrowed from the
civilisation and influence of Rome. There was no evidence that they had any
literature whatsoever, other than heretical religious nonsense that occasionally
found its way across the sea to Gaul.

Mertinus drew himself upright; first he frowned, then he smiled. This is a
good sign, thought the Emperor; he's worried but he's faking pleasure.

'Yes, Imperator, most assuredly we do have a small collection of miserable
tales in my native country. But they are hardly suitable for such discerning and
august ears as your own.'

Just as I thought, the Emperor smiled almost openly. 'Poor though they may
be, I expect that they will have a certain remote and bucolic charm. Perhaps you
can find one suitable to my needs . . . do you require time? I can allow you the
turning of a sand-glass to prepare any scrolls or clerical assistants who can read
and prompt.'

'Oh indeed not, most refulgent and opulent ruler,' came the instant reply. 'If
your Imperial person will permit I am able to proceed directly from memory.'

'Ah, yes. Well . . . proceed . . . do you require a stool? No? Good, carry on as
directed.' And the Emperor flicked the third finger of his left hand, upon which
sign the guard captain hurried out to stop the drilling and crunching and
grinding and shouting from outside. The march of boots turned into scurrying
and scampering, and a few lewd shouts floated over the night wind. Then there
was silence, and the bard began to speak softly in his perfect rhythmic Latin. As
he spoke the guards made signs to ward off spirits, but they crowded round the
chamber door to listen.

'Let all who have ears listen, and may the tale be remembered forever. This
is the tale of the Beheading Game and the Warrior from the land of Summer, told
this day by Myrddin of the Cymri in the Imperial hall at Ravenna.

'Once long ago in the land of Britain there was a great king who held his
warriors to a yearly pact; every year they must come to the royal hall for
feasting, games, combat, and a competition to establish the king's champion for

the year to come. And the king was called Bran in the British tongue, which is of course Brennus in Latin, and simply means "leader".

'As evening drew on, the company were seated in the hall eating and drinking and boasting. The doors flew open with a loud blast of howling wind and the door pins shattered and flew across the room to impale a Greek physician who stood mixing remedies for the wounded champions after the games. With a trembling of the floor from the great weight of his bear-skin clad feet, a horrible ugly giant of a man strode in and glared all around. He was wrapped in a mottled bull-hide and carried a living green tree in one broad hand, with its roots in the dark earth and its crown reaching up almost to the roofbeams of the hall. In his other hand, with fingers as broad as a warrior's wrist, he held an axe with a bronze head greater than the doors of the temple of Minerva in Rome itself. The handle would have taken a team of six great ploughing oxen to move it, but the sharpness of the blade-edge was so keen that a mere hair blown against it in a gentle breeze would be instantly split into two parts.

'This towering warrior burst through the assembled ranks, and trampled upon a masseur who had tried to hide under a bench. He took his stance right beside the great roof-support in the centre of the hall, where the undying fire burned winter and summer through.

'The king's house-master and steward spoke up saying: "Why do you burst in here and stand by the roof pole, blocking the fire? Do you wish to be burnt to death? I fear that the heat of your anger will destroy this hall rather than benefit it!"

' "Well spoken, little man," rumbled the warrior, shaking his green tree over the cowering heroes, "Whatever my powers are, you will all soon agree that I come to enlighten rather than to incinerate; no matter how much I glow, the hall of this king will never be destroyed. But light is not my only power, I have others also, but even the powers that I have cannot satisfy my quest."

'At this the king spoke up: "If you come as supplicant, I bid you tell of the nature of your quest, for this is the annual gathering of champions, where all great deeds may be performed with honour."

'At this kingly statement the green-branched warrior smiled and radiated heat . . . "I have been in Erin, in Alba, in Gaul and in Europe; in Africa and Asia and Greece and Scythia; in the Islands of Gades, the Pillars of Hercules, in the Tower of Bregon and the mountains of India; I have been in Summer Lands, and over Earth, and under Sea; my intelligence has reached to the furthest lights set by the Creator in the vault of Heaven, but never have I found a man who understands fair play." At this the company roared and protested and shouted and blustered that they were heroes all, and any one of them could show fair play, even to a giant who shed light as easily as a procuress sheds fleas.

'"Very well," rumbled the warrior, and his breath blew away a procession of cooks who brought meat to the royal table. "As you men of Britain excel all others in strength, prowess, valour, nobility, generosity, excellence, wit, dignity, honesty, truth and worth, you shall select a champion from among yourselves to satisfy my quest. But because of the sacred nature of his kingship, Bran shall be spared this test, for he shall act as a bridge across stormy waters in the times to come. Let a hero stand forth to prove he understands fair play."

'The warriors were silent, fearing some kind of trick. Finally, a great fat-necked, muscular, thick-skulled warrior asked as to the nature of the proof.

'"Easy is the answer to that question, little man, for I seek merely a bargain of fair play in which I cut off your head tonight and you in turn cut off mine tomorrow night." The fat-necked warrior, renowned for his strength at wrestling and his ability to think no thoughts for long periods of time, turned pale and said: "I'll take the challenge on the condition that you turn it the other way around, and let me have first blow."

'"So the men of Britain are as flatulent and soggy as the rest of the world," roared the giant, shaking his tree and blasting the company with the heat of his face. "Nevertheless I will turn the bargain around and agree to take the first blow." And he immediately lay down with his head on the chopping block, and pushed his axe into the hands of the fat-necked warrior. The blow was struck with great enthusiasm, straight through the giant's neck and on into the block did the huge sharp axe fall. The fountain of blood sluiced across the floor of the hall and flushed away two bishops who had but recently come into the land to preach.

'For an instant the giant corpse lay still, then, clutching his green tree as if it were a staff, the headless body slowly drew himself upright. He snatched at his fallen head, and stuck it back upon his shoulders, and taking tree, axe, chopping block and all, hurled himself from the hall of the king, straight out through the stout wall, which ripped apart like cloth.'

Suddenly Walu Mertinus paused, and seemed to mop his brow as if he too had felt the heat of the green warrior. The Emperor of the West sat rigid upon his throne; the symbolism of the tale had not been lost on him, and he saw it as an allegory of his futile wars against the invading tribes from the North and north-east. He also knew that there was some other subtle meaning to the tale just beyond his reach.

The German guards grinned at one another; they had liked the scene where the bishops were flushed away by blood . . . as for the rest it was a typical magician's story and was certain to have a tricky ending. The shaman was not chanting, however, and seemed suddenly to look around the room as if he had lost something. Just as the Emperor was about to lift a finger, Mertinus gave a visible start and rushed back into the telling.

'Yes . . . when the mysterious giant warrior returned the following evening, the fat-necked one had run away and broken his covenant. But with furious words and taunts he made another stout veteran strike off his head; once again he recovered from the blow, and once again the covenant was broken by a Briton who dared not receive his blow in fair play. On the third night of this contest, the king's personal champion returned from hunting, bearing a fine stag with ten points. The quality of this man was that he could grow short and broad or long and thin at will, and with his skill at arms and his speed in hunting, he had never lost a battle.

'The hero took one look at the green warrior stretched out upon the blood-stained block, and leaping forward snatched up the great axe. High he lifted it until it touched the roof of the hall; hard he hefted it until it clove through the air, neck, bone, block and floor. To this very day there is a cleft in the ground in that place where the River Avon flows into the Severn sea, and a sacred cavern dedicated to the giant may still be seen by those brave enough to climb up to it.

'But even this blow did not prevent the glowing warrior from picking up his head, clapping it onto his blood-clotted shoulders, and stamping off into the night. "I shall be back tomorrow, little man," he bellowed, "and I will have sharpened my axe!"

'All the next day the king's personal champion sat in dread, and a few unkind members of the court started singing funeral songs. When night fell there was no feasting in that hall, and the fire burned dim. Just at midnight the doors crashed open and the fearsome warrior made his presence felt with a blast of heat and the smell of green leaves and growing plants bursting from the earth.

'"Stretch out your neck, little man," he bellowed, flinging down the chopping block.

'The champion slowly stepped up to the block and laid his head upon it; a gasp went round the assembly.

'"Not long enough, little short neck . . . stretch further still." And the champion stretched his spine so that a warrior's full grown foot would have fitted between any two of his ribs, and his skin was pale with the stretching and his face red. But now his neck lay full across the death block, and the giant raised his axe . . . '

Now in the very midst of this drama, the Emperor of the West biting his knuckles and the guards climbing over one another to peep through the curtain, Walu Mertinus coughed again, and uttered a muffled word or two breaking up the metre of the verse as if he had lost the next line altogether.

Immediately a servant leapt forward with chilled wine and sugared fruits, but the bard waved these refreshments away. The Emperor could hardly contain himself from asking what would happen next . . . but it would be too much to show curiosity to this pedlar from over the western sea ... this supplicant for aid in the midst of chaos and ruin. The Emperor signed the servant to his dais, and took wine to mask his eagerness for the tale to continue. As he drank, he studied the bard over the rim of his goblet. Was his face flushed red again? Surely he was blushing; had he actually *forgotten* how to begin the next verse? But his powers of memory were supernatural ... or so he had posed and postured earlier in the evening.

With a deliberate show of imperial impatience, the Emperor allowed his fingers to drum lightly upon the arms of his throne. The servants turned pale, the house-master lifted his eyebrows several inches and began to sidle towards the chamber door. Behind the curtain, the German guards looked at each other in slow puzzlement; they knew that these western shamans had magical powers of memory and could not understand this embarrassing incident which would surely lose Walu Mertinus much prestige.

Once more the Walu cleared his throat and looked about him; the Emperor could resist no longer.

'So your powers of recollection are not as great as you would have us think, man of Britain. Perhaps it is the change of climate or the intimacy of the situation. It seems that you lose your wager with us; for if you cannot keep a simple boast, how can you keep a bargain concerning arms and materials? How do we know that your *dux bellorum* will not forget how much he has to pay?' The Walu grew dark red in the face and gasped for breath, as if indignant and outraged. But the Emperor was on sure ground now ... 'Enough play-acting, Mertinus Walu, we will revise our bargain. If you can complete the tale as agreed, you will live. If not you will have your head cut off at one blow by the captain of my guard ... and no power in the world will bring *you* back to strike a return blow!'

Behind the curtain the guards pushed and elbowed to be out from under the touch of their captain, who up to now had leant in a comradely fashion upon their shoulders. If he had to kill the shaman he would be the most unlucky man in Ravenna, perhaps in the whole world. Just as it seemed likely that the captain's luck had finally turned for the worse, the shaman cleared his throat again, and fumbled his way through a few lines from the previous verse of the tale. Suddenly he launched into the final scene with great power and a fine sense of rhythm. The German guards sighed and settled down to listen.

'The sound of the axe rising and the giant's bull-hide coat creaking were as loud as the tempests that toss the forest of Calydon on a winter night. There was a sound such as is made by a hundred eagles plunging for the kill with air whistling through their pinions, and the invincible axe came down upon the champion's neck; halting short, blunt side first.

'"Rise up, little man," roared the green warrior, his face glowing with pleasure. "You are incomparable for valour, for courage, and for fair play; henceforth let all the men of Britain look to you for an example, and if your totem is the boar, as I see it is from your round shield, then a bear will bear the boar as an example to the world."

'And with these enigmatic words, the mysterious warrior vanished.'

At dawn the Emperor drank a draught of watered wine mixed with a mild purgative, and wondered what the Emperor of the East had been prescribed by his physician. Secretaries and advisors gathered around armed with papers and petitions and information, while the churchmen muttered crossly to one another with much waving of arms and citing of references.

Just as he lifted a finger to commence the day's business, his favourite guard captain lumbered into the hall and whispered loudly in the Emperor's ear.

'The magician has vanished just like his giant.' The Emperor of the West was not good at riddles before noon, and stared blankly at his captain, trying to recollect if this was perhaps a code word for the day or for covert action against some group of dissidents.

'The Britisher, the Walu; he charmed himself over the guest-block walls into the night. He has taken three Imperial post horses!' For a short moment there was silence, then pandemonium broke loose as the Emperor of the West grew red then black in the face, stood up and gasped for breath. Slaves, doctors, advisors, clerics and burly warriors started running hither and thither, smashing into one another, trampling upon bare toes with studded boots, knocking over maps and inks and scrolls and stylii. But rage as he might, the Emperor of the West never saw a bard again.

The bard who bore the honoured title of Myrddin relaxed for the first time in seven months. The journeys through the restless vicious lands had been tedious and dangerous, but now he was on a ship from Little Britain, heading westwards into the refreshing sea rain and mist. The angelic British tongue was spoken all around him, and he was given some genuine respect and privacy. Not that he was a proud man, but it had been hard indeed to be treated as a mere entertainer and clown. How degenerate the Empire had grown; perhaps Britain really was the last haven of the light, just as Ambrosius insisted during his fiery speeches.

Telling the head-severing tale to that ridiculous puppet Emperor had been hard; Myrddin knew that he had overdone the loss of memory, but these barbarians were used to overacting and were often unable to detect subtleties . . . so the crude and obvious had to be employed openly. The Greek had worried him; they were a cunning people and probably had British ancestry somewhere in them before they had declined, or so it seemed from their literature. But the physician had understood the open threat in the tale, as had the old witch of a procuress. And the masseur would have said nothing anyway, being already well paid for information. Pity that the crack about the bishops was wasted, though it served to amuse the guards for a while.

A bard's memory was indeed as Myrddin had claimed for himself: perfect. In addition to the great works of Greece and Rome, Egypt, Chaldea and the vast Eastern lands beyond the known world, the Christian gospel (in all sectarian variants), modern historians and geographers and the vast oral repertoire of his own national poems, wisdom tales, initiatory dramas, alphabets, animal and bird lore, astronomy, cosmology, and extensive genealogy, Walu Mertinus now knew the strength of the Imperial armies in the West. He also knew the weaknesses of the officers, and what revolts were planned; what tribes were about to invade by land and by sea, and which of the savages had blood relatives in the Imperial court. He also knew a name-list of informers and the means to contact them, and a network of seamen and fisherfolk who would not hesitate to warn of a forthcoming fleet of barbarians . . . be they Imperial or otherwise.

He, Myrddin, would take this store back to the *dux bellorum*, who would use it not only to defend Britain, but to take as much of Europe as he could to declare a new Roman Empire. But the bard was uncertain about these greater ambitions; he knew that the strength of the Britons was also their weakness, the love of poetry and images over attention to facts and details. Ambrosius might be able to organise in the old Roman style, but it would not be likely to reach beyond the shores of the Island of the Mighty into neighbouring Gaul, other than through the present network of trade, friends and relatives, and of course spies. The British warriors lived as much in the land of the Fair Folk or the mysteries of Light as they did in the saddle or at the tower of a fighting ship. Even if Ambrosius did not sweep through Gaul into Germany and perhaps on even to Rome itself, the bards would eventually sing as if his dreams had become history. And then compose verses about some unborn son who would follow in his father's path.

As the salt spray washed across his face, Walu Mertinus, Myrddin by title in the ancient manner, pulled his high pointed hood down over his head, relaxed into the hard wooden bulwark of the vessel, and prepared to sleep in safety. What, he thought, was truth?

6 · Celtic Frenzy

Tri Lledrithiog farchawg oedd yn Llys Arthur: nid amgen, Menw ab Teirgwaedd; Tryfean ab Tallwch; Eiddilig Gorr; (neu Cai hir ab Cynyr farfog:) canys ymrithio a wneynt yn y rhith i mynnynt, pan vai galed arnynt, ac am hynny ni allai neb eu gorfod, rhwng eu cryfder, a'u dewrder, a'u hûd a'u lledrith.

Three Magical, or Necromantic Knights, were in King Arthur's Court: *Menw*, the fon of *Teirgwaedd*; *Tryftan*, the fon of *Tallwch*; and *Eiddilic Gorr*; for they could metamorphofe themfelves into what fhape or character they pleafed, and act accordingly, when they were reduced to extremity; and therefore, no man could overcome them.

ARTHUR THROUGH TIME

HE FORTUNES WHICH have attended the transmission of the Matter of Britain from its inception in the so-called Dark Ages have been as varied as possible. With the changes of attitude which have accompanied each succeeding age, so the figures of Arthur and his warriors have altered, sometimes subtly, often radically. Almost from the moment of Arthur's disappearance, reality began to be shaped to fit the needs of the time.

Thus in the year which followed the defeat at Camlan, Arthur and his followers already seem to have begun the metamorphosis which will turn them, ultimately, into figures of myth. The stories, whispered at first we may suppose, began to gather momentum until the successors to Arthurian Britain, the Anglo-Saxons, themselves began to appropriate Arthur as their own. When they, in turn, were overcome by the Normans, it was to find that the name of Arthur was already known. Refugees, fleeing from the Saxons years before, had crossed the sea to Armorica, which began soon after to be known as Little Britain, or Brittany. From there the stories of Arthur spread, finding fertile soil in a still largely Celtic-based land. The Norman French took Arthur to their hearts and further embroidered the tales in their retellings.

This is, of course, a vastly oversimplified version of what occurred, a thumbnail sketch of 500 years of history and cultural exchange. Yet, by the beginning of the Middle Ages, Arthurian 'relics' abounded. To the people of the period, who had little real notion of vast extents of time, let alone of archaeology, there was nothing strange in possessing, for example, the Mantle of Isolt, said to be kept at the church of St Sampson in Cornwall. In fact, any garment dating from the sixth century, would have long since crumbled away.

167

ARTHURIAN MIRACLES

HERE WERE, TOO, the miraculous objects: Gawain's skull, still on display at Dover Castle in Caxton's day; or Arthur's Sword, given by Richard I to the Sicilian King Tancred in 1191. Or, perhaps the most interesting and possibly the only real relic – a crystal cross said to have been given by Arthur to Glastonbury Abbey, after he had attained it in supernatural circumstances during a mass at which the Virgin herself presented her Child at the offertory. All of these were accepted matter-of-factly as splinters from the True Cross or nails from the Crucifixion.

Later, The Sword of Tristan appears in a list of King John's regalia for 1207, and has been tentatively associated with the sword Curtana, symbolizing the King's clemency. Because it was a shortened or blunted sword, R.S. Loomis identified Curtana with Tristan's sword, damaged during his combat with the Morhalt, Ireland's champion.

Other artefacts had a more directly political bearing – like the Crown of Arthur, which was presented to Edward I in 1283 by the Welsh in token of their submission after the death of Llewellyn II at Builth Wells – and which became a physical indication of their defeat at the hands of the English. The supposed grave of Arthur, discovered at Glastonbury in 1190 was, as already discussed, a very useful piece of propaganda to bolster the claim of Henry II to the throne of Britain.

Supposedly kept at St Edmund's shrine, Westminster, was the imprint of Arthur's Seal. It was described by Leland in 1540 as showing the figure of Arthur crowned and in royal robes, bearing in the right hand a sceptre with fleur-de-lys, in the left an orb with cross. The legend on the seal read 'PATRICIUS ARTURIUS BRITTANNIAE, GALLIAE, GERMANIAE, DACIE IMPERATOR'. While at Winchester stood the round table – actually dating from further back in time than the reign of Edward I. It can still be seen there today, painted with the names of Arthur's greatest knights, and bearing a Tudor rose in the centre, placed there as another point of Arthurian interest and propaganda.

ARTHUR IN POLITICS

HUS THE NAME AND status of Arthur can be seen to have had a lengthy history of political use which has as yet to be fully chronicled. It is clear that for the English monarchy of the Middle Ages, Arthur represented a figure of such eminence and nobility that to claim descent from him enhanced their own nature – as well as their claim to the throne. Just as the Normans regarded themselves as successors to Arthur, so the Welsh Princes, in their long

struggle against their overlords, claimed direct descent from Arthur, through
the line of Cadwalader, who was considered the last true king of Britain.

The historian Mary E. Giffin has pointed out that:

It has been shown by scholars that Henry VII, making the most of a slender claim to royal
prestige, traced his descent from Brutus in five score degrees, and was hailed by the Welsh as
their King, the Bull of Mona, the resurrected Arthur come at last to rule over all Britain.

(Cadwalader, Arthur, and Brutus in the Wigmore MS, Speculum, 1941)

169

and that at his coronation the red dragon of Cadwalader (and of Arthur) was born in procession.

The Wigmore MS, preserved at Chicago University Library, has also been cited as proof of the use of Arthurian material for political ends. This MS, which belonged to the powerful Welsh family of Mortimer, contained material from Geoffrey of Monmouth as well as other ancient sources; in the parts referring to Arthur, Brutus or Cadwalader, there are marginal notations which make it clear that the marriage of Ralph de Mortimer to Gwladusa, daughter of Iorwerth Prince of Wales, in 1228, was understood as a joining of the Norman family to one which stood in direct descent from Arthur.

The convocation of Merlin. The seer perceives the doom of the warriors of Arthur; his vision reaches far into the future.

NATIONALISM

LL OF THIS CAN be seen to reflect another important aspect of the Celtic soul – its intense and sometimes overwhelming nationalism, which not only fuelled the strength of purpose enabling Arthur to keep the Germanic invaders at bay, but actually generated the kind of heroic battle frenzy which we have noted as an aspect of the Arthurian warrior. Indeed Geoffrey's *Historia* can be said to be the first literary example of Celtic nationalism we still possess, and which provided material for several generations to build upon.

So it has continued right up to the present, where so-called Arthurian themes have been re-invoked to support more sinister racial tendencies. Thus in Germany, for example, at the height of Nazi domination, Hitler sent the highest-ranking members of his SS to Montsegur in the Pyranees to seek the Grail. Fortunately, if not surprisingly, they were unsuccessful, but belief in matters Arthurian sustained their search. Such belief indeed as has kept the legends alive, and with them a continuing tradition of the verities represented by Arthur's warriors and the Celtic culture which they in turn represent.

PARADOXES

FEATURE OF ARTHURIAN lore is that it is paradoxical; this paradox runs through many aspects of Celtic culture even today. History, legend, fact and fiction are fused together in a strange yet often potent manner; the warriors of Arthur were brutal yet honourable, savage yet otherworldly. Such qualities came to the fore during the medieval period, sometimes stylised to ridiculous extremes, but their roots were in the Celtic culture of an earlier age...earlier than that of Arthur and in some ways-difficult to pinpoint historically. Against enormous odds, the Britons of the fifth and sixth centuries

170

forged a short cultural period which had a remarkable effect upon Western history – religious, artistic and idealistic. Many of the essential concepts of natural law or justice seem to have their origins in 'Arthurian' ethics; the epitome of civilisation is a society in which the strong defend the weak rather than prey upon them, and in which, worldly enemies subdued, the vision turns to transpersonal or religious and spiritual quests. Such ends, both literal and poetical, are radically different to the materialist Roman-based culture that dominates the world today . . . yet the kingdom of Arthur was forged out of both Roman and Celtic components.

If we look for the origins of the role of strength defending weakness, or of the apparently worldly warrior suddenly seeking mystical enlightenment (and the two concepts are very closely connected indeed) we cannot trace it directly to the sixth century. While certain powerful expressions of the Celtic Church and of British post-Roman organisation may be defined through historical sources, the concepts themselves are founded upon an ancient religious and magical worldview which is essentially Celtic. When we describe such a worldview in broad terms it is open to abuse, both in the sense of vapid idealistic romanticism, and in the more pernicious sense of political racial manipulation. The worldview itself is derived from a heroic tribal society or culture in which such foundational values were not called into question; indeed many of them survived well into historical times and were only broken through force of arms. In the primal culture or cultures which remain shrouded in the distant past but approachable by a number of disciplines, political abuse of foundational values would have been unlikely . . . and perhaps impossible for individuals to contemplate. In other words modern readers and thinkers should be very cautious when considering such values or their magical-religious worldview in retrospect.

Despite the mysterious cultural origins, both known and unknown, certain Celtic characteristics appear strongly even today. In military practice the courage and strength of Celtic regiments has been frequently employed by ruling powers; in Britain this represents a particularly ironic twist of politics, in which the very qualities destroyed culturally by force of arms are restored for purely political militaristic reasons. Such abuse is based upon both the valour and the romantic weakness of the Celts; a Celt, it seems, must have a cause.

An idealised Arthurian culture is founded upon concepts which have their origins in the Celtic past, and it is worth summarising such concepts briefly. The list is by no means complete, but the reader will see a number of connections between the qualities listed and the legends and history of Arthur.

1) The value of the individual is ultimately less than that of the clan, tribe or race. Individual death is meaningless.
2) Warriors have a strict obligation to defend and support weaker or differently orientated sectors of the community or culture.
3) Kings and chieftains hold both power and land in trust rather than legal ownership. They are personally responsible for the health of both land and people.

Three soldiers from Croy Hill, Dumbartonshire.

4) Patterns of living are based upon a series of magical-religious beliefs and practices which are often unspoken or deeply intuitive rather than intellectually formulated or defined.

5) The arts of the imagination are held in high respect and act as an enabling force within the community, spanning generations and linking them through both inspiration and collective education. Originally this aspect of Celtic culture was perpetuated by specific sectors of the culture, in the form of druids, seers, and bards.

6) The fusion of 4 and 5 above in the life of any individual leads to occasions of remarkable heroism, idealism and achievement. The temporal individuality is

subsumed by an imaginative higher order; this may be expressed as valour in arms or as artistic or religious perception and dedication. Both are hallmarks of Celtic culture through the centuries.

7) The hard facts of survival are mixed with a deep flow of dream-like otherworldly symbolism which is very distinct and definite; it is derived from environmental relationship between land and people over prolonged periods of time. Expressed as poetry, songs, music or tales, it forms a collective foundation for all aspects of life.

8) Celtic culture has strong tendencies towards decentralisation, individualism and radical opposition to enforced authority. This may seem at first to contradict some of the previous points, but it is based upon an intuitive value in which government must be by consensus (the king holds the land for the people, in ancient terms) rather than by decree.

9) An enduring importance is placed upon the role of woman in Celtic culture. This varies in modern expressions from region to region, but is derived from an early worldview in which the feminine principle was worshipped as divine. The theme runs through religion, but also appears strongly in tradition; we discovered in an earlier chapter that warriors were taught by warrior-women (the tradition of Scathach) according to Irish legend deriving from a fierce war-goddess. Even today the fury of a Celtic woman is something to be wary of, a power shared by certain Iberian peoples, but by no means universal.

We have assembled in these pages evidence of sixth-century warriors, told tales which demonstrate their values and adventures, and tried to show how closely history and legend actually depend upon one another.

In conclusion it must be stated that the qualities or elemental characteristics

The passing of Arthur. The wounded king is carried to the Fortunate Isle by the Otherworld ferryman, Barinthus. In time he will be cured by the magical healing arts of Morgen, the ruler of that mysterious blessed realm. The prophet Merlin and the bard Taliesin have carried the king's body to the sea shore, and watch his departure. (From the description in the *Vita Merlini* by Geoffrey of Monmouth, written in AD 1150)

Galahad and Perceval, from a fourteenth-century manuscript.

which created the Arthurian warrior, both historical and fictional, may be traced through a long period of time, from the earliest records of the Celts to the twentieth century.

From the early descriptions of Celtic warriors, such as Livy, who described the habit of yelling and singing, Diodorus who described the fearsome long hair and moustaches, Caesar who also noted that noise, in his example from chariots, was used in the battle charge, we can leap an immense time span to the nineteenth- and twentieth-century Scottish regiments. They too charged into battle without benefit of armour, to the sound of yelling and bagpipes, and were renowned for heroic actions of dramatic proportion. Indeed, the early Scottish regiments in the eighteenth century were composed of Gaelic-speaking men from wild Highland regions . . . their long hair and beards, kilted costume, and use of national music would not have been totally unfamiliar to a sixth-century tribal chieftain.

The courage of the Celtic warrior sometimes seems mad to the modern reader, yet an example from the First World War reads just as if it came direct from an ancient legend:

The gallantry of the Highland Regiments engaged – men wearing the tartans of many a famous clan – would be unbelievable were it not so entirely traditional. In one of their actions a Gordon battalion crossed the parapet and marched to the attack in extended order as if on parade . . . capturing and holding a position which had defied all previous efforts.

This seems innocuous enough until we remember that the parapet was that of the trench front line, and such advances were made under a destructive hail of opposing weapon-fire. The image of kilted soldiers marching as if on parade under such circumstances is either the height of folly or an order of courage and indifference to death quite alien to modern culture.

The Celtic warrior, from the earliest conflicts with the Greeks and Romans to the modern wars in twentieth-century Europe, seems to derive his courage from a deep rooted indifference to death . . . not a languid or materialist indifference or apathy, but something drawn from that mysterious depth of the Otherworld, once the source of worship and mystery to our ancestors. We know from Julius Caesar that one of the most important religious beliefs of the Celts was that souls passed from one body to another after death; we also know that the Celtic faith was based upon ancestral worship. Something of this concept of cyclical immortality seems to remain hidden within the modern Celt; it certainly manifests as remarkable courage in modern warfare.

There is, of course, another side to this which must not be overlooked. It is summed up admirably by Mark Girouard in his study of the changing patterns of chivalric behaviour, *Return to Camelot*. Describing the carnage of the front line during the First World War, he says:

The chivalry of England, young, brave, dashing and handsome, line up to process to the tournament. They are filled with ardour for the fight . . . and longing to do great deeds and win honour for themselves and their lady loves . . . Then the rain starts falling. The shining knights cannot charge, for their horses are bogged down and they themselves are wallowing in mud up to

Glastonbury Tor, Somerset. Legends abound about this ancient site. It is associated with both Arthur and with the mystical Grail, which in later stories became the object of quest for Arthur and his knights.

the groin . . . They fall over, their armour splits open and their blood and entrails spill out into the mud.

It is the same, whether the battle is called Badon, Crécy, Waterloo or Ypres — the splendour cannot disguise the agony of the dead and dying.

For good or ill such deeds of valour remain in the consciousness for long ages after their originators have perished. The warriors of Arthur, who became in time the Knights of the Round Table, preserved the ideals of personal bravery, protection of the weak, and above all of a wild and unequivocal daring in the face of adverse conditions. They were transformed from ordinary men into larger-than-life figures — into heroes in fact — thus warranting the re-titling of the Arthurian period as 'the Heroic Age'. We have tried to show something of their magnificent qualities, bringing them out of the shadows and once again clearly before our eyes. In this way we also see the magical event take place — names suddenly take on the faces, characters and qualities of real people. It took the qualities of an Arthur to bring forth the best of the age, but without the warriors who supported him it is more than likely that we should not, now, be celebrating his name at all.

Owein of the Ravens

The story of Owein of the Ravens, or as it is more properly called *Rhonabwy's Dream*, comes from the premier source of ancient Welsh lore and legend collected under the title of *The Mabinogion*. It is here that we find perhaps the most significant descriptions of Arthur's warriors; not, as one might expect, couched in the language or fashion of the twelfth century, when it was first written down, but bearing all the hallmarks of the sixth-century warriors upon whom so many of Arthur's knights are based.

The intricate and detailed descriptions of clothing and weapons are unparalleled anywhere else, and are the reason why this story is said to be impossible to tell from memory, as the ancient bardic story-tellers once did with all their lore and history.

Owein himself appears in the medieval romances as Sir Uwain, the son of Arthur's greatest adversary King Urien of Gore. In fact, both Urien and Owein are historically attested figures, who had bardic laments written about them which are still extant. Urien was king of the Strathclyde area of northern Britain, either in the same period or shortly after that of Arthur. There is an extant early Welsh lament commemorating Owein's death in which he is described as a 'reaper of foes' and 'a despoiler'.

Of the strange game played by Arthur and Owein in this story, much speculation has gone into its nature. It is clearly a board-game related to chess, though scholarly consensus is that it is *not* chess. Another speculation points to the Irish game of fidchel. Little more is known about this game than about gwyddbwyll, but it does offer one clue to the nature of the conflict between Arthur and Owein. In fidchel, as in chess, the king is the most important piece and is defended by a series of knights; however, significantly, the king's defenders are less in number to that of his adversaries, whose task it is to capture him. If we assume for the moment that gwyddbwyll was a similiar kind of game and that Arthur was the King (in both senses of the word) and Owein's Ravens his opponents . . . then we may begin to see aspects of the story in a new light.

In our story, as in the original version, the battle between Arthur and his nephew is a symbolic or magical struggle carried on within the framework of a dream. We have chosen to suggest that the Ravens were an actual group of fighting men, although in the original this is ambiguous enough to give one pause. However, the raven was the symbol of the Celtic battle goddess, the Morrigan, and there are enough literary references to the bloody work of these battleground scavengers to suggest the underlying nature of the tale. Perhaps also, buried deeply within the old text, is a reference to the difficulties experienced by Arthur in trying to weld the proud, wild, passionate-natured Celtic tribesmen into a fighting unit alongside the Romano-British descendants of the Legions which had always been the tribesmen's enemy.

There was once a man called Iorweth ap Maredudd who desired greatly to be overlord of Powys instead of his brother Madawg – however, this story does not concern him at all and so we shall not hear of him again. It concerns rather one of his men who was called Rhonabwy, and a certain dream that he had while sleeping on the skin of a yellow ox in the house of Heilyn the Red, son of Cawgawn, son of Iddon, son of . . . well, never mind who he was the son of – let us hear about Rhonabwy's dream.

This was the way of it: Rhonabwy thought that he was riding towards the Ford of the Cross at Havren in the Kingdom of Powys and that he saw coming towards him a figure that gave him cause to feel fear. The figure was of a warrior dressed in green from the waist down, with a tunic of gold brocade sewn with green thread, and at his thigh a gold-hilted sword in a sheath of best cordovan leather. Over all he wore a mantle of yellow brocade with patterns upon it sewn with green silk, and he rode a spirited, high-stepping horse which covered the ground so swiftly that he overtook Rhonabwy in two breaths. Such was the size of the warrior that Rhonabwy, even when mounted upon his horse, reached only to his thigh.

And Rhonabwy gave him very polite greeting and asked to know who he was.

'Iddawg is my name, son of Mynyo. But I am better known by my nickname which is the Church of Britain.'

'Why arc you called that?' asked Rhonabwy.

'Because I was one of the messengers between Arthur and Medrawt before the Battle of Camlan, and every good word that Arthur spoke I made to sound like an insult, for I was young and eager and I desired very greatly that there should be battle between the two of them.'

Now, even in his dream, Rhonabwy knew that the Battle of Camlan had taken place many hundreds of years before and that all these men had died there, including Arthur and Medrawt – though some still told a tale about Arthur being taken away by three Royal Women to a mysterious island somewhere in the West. Rhonabwy knew of course, as all sensible people know these days, that such things were merely fables designed to entertain men of simple minds –

yet here he stood in the presence of a giant warrior who claimed he had been at Camlan, and this did not seem like a fable.

'Three days before the battle ended, I went to Scotland to do penance for my wicked deeds, but now I am returning to the Camp of Arthur to join in the hosting of the Ravens. If you wish, you shall ride with me. . . .'

This seemed to make even less sense to Rhonabwy, because if Arthur had been killed at Camlan along with all his warriors, then how was it possible for Iddawg to be going to *visit* him?

While he was thinking this, another warrior upon a great black horse rode towards them. He was clad in red brocade sewn with yellow silk, and his mantle was fringed with gold. He swiftly overtook Rhonabwy and Iddawg and asked who was this little fellow that Iddawg had found; and though he did not much like being called a 'little fellow', Rhonabwy had to admit the truth of it and so he kept silent while the two warriors conversed.

And Iddawg explained that he had found Rhonabwy upon the plain, and that he had invited him to ride to the hosting of the Ravens. And the two fell to talking of who would be present and Rhonabwy listened in astonishment to the names of the heroes who were believed long dead in his time but who, it seemed, were coming together to fight a great battle against Osla Big-Knife at a place called Caer Faddon. And he heard much of one Owein, nephew of Arthur, whose warriors were called 'Ravens' and from whom he might look for 'entertainment' when he arrived at the camp.

And so the two huge warriors, with Rhonabwy riding between them (struggling to keep up, if the truth be told) crossed the plain of Argyngrog and came to the ford of Rhyd y Groes on the Hafren; and there they found the tents of Arthur set up along the side of the road. And on a little flat islet in the centre of the river, the pavilion of Arthur was set up. And Arthur himself stood before it with a bishop upon his one side and a slender dark youth upon his other.

Rhonabwy stood in the presence of one already deemed fabulous and who, from his great size alone, could never be taken for a mortal. For Arthur was like a man of bronze, with his ruddy skin and red-gold hair, and beard streaming down upon his breast. So powerful was he indeed that it seemed to Rhonabwy that he almost emitted a glow of light.

Iddawg and his companion (who was called Rhufawn) got down from their horses and splashed across the river to greet their lord. Rhonabwy hung back until Arthur saw him and demanded to know whence he came. When Iddawg explained, Arthur looked down at Rhonabwy and was silent. At length he sighed and said: 'To think that men of this kind shall come to rule this land, after

A contest of skill. Arthur and his nephew, Owein, fight a strange game while their armies battle against each other.

those who ruled it before them,' which confused Rhonabwy deeply since it seemed impossible to him that he should be in the presence of so great and ancient a figure who yet addressed him as a man of the future.

While this exchange had been taking place a great commotion began along the river, and looking in that direction, Rhonabwy saw a second host of men approaching. They were dressed in black from head to foot, except for the fringes upon their mantles, which were of pure white, and they each had a tuft of ravens' feathers upon their helmets or about their persons, and the banner they bore was a raven upon a white ground.

Arthur stood up then and called: 'Welcome, Owein, son of Urien – welcome to the Ravens.' And one rode forward into the water upon his high-stepping black horse and called back: 'Greetings to the War-Lord, Arthur; greetings, uncle.' And Rhonabwy looked with keen interest to see this famed figure whose death-song had been sung by no lesser bard than Taliesin Pen Beirdd. He saw a tall slender youth with shining black hair and eyes the colour of cornflowers, and a look of confidence about him that warned of a high-metalled spirit. And he saw that although many of the warriors of Arthur greeted the Ravens of Owein, yet the latter chose to make camp on the further bank of the river. But he was distracted from thinking such thoughts by Iddawg, who called to him to come and watch the arming of Arthur. 'For', said he, 'the Host must be at Caer Faddon by midday to meet with Osla Big-Knife, and the Lord must first be armed for battle.'

Then Rhonabwy saw a small hairy man with a great scarlet face come forward, and he had in his arms the sword of Arthur, that was named Caledfwlch, having a design of two serpents upon the hilt. When the sword was drawn it was as though fire came from the mouths of these creatures in two flames, and the light was such that no one might look at it. Then from a great pack, the small man drew forth a scarlet mantle with an apple of red-gold at each corner, and placed it about the shoulders of the Lord, and Rhonabwy remembered that it was said of this mantle, which was called Gwenn, that when it was wrapped about the body of the man who wore it, none might see where he walked, though *he* might see all that he wished.

And so the arming went on, with Arthur's shield, Prydwen, with its magical likeness of the God's Mother painted upon it, and Arthur's knife, Carnwennan, that could cut the very air, and his mighty spear Rhongommiant, that no amount of living men could turn aside – until at last the warrior stood ready and the Great Dragon standard was unfurled at the head of its staff and the whole host stood ready to depart. And at that moment Owein came forward from the press of men gathered about their Lord, and said loudly: 'Uncle, will you play a game of gwyddbwyll with me?' and there was a sudden silence over all the throng.

Rhonabwy waited for Arthur to speak angrily to his nephew, but instead he merely smiled and said to the small man who carried his weapons, 'Eiryn, fetch me the board and the pieces.' And he called for two chairs and sat down and, when the gwyddbwyll board had been brought, Arthur and Owein began to play, while the rest of the host sat down to await the outcome of the game.

Now, when they were deeply into the game, a messenger hurried up to Arthur and said: 'Lord, the Ravens are attacking your men and are killing them with beak and claw!' And Arthur paused in his play and said: 'Nephew, call off your Ravens!' But Owein merely looked at the gwyddbwyll board and said, 'Your move, Lord.'

And so they continued to play, and all the time Rhonabwy, who did not quite dare to go and look, could hear the sound of a great commotion coming from the far side of the river.

Presently, when Arthur and Owein had finished one game of gwyddbwyll, and had begun another, a second messenger rode up in a lather of sweat and cried out to Owein that Arthur's warriors had turned upon the Ravens and were inflicting terrible slaughter upon them; then it was Owein's turn to ask that Arthur call off his men. But Arthur merely said: 'Play on, nephew.' And so they played, until a third warrior rode up and he was dressed all in green and gold, with a helmet with a dragon's crest the eyes of which blazed so furiously that no one dared look at them. And this messenger cried out that there was terrible slaughter between Arthur's warriors and Owein's Ravens, and that soon there would be a scarcely a whole man among either host. Then Arthur stood up and took four of the pieces in each of his great hands and crushed them to golden powder, and Owein looked at that work and, calling forward one of his retinue, told him to lower the standard of the Ravens. And at that there was peace between both sides and Arthur and Owein shook hands.

Rhonabwy, who had watched all this in some astonishment, shook his head over the strange actions of heroes (mythical or not) and turned to look for Iddawg for clarification. But the giant warrior only smiled and shrugged, and pointed to a ring that sparkled upon Arthur's finger. 'See that,' he said, 'that is the ring of Arthur, and it has the property that will enable you to remember all that you have seen tonight.'

At that moment a warrior came up to Arthur and said that Osla Big-Knife had asked for a truce until a fortnight hence and what should be his answer? And Arthur said that he would grant the truce, so that both he and Owein might have time to reassemble the fragments of the host and be ready for the battle. And he got upon his great war steed from which he towered above all men there, and in a great voice said, 'Let all those who would take part in this battle with me meet upon the field of Caer Faddon in a fortnight in the morning. And those who shall not, need not.' And he gave a great laugh and looked (Rhonabwy thought) straight at him. Then the camp began to break up, and in the noise and bustle of that Rhonabwy awoke; and whether he was a wiser man for the dream that he dreamt upon the yellow ox-skin, or whether he was not, I cannot say, but I believe that he went away and spoke long and deeply to the two brothers who wished to be kings of Powys. Though whether they listened to him or not, I know not, for this is the end of the tale of Rhonabwy's dream and nothing else need concern us.

Envoi

Go, litil book, and humbilly beseche
The werriourys, and hem that wil the rede,
That where a fault is or impropir speche,
Thei vouchsafe amende my mysdede.
Thi writer eek, pray him to taken hede
Of thi cadence and kepe Ortographie,
That neither he take of ner multiplye.
Knyghthode and Bataile (fifteenth century)

The Hunter. A modern illustration by Miranda Gray of the Celto-Arthurian Warrior.

Bibliography

Alcock, L., *Arthur's Britain*, Allan Lane 1971.

Alcock, L., *By South Cadbury is that Camelot...*, Thames & Hudson 1972.

Anderson, A. S., *Roman Military Tombstones*, Shire Publications 1984.

Anglo-Saxon Chronicle, Trans. A. Savage, Papermac 1984.

Armes Prydein (The Prophecy of Britain), ed. Sir I. Williams, Dublin Institute for Advanced Studies 1982.

Ashe, G., *A Certain Very Ancient Book*, in *Speculum*, Vol. 56, 2 1981.

Ashe, G., *Discovery of King Arthur*, Debrett's Peerage 1985.

Ashe, G., *From Caesar to Arthur*, Collins 1961.

Ashe, G., *Guidebook to Arthurian Britain*, Longman 1980.

Ashe, G., *King Arthur's Avalon*, Collins 1957.

Ashe, G., ed., *The Quest for Arthur's Britain*, Paladin 1971.

Barber, R., *The Knight and Chivalry*, Longman 1970.

Barber, R., *The Reign of Chivalry*, David and Charles 1980.

Bartrum, P. C., *Welsh Genealogies*, University of Wales Press 1974.

Bede, *A History of the English Church and People*, Penguin 1955.

Binchy, D. A., *Celtic and Anglo-Saxon Kingship*, Oxford University Press 1970.

Brewer, D., and Frankel, E., *Arthur's Britain*, Pevensey Press 1985.

Bromwich, R., *Celtic Dynastic Themes and the Breton Lays* in *Etudes Celtiques*, Vol. 9, 1960–1, pp. 439–74.

Bromwich, R., *Scotland and the Earliest Arthurian Tradition* in *Bulletin Bibliographique de la Société Internationale Arthurienne*, Vol. 15, 1963, pp. 85–95.

Bromwich, R., *Trioedd Ynys Prydain: The Myvyrian Third Series*, Parts 1 and 2, in *Transactions of the Honourable Society of Cymmrodorian*, 1968–69.

Bromwich, R., *The Twenty Four Knights of Arthur's Court* in *Trans. of the Hon. Soc. of Cymmrodorian*, 1957, pp. 116–32.

Bruce-Mitford, R., *Sutton Hoo Ship Burial*, British Museum Publications Ltd 1972.

Capellanus, A., *The Art of Courtly Love*, W.W. Norton and Co 1941.

Chambers, E.K., *Arthur of Britain*, Speculum Historiale 1964.

Collingwood, R. G., and Myers, J.N.L., *Roman Britain and the English Settlements*, Oxford University Press 1936.

Collingwood, W.G., *Arthur's Battles* in *Antiquity*, Vol. 3, 1929.

Crawford, O.G.S., *Arthur and his Battles* in *Antiquity*, 1935.

Crawford, O.G.S., *Topography of Roman Scotland*, Cambridge University Press 1949.

Crowl, P.A., *The Intelligent Travellers Guide to Historic Britain*, Sidgwick and Jackson 1983.

Cunliffe, B., *The Celtic World*, Bodley Head 1979.

Ditmas, E.M.R., *The Cult of Arthurian Relics*, in *Folklore*, Vol. 85, 1, 1964, pp. 19–33.

Ditmas, E.M.R., *More Arthurian Relics* in *Folklore*, Vol. 87, 2, 1966, pp. 91–104.

Eade, J.W., *The Development of Roman Mailed Cavalry* in *Journal of Roman Studies*, Vol. 59, 1967.

Edel, D., *The Arthur of 'Culhwch and Olwen' as a figure in epic-heroic tradition* in *Reading Medieval Studies*, Vol. 9, 1983, pp. 3–15.

Edel, D., *The Catalogues in 'Culhwch and Olwen' and Insular Celtic Learning* in *Bulletin of Board of Celtic Studies*, Vol. 30, 1983, pp. 253–67.

Embleton, R., and Graham, F., *Hadrian's Wall in the days of the Romans*, Frank Graham 1984.

Fairbairn, N., *Travellers Guide to the Kingdoms of Arthur*, Evans Bros 1983.

Ford, P.K., *On the Significance of Some Arthurian Names in Welsh* in *Bull. Brd. Celtic Studies*, Vol. 30, pp. 268–73.

Gamber, O., *The Sutton Hoo Military Equipment* in *Journal of the Arms and Armour Society*, Vol. 5, 1966.

Geoffrey of Monmouth, *History of the Kings of Britain*, Penguin 1966.

Gildas, *The Ruin of Britain*, Phillimore and Co. Ltd. 1978.

Girouard, M., *The Return to Camelot, Chivalry and the English Gentleman*, Yale University Press 1981.

Goodrich, N.L., *King Arthur*, Franklin Watts 1986.

Gwynne, T., *Some Arthurian Material in Keltic*, in *Aberystwyth Studies*, vol. 8, 1926.

Jackson, K., *Nennius and the 28 Cities of Britain* in *Antiquity*, Vol. 12, 1936.

Jackson, K., *The Britons in Southern Scotland*, in *Antiquity*, Vol. 29, 1955.

Jones, E., *The Bardic Museum*, A. Strahan 1802.

Jones, G., *Kings, Beasts, and Heroes*, Oxford University Press 1972.

Keen, M., *Chivalry*, Yale University Press 1984.

Kennedy, B., *Knighthood in the 'Morte d'Arthur,'* D.S. Brewer 1985.

Kruta, V., and Forman, W., *The Celts of the West*, Orbis 1985.

Laing, L., *Archaeology of Late Celtic Britain and Ireland*, Methuen 1975.

Lewis, T., *Bolg, Fir Bolg, Caladbolg*, in *Essays and Studies presented to Prof. E. MacNale*, Three Candles 1940.

Mabinogion, Trans. J. Gantz, Penguin 1976.

Mabinogion, Trans. Lady C. Guest, David Nutt 1910.

Matthews, C., *Mabon and the Mysteries of Britain*, RKP Arkana, 1987.

Matthews, J., *The Grail, Quest for the Eternal*, Thames and Hudson 1981.

McGrail, S., *Ancient Boats*, Shire 1983.

McKisack, M., *The Fourteenth Century, 1307–1399*, Oxford University Press 1959.

Melville-Richards, G., *Arthurian Onomastics*, in *Trans. Hon. Soc. Cymmroddorian*, 1969, pp. 250–64.

Morris, J., *The Age of Arthur*, Weidenfeld and Nicholson 1973.

Newark, T., *Celtic Warriors*, Blandford Press 1986.

Nickel, H., *The Dawn of Chivalry* in *From the Lands of the Scythians*, catalogue of Metropolitan Museum of Art.

Nicolle, D., *Arthur and the Anglo-Saxon Wars*, Osprey 1984.

Nitze, W.A., *Arthurian Names: Arthur*, in *Proceedings of the Modern Language Assoc. of America*, Vol. 64, 1940.

O'Hogain, D., *The Hero in Irish Folk History*, Gill and MacMillan 1985.

Pearce, S.M., *Cornish Elements in the Arthurian Tradition* in *Folklore*, Vol. 85, 1974.

Piggot, S., *The Sources of Geoffrey of Monmouth* in *Antiquity*, Vol. 15, 1941.

Richmond, T.D., *The Sarmatae Bremetennaeum Veterandum* in *Journal of Roman Studies*, Vol. 35, 1945.

Ritchie, G. and A., *Scotland; Archaeology and Early History*, Thames and Hudson 1985.

Ritchie, W.F. and J.N.G., *Celtic Warriors*, Shire 1985.

Rivet, A.L.F., and Smith, C., *Place-Names of Roman Britain*, Batsford 1979.

Russell Robinson, H., *The Armour of Imperial Rome*, Arms and Armour Press 1975.

Russell, J.C., *Arthur and the Romano-Celtic Frontier*, in *Modern Philology*, Vol. 48, 1950–1.

Saklatavala, B., *Arthur, Roman Britain's Last Champion*, David and Charles 1967.

Senior, M., *Myths of Britain*, Orbis 1979.

Sidonius Apollinaris, *Poems and Letters*, Heinemann 1936.

Simkins, M., *The Roman Army from Hadrian to Constantine*, Osprey 1979.

Spence, L., *Arthurian Tradition in Scotland*, in *The Scots Magazine*, April 1926.

Stewart, R.J., *The Prophetic Vision of Merlin*, RKP Arkana 1986.

Stewart, R.J., *The Mystic Life of Merlin*, RKP Arkana 1986.

Stewart, R.J. (editor), *The Book of Merlin*, Blandford Press 1987.

Stoker, R.B., *Legacy of Arthur's Chester*, Covenant 1965.

Stuart-Glennie, J.S., *Arthurian Localities*, Edmonston and Douglas 1869.

Tacitus, *The Agricola and Germania*, Penguin 1948.

Tolstoy, N., *Nennius, Chapter 56* in *Bulletin of Celtic Studies*, Vol. 19, pp. 118–62, 1961.

Wace and Layamon, *Arthurian Chronicles*, trans. E. Mason, Dent 1962.

Watson, W.J., *The History of Celtic Place Names of Scotland*, Wm. Blackwood and Sons Ltd 1926.

Welsh Triads, The (*Trioedd ynys Prydain*), trans. R. Bromwich, University of Wales 1981.

Westwood, J., *Albion, a Guide to Legendary Britain*, Granada 1985.

Williams, M., *King Arthur in History and Legend*, in *Folklore*, Vol. 73, 1962.

Index

Alternative Celtic and Medieval names of Arthurian characters are given in square brackets. Page numbers in **bold** type refer to the colour plates.

Abduction & Rescue of Gwenhwyfar the Queen 94–5
Aeneas 17
Aetius 47, 48, 50
Agincourt 34
Aife 88
Alaric the Goth 44
Alexander the Great 16
Alfred the Great 108
Ambrosius 48, 53–4, 60, 112, 114, 116, 130, 150
Ammanius Marcellus 79
Andraste 86
Andreas 26
Aneurin 58
Anglo-Saxon England 11, 18, 52
Annales Cambriae 51, 116
Aquae Sulis [Bath] 83
Arianrhod 90
Art of Courtly Love 26, 80
Arthur 11, 15, 16, 24, 26, 29, 30, 34, 35, 42, 48, 53, 57, 60, 79, 93, 128, 130, 152, 153, 178, 180; as Ambrosius' protegé 54; as Christian King 11, 46, 57, 58, **111**; as Riothamus 60; as 'tyrant' 47; as undying hero & mystical leader 16, 22, 26, 116, 153, 166; battles 98–107, 112; crown

168; 'grave' 26, 27; genealogies 138, 139; seal 168; weapons 135–7; historical (Dark Age) 18, 43, 44, 58, 61, 98, 125, 128, 130, 150; passing **175**
Arthur, Prince of Wales 27
Arthurian arms and armour 132–137
Arthurian Britain 42–59; as Celtic propaganda 126–7; as Norman propaganda 168–170; magical traditions underlying 126
Arthurian civilization 14, 15, 28, 32, 56–7, 128; influence on Medieval ethos 30, 32
Arthurian heroes 136–149; enduring traditions of, 170; magical properties of, 136
Arthurian relics 167–8
Arthurian legends: *see* Matter of Britain
Arvandus 59
Ashe, Geoffrey 59
Athena 82
Avalon 16, 22, 27

Badbury Rings 104
Badon, battle of, 58, 98, 101, 102, 106, 116, 132, **105**

bards and oral tradition 150, 153
Barnet, battle of, 133
Bede 50, 57
beheading game in Arthurian tradition 86, **157**
Beheading Game 130, 155–166, **157**
Bernard of Clairvaux, St, 22
Black Book of Carmarthen 106
Bladud 82
Blodeuwedd 93
Blundering Hero, 64–77
Boorman, John 11, 149
Bors 22
Bosworth Field, battle of 32
Boudicca 85–6
Bran mac Febal 35
Brent Knoll 102, 104
Brigantia 92
Briggidda 83
Brigit 83
Britannia 92
British navy 108
Britomart 92
Britomartus 79
Brittany 18, 108, 112, 113, 167
Broceliande 20
Brutus 17, 30, 169, 170

Cai, *see* Kei
Cain Adamnan 79
Camelot 16, 32, 36, 93, **49**
Camlan, battle of 16, 108, 114–6, 167
Carausius 112
Castus, Lucius Artorius
Cat Coit Caledon, battle of 98, 101, 104
cataphracti 56, 134
Caw 104
Caxton, William 22, 32, 34
Celtic church 46, 61
Celtic gods 80–5
Celtic kingship 128–132
Celtic warriors 78–9; inherited codes and practices 170–7
Chapel of St George, Windsor 30
Charlemagne 17, 24
Charles II 154
chivalry 15, 16, 20, 14, 32, 34, 90, 176
Chrétien de Troyes 19, 20, 21, 25, 26, 35, 93, 132
Christ 21, 22
Christian influence on Arthurian legends 21
Christianity in Britain 46, 58; fusion with paganism 61, 155
Cid, the, 24
Civil War 133
clan system 128
Clastidum, battle of 78
Cliges 20
conteurs 16, 18
Collingwood, R.G. 100, 101
Constantine III 44
Council of Arles 46
Count of the Saxon Shore 44
courtly love 24, 26, 80, 93
Cradoc of Llancarven 93
Crecy 30, 34
Cromwell, Oliver 46
crusades 16, 26
crystal cross 168
Cu Chulainn 86, 87, 88, 89
Culhwch and Olwen 127, 141, 144
Cunedda 46

De Exicidio Britonum 47
De Ortu Waluuanii 50
De Re Militari 114
dindshencas 141
Diodorus Siculus 150
Discovery of King Arthur 59
dragon-standard 134
Dream of Rhonabwy 136, 137, 178
druids 53, 82, 84, 150, 153; advice from **151**; suppression of, 150
Dux Britanniarum 44

Ebissa 50, 101
Edmund of Rutland 32
Edward I 168
Edward II 28, 30
Edward III 30, 32
Edward IV 32, 34, 133
Edward, Black Prince 32
Edward, Duke of York 32
Edward, Prince of Wales (1471) 32
Eleanor of Aquitaine 26
Elizabeth I 92
Emrys [Merlin] 54, 152
Enide 20
Erec 20; *see also* Gereint
Erec and Enide 19, 132
espionage as magical intelligence 154–5
Euric, King 59
Excalibur 80, 90, 133
Excalibur (1982) 11, 12, 149

Faerie Queene 90
faery 35
female military service 79, 92, **81**
feudal system 28
fidchel 178
Field of the Cloth of Gold 34
Finnian of Clonard, St 102
Fisher King 21
France 16, 18, 19
Franks 42, 51
Frisians 51

Galahad 22, 35
Ganieda 152
Gareth 16
Gaul 44, 48, 61, 110
Gawain [Gwalchmai] 16, 22, 35, 86; as Roman legionary 60; his skull 168
Gawain and the Green Knight 130, 132, 155
Gawain and Ragnell 86
geas (pl. *geise*) 62, 90
Geoffrey of Monmouth 17, 18, 20, 54, 59, 82, 106, 108, 112, 125, 126, 132, 133, 142, 150, 152, 170; criticized as unreliable chronicler 125
Gereint [Erec] 106
Germanus of Auxerre, St 46
Germany 16, 19
Gildas 46, 47–8, 50, 53, 56, 58, 104
Glastonbury 26, 27, 102, 168
Glein, battle of 98, 104
Goddess, the Celtic 80–2, 92; hag-aspect of 86
Godfrey of Bouillon 25, 34
Gorlois 143, 152
Grail 14, 16, 20, 21, 22, 25, 26, 61, 62, 170

Green Knight 16
Guest, Lady Charlotte 137
Guinevere [Gwenhwyfar] 11, 15, 16, 20, 22, 26, 93, 142, 154; adbution and rescue 93–97, **95**
Guinnion, battle of 98, 101, 104
Gwenhwyfar, *see* Guinevere
gwyddbwyll 178

Hadrian, Emperor 45
Hengist 50
Henry II 15, 17, 26
Henry VII 169
Henry VIII 34
highland regiments 176
hillforts re-fortified 52, 54
Historia Brittonum 98
History of the British Kings 13, 17, 108, 125, 142
History of the English Church and People 57
Hitler 170
Holy Grail, *see* Grail
Homer 141
Honorius, Emperor 44
Hueil, son of Caw 104
Hunting of Twrch Trwyth **131**

Iceland 18
Irish pirates 44, 48, 101, 114
Isabel of France 30
Isolt 15, 16, 22, 168

Janus 116
Jerome, St 44
Joseph of Arimathaea, St 22
Julius Caesar 32, 82, 85, 110, 130, 150, 176

Kay [Kei] 93
Kei 35, 93, 117–120, 137; as Arthur's butler and gatekeeper 117
Kei and the Giant 120–124, **123**
knights, medieval, 34, 35
Kundry 80

Lady of the Lake 80, 90.
Lady of Shalott 36
Lancelot 11, 15, 16, 22, 24, 32, 35, 93, 154; mythical descent from Lugh 138
Lancelot or *The Knight of the Cart* 20, 93
Layamon 18, 134
Leo I 59
Life of Gildas 93
Livy 176
Llewellyn II 168
Llongborth 106
Llwch Lemineawg 35

Llwywarch Hen   58
Llyr Marini's genealogy   143
Logres   28
Lugh   35
Lugh Loinbheimionach   35
Lugh Strong Arm and the Three Queens   36–41, **37**
Lunet   16

Mabinogion   13, 61, 88, 90, 126, 128, 136, 137, 178
Macsen Wledig's genealogy   141
magical weapons   12, 124, 126–8
Magnus Maximus   48, 108, 112
Malory   22, 24, 28, 32, 34, 36, 93
Marcellus, Marcus C.   78–9, 90
Marie de Champagne [de France]   26
Mary, Blessed Virgin,   58, 98, 132
Math, son of Mathonwy   90, 93
matriarchal society   35
Matter of Britain   16, 17, 18, 21, 22, 167
Medrawd(t) [Mordred]   104, 116
Meleagrance   93
Melwas   93
Merlin   11, 14, 15, 18, 82, 104, 126, 130, 149–53, **171**; as child prophet 53–4; madness 150; Enclosure 154; name 152
middle ages   15, 16, 24, 30, 32, 61, 93, 149
Minerva   82–5
Mordred [Medrawt]   16, 34
Morgan le Fay   35
Morgana   35
Morholt   168
Morrigan   80, 85, 180
Morris, John   107
Morte d'Arthur   22, 14, 32
Mortimer, Roger   30

Nennius   50, 53, 57, 58, 98, 100, 101, 104, 106, 112
Niall of the Nine Hostages   45
Nickel, Helmut   134
Night of the Long Knives   **31**, 50
nine hags of Gloucester   88
Nine Worthies   16, 24–5
Ninian, St.   46
Notitia Dignitatum   134

Octa   50, 101
Order of the Garter   30, 32
Order of the Golden Fleece   31
Orion   118
Orkneys   50, 102
Ostrogoths   42
Owein   16, 104, 178; his Ravens 179–80
Owein of the Ravens   180–4, **181**

Palladius   46
Parzival   25
Patrick, St   46
Pausanius   79
Perceval [Peredur]   80
Perceval, or the Story of the Grail   20
Peredur [Perceval]   20, 61, 62, 90, 144; as blundering hero 61, **69**
Picts   42, 45, 46, 48, 50, 52, 98, 101, 104, 114
Plantagenet dynasty   26
Pleiades   118
Polibius   78
Posidonius   85
Prophecies of Merlin   14, 20, 152

Queen of Norgalles   35
quest   21

reincarnation as Celtic belief   85
Rheged   104
Richard III   32
Richard Lionheart   15, 168
riddles as traditional teaching   90–1
Riothamus   59
Robert II   117
Roland   24
Roman de Brut   18
Roman legions   11, 53, 134, 180; withdrawal of from Britain 43
Romano-British culture   13, 42 et seq, 130, 153, 172
Rome   18, 48; fall of 16, 44, 45
Round Table Fellowship   14, 15, 18, 28, 30, 32, 34, 35, 154, 177

Sarmatian cavalry   134
Sarras   16
Scathach   86, 87, 88, 174
Saxon armour   133
Saxons: as federate troops in Britain 50, 52; as invaders 42, 44, 45, 51–3, 79, 100, 107, 108, 110, 112
sea-battles   106–114, **111**
severed head in Celtic belief   61, 62
Shakespeare   17
ships: Arthurian   108, 112; Roman 112; Saxon 110
Sidonius   51, 110
Spain   16
Spenser, Edmund   90
spiritual chivalry   21, 24
Stephen, King   27
Stonehenge   15
Stories: *Abduction & Rescue of Gwenhwyfar the Queen* 94–5; *The Beheading Game* 155–166; *The Blundering Hero* 64–77; *Kei and the Giant* 120–124; *Lugh Strong Arm and the Three Queens* 36–41; *Owein of the Ravens* 180–4.
storytelling   12–14, 16
Strabo   78
Stuart dynasty as stewards   117
Suetonius Paulinus   86, 150
Sul   83
sword in the stone   15, 128

Tacitus   86
Taliesin   58, 82, 152
Tancred of Sicily   168
Tara   79
Templars   25
Tennyson, Alfred Lord,   36
Thirteen treasures of Britain   136
Tintagel   58
Tolstoy   104–6
Triple Goddess   35, 80
Tristan   15, 16, 22; sword 168
trouvères   19
Trystan ac Essyllt   93
Twenty-four Knights of Arthur's Court   137, 144
Twrch Trwyth, hunting of   **131**

Underworld   62, 83, 90
Urien of Rheged   164, 178; genealogy 143
Uther   152
Uwain [Owein]   178

Vegetius   114
Venus   80
Virgil   16
Visigoths   42
Vita Merlini   82, 120, 153
Vortigern   48–51, 53, 58, 112, 130, 31; genealogy 142; Tower 53
Vulgate Cycle   22

Wace   18
Wales,   45, 46, 53
Wansdyke   52
Wars of the Roses   22, 32, 133
Waste Land   21
Welsh Triads   136, 144
White Stag   19
White, T.H.   34
William of Newburgh   125
Winchester   168
Wolfram von Eschenbach   25
women warriors   12, 79–92, **81**, 174; as instructors in battle skills 85
World War 1   176
World War 2   134

Yvain, the Knight of the Lion   20

ILLUSTRATIONS

Colour plates painted by Richard Hook.
Colour photography by John Rogers.
Line illustrations by Chesca Potter, except page 99 by Caitlín
Matthews and pages 6 and 185 by Miranda Gray.

Other illustrations and photographs from the author's collection or courtesy of:

Leslie Alcock/British Academy (page 56)
Ashmolean Museum, Oxford (page 91)
Bodleian Library, Oxford (page 109)
BBC Hulton Picture Library (page 33)
The British Library (page 32)
The British Tourist Authority (page 52)
Fogg Art Museum, Harvard University (page 102)
Hermitage Museum, Lenningrad (page 101)
Mansell Collection (page 43)
Royal Commission on Ancient Monuments, Scotland (page 173)
Royal Museum of Scotland (page 103)
Michael Simkins (page 153)
Trinity College Library, Dublin (page 53)
Trustees of the British Museum (pages 144, 148)
Apologies to any source erroneously credited or inadvertently uncredited.

192